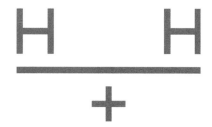

HEMSLEY HEMSLEY

GOOD + SIMPLE

JASMINE AND MELISSA HEMSLEY

EBURY
PRESS

DEDICATED TO DAD

CONTENTS

INTRODUCTION

Food should be good for you, it should be delicious and nutritious, and it should be simple and sustainable.

DELICIOUS

Tasty, impressive dishes that you enjoy cooking, eating and sharing

NUTRITIOUS

Food that provides you with the building blocks to keep you at your very best

SUSTAINABLE

Quick, easy and affordable cooking for every day with ingredients that are thoughtfully sourced

We started our family business with good food and good health at its heart. Our aim was to coach people away from fad diets and unhealthy eating towards an appreciation of the power of real food, properly sourced and correctly prepared. Our clients felt happier, healthier and more energised and couldn't believe how easy it was to adopt the Hemsley + Hemsley principles for better living. Eating well is one of the most important ways to keep in good health and it is also one of life's pleasures. Working out how to combine the two culminated in our first book, *The Art of Eating Well.*

In *Good + Simple* we want to show that healthy eating doesn't have to be complicated: eat good food and good things will result. If the food you eat is delicious and simple to prepare, then you can maintain a healthy diet without difficulty. To prove this, we've developed over 140 recipes for their great taste, ease and versatility, stripping back our principles to make eating well even simpler. We've created dishes that

are packed with flavour, work for us every day, are straightforward and quick to make and use ingredients that are readily available.

We take a holistic approach towards well-being, because for us it's not just about healthy eating. Food should be good for you but it should also taste good, make you and your family feel good, be good for the environment *and* your pocket. Food culture today is complicated by too much choice and too many fake foods: rows of highly refined packaged products flanked by adverts for the latest fad diet or quick fixes for weight loss – approaches that rarely work in the long term. Knowing how best to feed yourself is a skill for life and means that you'll be healthier, more contented and better prepared to take on the ups and downs of daily life, and you'll be setting an inspiring example to those around you too. Anyone can be a good home cook and nothing beats delicious, nourishing home-cooked food made with love.

THE HEMSLEY + HEMSLEY PHILOSOPHY

We've been developing and growing the H+H way of eating for over ten years, through research, study and self-practice. It's been six years since we turned this knowledge and passion for good food into a bespoke service to help people improve the way they eat, enjoy their food and understand why digestive health is so important.

We believe in back-to-basics nutrition. Avoiding processed, refined or sugary foods, we instead enjoy a wide array of vegetables, as well as good-quality meat, fish, legumes and pseudocereals. Here you'll find easy and delicious recipes for everyone, whether you eat meat, are vegetarian, vegan or on a Paleo, primal or raw-food diet, and for those with allergies or intolerances we suggest alternatives to nuts, dairy and eggs where possible (see also page 17).

Our motto is 'Good food, good mood, good digestion, good health!' and we are always telling our clients to 'get with your gut' because gut health translates to overall health. Our secret weapons for nourishing the gut are bone broth – a frugal and time-honoured food that's packed with protein, vitamins, minerals, collagen and keratin – and probiotics that we culture cheaply and easily ourselves, such as sauerkraut and other condiments. Combine this with our principles of low-stress and low-chemical living, chewing well and basic food combining and you have a recipe for optimum digestive health.

Using natural fats (including animal fats), being thoughtful about the ingredients you buy and keeping even natural sweeteners (including fruit and raw honey) to a minimum are other key principles of the H+H philosophy. Most importantly, our approach has to work for you – it has to be practical in the kitchen, fit with your schedule and, of course, make you look and feel your very best.

FAST FOOD THAT'S GOOD FOR YOU

What are our go-to recipes when we've had a day of it? Running our business means we have no set routine. We don't get to eat the food we make for other people(!), so, just like everyone else, we have to put some effort into planning ahead. In this book, we share the recipes that we return to time and again, from our old faithful standbys – soups and stews – to quick 10-minute suppers, as well as the easiest snacks for food on the go.

For those who don't really enjoy vegetables, or struggle to eat enough of them, we say: Soup! Stew! Spiralize! The three 'S's are our way of packing plenty of nutrient-dense and refreshing veggies into meals. They are an easy and affordable way to feed friends and family with real wholefoods from one day to the next, with leftovers for tomorrow's packed lunch.

There is a misconception that healthy food is boring: it is anything but! Even when keeping things simple, we use different flavours and textures to make a recipe interesting. We love to try out local dishes on our travels, experimenting with new ingredients and traditional techniques, and have fun in the kitchen reinventing culinary classics – from pasta and pizza to cakes and sandwiches – using wholefood alternatives.

Our clients and readers also like to challenge us to recreate their favourite takeaways or childhood meals. Our advice is to combine variety with a fuss-free kitchen routine and a methodical approach to cooking to keep it enjoyable and never a chore, especially when life is busy enough anyway.

Only a few generations ago, meals conformed to more of a weekly schedule and nothing went to waste: roast chicken on a Sunday, leftovers on a Monday and a pot of nutritious bone broth for making other dishes later in the week. This made preparing food easier and more economical: you know what to shop for – no need to dig deep for inspiration after a full day at work. These days we're spoilt for choice, but getting back into a way of eating that looks ahead and uses

food economically – from the fridge and store cupboard – will help you plan and eat well every day.

With this in mind, we have put together some mouth-watering and simple weekly menus, including shopping lists, to help you plan ahead so that you're always prepared when hunger strikes (pages 334–7). You'll find a section on our favourite ingredients and useful kitchen equipment, tips on how to stock your kitchen, and how to make our philosophy work in a variety of situations, from work lunches and late-night suppers, to on-the-go snacks and packing food to travel.

Planning ahead needn't be a chore either; it's empowering and makes life easier and more enjoyable in the long run. And of course, if plans change, dip into your freezer – our freezer is our best friend! Eating well every day does not mean having to cook every day.

As you kick-start this new way of eating, things will take a little longer initially, but you'll very quickly get

the hang of it; you'll soon feel the difference and find you've made positive changes to last a lifetime.

For those who want to hit the ground running, we've included our top ten recipes to get you started (page 19) and a one-week restorative reboot to reset your taste buds and relationship with food (page 21).

15 H+H PRINCIPLES FOR EATING WELL

Here's an overview of our key philosophy.
Use these 15 principles as a quick guide.

1 **GUT INSTINCT**
2 **BOIL YOUR BONES**
3 **FORGET CALORIES, THINK NUTRIENTS**
4 **MEAT AND TWO VEG**
5 **GOING AGAINST THE GRAIN**
6 **FAT IS YOUR FRIEND**
7 **SWEET ENOUGH**
8 **DRINK TO THINK**
9 **THE REAL DEAL**
10 **KNOW YOUR ONIONS**
11 **PREPARE, CHEW AND COMBINE**
12 **BE MINDFUL**
13 **STRESS LESS**
14 **TUNE IN**
15 **THE 'BETTER THAN' RULE**

1 GUT INSTINCT

The gut is the centre of our immunity. A healthy gut, rich in beneficial microflora, leads to a healthy body and mind.

Without a healthy gut, your body will not be able to efficiently digest and absorb vital minerals and nutrients from your food. Because of this, it's imperative to focus on the foods that enrich your immunity, reduce inflammation caused by internal and external stressors on your system and nourish you from within.

The gut is looked after by microflora (an internal ecosystem living together in harmony, geared to keeping you healthy). Your microflora is made up of 100 trillion bacteria, ten times more than there are cells in your entire body. For good digestive health we like to eat naturally fermented or cultured foods – full-fat yoghurt, sauerkraut, unpasteurised miso, kimchi and kombucha – rich in probiotics that keep our microflora diverse and topped up, such as our BBQ Ketchup (page 278) or Pink Chilli Kraut (page 130). We avoid refined and chemically

processed foods and try to reduce stress levels that upset our system. We drink bone broth, eat slowly, chew thoroughly (see page 14) and practise proper food preparation, such as activating and gentle cooking, to help keep the gut healthy. (For more on activating, see page 341.)

2 BOIL YOUR BONES

Frugal, nourishing and tasty, bone broth is the age-old superfood at the heart of the H+H philosophy.

Thanks to its nourishing, easily digestible nutrients, bone broth is often used to treat ailments and nurture the sick. Just as green juice is the super concentrate of green vegetables, bone broth provides the essence of goodness that only animal foods can offer. The key to a good broth is the quality of the bones and a really long simmer to extract the nutrients, making it different from a classic stock, which is simply about flavour. A soup made with bone broth is tastier, more nutritious and satisfying than one made without it. For how to prepare bone broth, see page 63.

3 FORGET CALORIES, THINK NUTRIENTS

Counting calories is not a natural or sustainable way to live. Focus on nutrients not numbers.

All calories are not created equal and the body deals with different sources of energy differently. Rather, every calorie consumed should be packed with as many nutrients as possible, enabling you to feel satisfied with less food and for longer. Counting calories is not a natural way to determine the foods that you should be eating, and calorie-controlled 'diets' tend not to work in the long term or address the root cause of the problem. Nutrient-dense foods, such as broccoli topped with melted butter and a sprinkle of sea salt, will leave you feeling satisfied for longer, while a low-calorie 'diet' food, such as a low-fat or low-'sugar' cereal bar, might fill you up but leave you wanting more an hour or so later. Make the ingredients, not the calories, the first thing you check out when you encounter a new food.

4 MEAT AND TWO VEG

While vegetables take centre stage, eating food from both the plant and animal kingdoms makes sense.

Eating meat, fish and vegetables helps us feel our best. Vegetables, which are naturally high in fibre, are the star of the show, with non-starchy varieties making up the majority of the plate and featuring in as many meals as possible. But animal foods of good provenance are essential to a healthy balanced diet, offering nutrients that are hard to obtain from plants alone. Meat doesn't have to feature at every meal or in large quantities, nor does it have to be expensive. Make friends with your butcher and try the cheaper, less fashionable cuts, which are just as nourishing and often tastier. We like onglet, chicken livers, beef shin, lamb breast and, of course, bone broth.

5 GOING AGAINST THE GRAIN

Choose complex carbohydrates: vegetables, legumes and pseudocereals, as well as fruit.

Modern diets are often heavily reliant on grains – cereal or toast for breakfast; sandwiches, wraps and noodles for lunch; biscuits and crackers for snacks; pasta or rice for dinner; and not to mention pastries, puddings and desserts. The majority of these commercial crops are intensely hybridised, sprayed with chemicals and often served in refined forms, which convert to glucose at a faster rate when digested and can have a rollercoaster effect on your blood-sugar levels. This encourages you to overeat as you tend to feel hungry soon after a meal. Whole grains can be harder to digest for many individuals and can lead to other digestive problems.

We stopped eating meals based on grains such as wheat, spelt, rye, oats and rice, along with potatoes. Instead we like to keep things diverse, with tasty recipes that encourage a broader range of nutritious foods, such as vegetables, legumes and pseudocereals

(for example, quinoa, amaranth and buckwheat) as our main source of complex carbohydrates. These foods are naturally gluten-free, more nutrient- and mineral-dense and, with plenty of fibre for gut microflora, a better option than refined carbohydrates.

6 FAT IS YOUR FRIEND

Enjoy both saturated and unsaturated fats in their natural and unrefined forms.

We do not advocate foods labelled 'low-fat'. It's not natural fat that causes health problems – it's the processed stuff. We embrace the natural fats from both plant and animal sources – from olive oil, coconut cream, avocado and nuts to ghee, butter, egg yolk, bone marrow and dripping. Fat is an excellent source of sustainable energy that makes meals tasty and satisfying. It helps to stabilise blood sugar, optimises digestion and enables us to absorb vitamins. We cook with saturated fats such as coconut oil, ghee or butter and save the more delicate unsaturated plant fats, such as extra-virgin olive oil (which we always buy cold-pressed for its nutritional benefits) for drizzling on salads. Avoid all refined fats, especially hydrogenated ones (these are the saturated transfats): margarines, corn oil, processed vegetable oil, cooking sprays and vegetable suet.

FATS

SATURATED FATS – GOOD FOR COOKING

Typically solid at room temperature, the following fats are more heat stable and therefore more suitable for cooking, roasting and baking. Always choose full-fat varieties. Long-lasting if kept well – store in a cool place or in the fridge.

Animal fats (e.g. dripping and goose fat, either shop-bought or saved from roasts/skimmed from bone broth)

Butter (unsuitable for high-temperature cooking like roasting or stir-frying as the milk solids burn; great for baking and sautéing)

Coconut oil (virgin, unbleached)

Ghee (clarified butter)

UNSATURATED FATS – GOOD FOR DRESSINGS

Typically liquid at room temperature, the following fats are less stable in cooking, so save for drizzling, dressing, dipping and finishing dishes. Look for cold-pressed and unrefined varieties. Store in a cool place or in the fridge.

Extra-virgin olive oil (EVOO) (suitable for cooking at low temperatures, though we prefer to save it for finishing dishes)

Flaxseed oil (keep in the fridge)

Sesame oil (make sure to use plain, unrefined oil – also good as a body oil). Use toasted oil sparingly as a flavouring.

Macadamia nut oil

7 SWEET ENOUGH

Sweeten minimally for balance, keep it natural for nutrition and reawaken your taste buds.

When is a sweet not a treat? When it disrupts your metabolism. Sugar – in any form – activates the pleasure centres in the brain and it can become addictive. It is also now understood that even overeating fructose (natural fruit sugar) is a massive driver of obesity, along with fatty liver and heart disease. Sugar can promote inflammation in the body and also cause those well-known 'sugar rushes' (unwanted spikes in blood-sugar levels) that are usually followed by 'sugar lows'. Keeping your blood-sugar levels stable is key to good health; leading to increased energy, weight loss and better overall well-being – including having a positive impact on your general mood and also your quality of sleep.

Use small amounts of natural sweeteners (see table opposite), which are rich in vitamins and minerals, and let them enhance the natural flavour of the food, not overpower it. Balance sweet treats with protein, fats and fibre for better blood-sugar balance. Beware of snacking freely on dried fruit, as it is a concentrated source of sugars, and be sure that it is dried naturally and not treated with sulphur dioxide.

+   Stevia and xylitol are two sweeteners that people with diabetes or blood-sugar problems find useful because they do not have a direct impact on blood-sugar levels. They are helpful for anyone trying to cut down on the amount of sugar they use. Just be sure to check the labels for pure forms and don't be fooled into over-sweetening foods with these 'safe' sweeteners. Your brain still registers a 'sweet' sensation when you consume them so they are no substitute for weaning yourself off sweeter-tasting foods in the long run.

SWEETENERS

USE SPARINGLY	AVOID
Honey (raw/unpasteurised, unrefined)	Agave (very high in fructose and often highly refined)
Maple syrup (pure, Grade B for flavour)	High-fructose corn syrup (sometimes called glucose-fructose syrup and used in sweetened soft drinks and juices, processed biscuits and breakfast cereals)
Dried fruit (raisins, goji berries, figs, dates, apricots, etc. – sulphur dioxide-free)	Sugar (white or brown)
Fresh fruit (bananas, apples, peaches, pears, grapes, melons, berries, etc.)	Aspartame (and other synthetic sweeteners)

8 DRINK TO THINK

Cut caffeine, fizz and fruit juice. Drink water to help flush toxins, curb cravings and stay alert.

Without realising it many of us may be mildly dehydrated, which can lead to feelings of fatigue and loss of alertness, something that's worth bearing in mind before you reach for anything other than water. If you feel hungry between meals, check that you are properly hydrated. Drinking something with a bitter or sour flavour, such as ginger, lemon or lime water, will also help to beat cravings.

If you rely on a glass of wine or two at night to wind down, consider dropping this habit for a week to see if it affects your sleep and, in turn, your mood and stress levels the next day. Keep your caffeine intake to a minimum particularly during the first half of the day as caffeine, as well as sugar, can overstimulate you and aggravate existing health problems.

Remember that decaffeinated coffee (unless water-decaffeinated) is chemically processed and still contains some caffeine.

During sleep your body goes through a process of cleansing and repair. First thing in the morning, wake up your system with a glass of water to hydrate your body and get your system moving. We like to drink warm water with a squeeze of lemon juice to help this process. Don't down drinks in one because this can shock the system, especially cold drinks – drink them at room temperature or warm and savour them. Remember the old saying 'chew your drink and drink your food'.

+ Filtered water. It makes sense to ensure that you're drinking, cooking and even washing food with the most purest water possible, so we recommend using the best water filter that you can afford.

9 THE REAL DEAL

Rediscover whole, unprocessed foods. Pure apple juice from a carton is not the same as eating an apple. Choose delicious flavours from nature, not laboratories.

Eating real wholefoods, with all their natural nutrients and fibre and minimal processing for maximum nourishment, makes sense. This is food that delivers, with every delicious and nutrient-rich bite. Use processes that enhance the nutrients in your food and aid digestion, such as soaking, sprouting, fermenting and cooking. These days food is often highly processed to a point where your body may struggle to recognise it as food. If you look at the back of the packet and barely recognize the ingredients, your body will respond in the same way. Foods labelled 'pure', 'natural', 'healthy' or 'whole' might not have had anything added but can still have had plenty taken away, so find out what your food is and what it isn't. Eating seasonally offers the best value and flavour, and adds variety to your meals.

10 KNOW YOUR ONIONS

Where does your food come from? How was it grown? Choose naturally grown and reared food that has no artificial additives and hasn't been genetically modified.

How your food is grown is important both for you and the environment. Choose food produced by traditional rather than intensive farming methods, and use your spending power to champion local food that has been organically grown or humanely reared. Make it your business to know the provenance of your food so that you can avoid, where possible, putting toxins, chemicals, artificial additives or GMO ingredients into your body. Choose home-grown or naturally farmed foods, including organic and biodynamic-certified produce, or those from a sustainable wild source – especially for meat, fish and dairy (see also page 340).

11 PREPARE, CHEW AND COMBINE

Bump up your digestion to maximum efficiency and enjoy what you eat.

You are what you can digest – not simply what you eat – so as well as maintaining a fit and healthy gut and choosing real foods, we must properly prepare ingredients to get the best from them. Follow these three key steps for optimum digestion:

+ **PREPARE.** We soak, or 'activate', our nuts, seeds, pulses and pseudocereals to release nutrients and make them easier to digest (see also page 341 for more details). When you're cold, be sure to cook your foods and add warming spices. Enjoy refreshing salads and cooling yoghurt when you're feeling hot, and make easy-to-digest soups when you're feeling under the weather.

+ **CHEW.** Chew before you poo, which not many people do, boo hoo. Yes, we did just write that, because it is so important! Seeing and smelling your food is where digestion begins. Once it reaches your mouth, the enzyme amylase – present in human saliva – starts the process of breaking down food. Therefore chewing well and savouring each mouthful before swallowing is a crucial stage in digestion. Remember that there are no teeth in your tummy!

+ **COMBINE.** Since different foods are digested at different rates, we base our recipes on the simplest form of food combining – that is, avoiding substantial amounts of protein and starch (such as chicken and quinoa) in the same meal. This optimises digestion to get the most out of the nutrients, which leads to more energy and increased overall well-being. We also like it because it makes more room for green, leafy vegetables on the plate. Don't worry too much about this yourself, as all of the recipes in this book already fit the bill and include serving suggestions to go with each dish, so we've done the work for you!

12 BE MINDFUL

We advocate mindful eating – being conscious of what you are eating and how you are eating it.

Think about what you are eating – why you've chosen to eat it, as well as where it comes from (see left) –

and take your time to eat and truly appreciate your food. Your meal shouldn't play second fiddle to working, reading, writing or watching TV. Even if your food choice hasn't been ideal, stuffing it down quickly and pretending it didn't exist will only make things worse, not just for your digestive system but also your conscience. By connecting with your food, you'll be better placed to ask yourself what it is or isn't doing for you.

Eating is emotional. What food does to your state of mind is just as important as what it contributes to your physical health, so it's crucial to avoid the cycle of deprivation and guilt. Maybe you don't need to be eating banana bread and chocolate cake, but if you want to, you shouldn't feel bad about it. We always enjoy what we choose to eat and eating well is not about being perfect. If we see some gorgeous hand-made croissants and fancy eating one, we'll buy it and enjoy every mouthful. No guilt.

Knowledge is power, so in learning more about our food, going back to basics and getting into the groove with what suits, you can get back into a state of mind where you can say: 'I love my food and my food loves me!'

13 STRESS LESS

Reduce internal, external and environmental stress to enhance your sense of well-being.

Plan ahead so that you keep well fed; try to reduce toxic chemical products in your home and work environment, and value the importance of sleep. Make early nights a priority and daily downtime non-negotiable and you will soon reap the benefits. Try to reduce stimulants – keep coffee, sugar and alcohol to a minimum, try a cup of green tea in the morning or a couple of squares of dark chocolate as a pick-me-up instead.

Reducing both internal and external stresses, from what you put into your body to your worries and fears in life, will have a positive effect on both your mind and body and hence affect your food choices and how you cope with life in general. See our lifestyle section (pages 344–5) for tips and tricks for a new way of living and creating new 'good for you' habits.

14 TUNE IN

Your body needs you. We are all individuals, so get to know yourself better, understand what makes you thrive and be the best version of you.

Our aim is to help you navigate through the confusion and teach you to approach health and wellness in a more intuitive way. It's important to stress that there is no 'one size fits all' with nutrition. Eating well for you personally is key; your mood, surroundings and the weather can have just as much of an impact on your nutritional needs as your metabolism or general physical health. Be aware that your nutritional needs may change throughout your life too – such as during pregnancy, during times of intense activity or when you're unwell. This all might sound like hard work, but it's just based on tuning in to what your body responds to best. Turn to pages 344–5 in the lifestyle section for the good habits that work for us – plenty for you to try out and keep if they suit you or discard if they don't.

15 THE 'BETTER THAN' RULE

The one to remember: don't strive to be perfect – life happens. Do the best you can at the time.

Adopting a few healthy habits and making practical food swaps is better than not making any changes at all. Preparation is key, but of course we can't predict the future or control our circumstances; so when you're out and about, if hunger strikes and you don't have any good food to hand, go for the next best thing. For example, if you're stuck in an airport, with only high-street foods available, just look for the healthiest option on offer. It might not always be the most fun or the most appealing but it will be more sustaining. If options are very limited and you can only go for the 'unhealthy' choice, however, don't beat yourself up about it; enjoy it for what it is. Remember also that when you start to eat healthily, your taste buds will adapt, your cravings will diminish and you will *want* to choose the better option every time.

GOOD + SIMPLE COOKING TIPS

SPOON MEASURES. All spoon measures are level unless otherwise stated. (See also page 343.)

OVEN TEMPERATURES. All the recipes were tested in a fan-assisted oven. If using a conventional oven, set the temperature 20°C higher than stated in the recipes. Oven temperatures do vary, so practice makes perfect!

BUTTER is unsalted unless otherwise stated.

DRIPPING/ANIMAL FAT is a frugal alternative for cooking in place of butter, coconut oil and ghee. Save it from your roasting tray or skim off the top of cold broth and store in an airtight container.

EGGS ARE MEDIUM-SIZED. For baking, remember to use them at room temperature. Guidelines recommend that pregnant women, the elderly, babies and toddlers, as well as people who are unwell, should avoid recipes that contain raw or partially cooked eggs.

LEMON/LIME JUICE AND APPLE CIDER VINEGAR (ACV) are interchangeable in many of the recipes although the ratio varies depending on the dish. Please see individual recipes for recommended amounts.

FRESH OR DRIED HERBS. If you don't have fresh herbs, simply replace with dried ones – about 1 teaspoon of dried herbs for 1 tablespoon of chopped fresh. Keep dried herbs in a sealed container to retain their flavour.

KEEP THE STALKS. Don't waste the stalks of fresh, tender-stemmed herbs like parsley, coriander and basil. Instead, finely chop with the leaves for sprinkling over dishes, blend into dressings and pestos or blitz into soups. Save mint stalks for brewing mint tea.

PAPRIKA AND CHILLIES. Where 'smoked paprika' is given in a recipe, either sweet or smoked can be used. Dried chilli flakes, chilli powder and cayenne

pepper are interchangeable and you can swap them for finely diced fresh red chilli, if you prefer.

ACTIVATING. We 'activate' or soak pseudocereals, and certain lentils, nuts and seeds, and dried beans, before eating or cooking them. If you don't soak them, you will need to allow more liquid in a recipe and a longer cooking time. (See page 341 for more information.)

SPIRALIZING OR PEELING. If you don't have a spiralizer, you can use a julienne peeler or standard vegetable peeler instead where indicated in a recipe.

GLASS JARS. Store pestos/dips/sauces/dressings in a sterilised glass jar with a lid. For sauces or dressings made with fresh ingredients (such as pestos), cover with a layer of extra-virgin olive oil (EVOO) and store in the fridge.

STERILISING GLASS JARS. To sterilise your glass jar and lid, add boiling water and leave for 10 minutes then drain, or put through a dishwasher cycle.

REHEATING. We avoid microwaves and simply reheat food in a pan with a lid (ideal for soups and stews). Bring to the boil, then reduce to a simmer to heat through thoroughly without impairing the flavour. Alternatively, heat through in the oven in an ovenproof dish with a lid. Add a splash of water to whatever you are reheating as it will lose moisture as it heats.

BATCH COOKING. We like to batch cook and many of our recipes can be easily doubled in quantity, allowing you to store half in the freezer for later use.

FREEZING. Allow food to cool down before placing in the fridge or freezer, and get into the habit of labelling food with the date you made it so your freezer is nicely organised and you're more likely to use what you've made. Glass jars can also be used to store frozen foods, but they should not be used to store liquids. If you use glass jars, be sure to choose the wide-mouth, dual-purpose jars that are for freezing and bottling and leave 2.5cm of unfilled space for expansion.

STORING COOKED FOOD. We avoid storing food and drink in plastic wherever possible and use glass, ceramic or stainless steel jars instead. For any non-liquid foods, such as cakes, crackers, biscuits or burgers, you can line plastic containers with good-quality baking parchment (page 342).

STORING FRESH FOOD IN THE FRIDGE.
Keep raw meat, fish and eggs away from other foods.

WASHING FRESH PRODUCE. For advice on washing fruit and vegetables before eating, see page 340.

WAX REMOVAL. To remove the wax from a non-organic citrus fruit, place in a colander and pour over freshly boiled water. Scrub with a brush, then rinse under cool water and dry.

GINGER. If you don't like the texture of fresh ginger, try using a microplane for finer slices or wrap the chopped ginger in muslin or a clean tea towel and squeeze out the juice, then discard the pulp.

NOTES FOR VEGANS, VEGETARIANS AND THOSE WITH ALLERGIES

Our recipes can be easily tailored to suit your dietary needs with simple substitutions. Wherever possible, we suggest alternatives within the recipe. The following apply throughout the book:

+ Coconut oil. In all recipes, whether sweet or savoury, coconut oil can be used to replace animal fats.

+ Coconut yoghurt can be used in place of cow's milk yoghurt.

+ Maple syrup can be interchanged for raw honey in every recipe.

Bone broth can be replaced by a good-quality vegetable stock in all recipes. In certain cases, where the bone broth or vegetable stock is not essential to the recipe for its flavour, water can be used instead – this is indicated in the recipe. Bear in mind that neither vegetable stock nor water will have the same nutritional value as a quality bone broth.

Eggs can, in some recipes, be substituted with a gel made from ground flaxseed and water known as a 'flaxseed egg'. It's not an exact 1:1 substitution in every recipe since it won't bind and stiffen during baking quite like an egg does, but it works where indicated in the book. Where a dish works equally well without using eggs (such as for Chestnut Pancakes – page 30), this is indicated in the recipe.

GETTING STARTED

Hippocrates said, 'Let food be thy medicine and medicine be thy food', and this rings true for us. We like our food – rather than the pharmaceuticals – to do the talking. Let's save them for emergencies instead! Eating is one of life's greatest pleasures, so what can be better than to enjoy eating our way to good health and a good life?

STARTER FOR TEN

Here are ten recipes to get you started
– a combination of our clients' favourites
and ones we rustle up all the time.

HUEVOS
RANCHEROS
WITH
GUACAMOLE
(PAGE 50)

SANDWICH
CLASSICS 3 WAYS
(PAGES 138–140)

GREEN
GODDESS
NOODLE SALAD
(PAGE 250)

BLUEBERRY
MUFFINS
(PAGE 308)

SLOW-COOKED
'NO FRY'
CHICKEN CURRY
(PAGE 197)

SUPER-CHARGED
STORE
CUPBOARD
SPINACH SOUP
(PAGE 83)

COURGETTE
AND CANNELLINI
BEAN LASAGNE
(PAGE 226)

SPICY MISO
SALMON WITH
BROCCOLI RICE
(PAGE 170)

COURGETTI WITH
QUICK CHICKPEA
TOMATO SAUCE
(PAGE 229)

BUTTERNUT AND
ALMOND BUTTER
PORRIDGE
(PAGE 34)

THE ONE-WEEK REBOOT

We started H+H as private chefs and all our clients begin with 'Soup Service', our one- or two-week reboot plan. The following is a simplified version of the reboot that you can make at home. Here we go back to basics using yummy, easy-to-make and easy-to-digest dishes, including hearty bone broth and vegetable-packed soups, hot porridges, smoothies and eggs for breakfast, and sweet and savoury snacks. During the reboot, you will enjoy only foods that will nourish your body, retune your taste buds and beat cravings. You'll feel more energised and brain fog will be a thing of the past.

Get yourself a 500ml stainless-steel vacuum flask for soups and a canteen for juices and smoothies. If you can, make some time to relax and get a bit of pampering in with your taste bud reboot. Turn to pages 344–345 for our ultimate reset guide, which includes info on salt baths, bedtime routines and how to make the most of your reboot. Taking time out to look after yourself will help counteract the effects of a busy lifestyle, allowing you to get back to functioning optimally. Don't be put off by the Sunday Cook-Off – kitchen time spent well will leave you more time to relax for the rest of the week.

Come back to the reboot any time you're feeling less than your best, in need of some nourishing support, a health boost or simply a break from the temptations around. Our clients regularly return to the reboot plan as they find the recipes restorative, comforting, delicious and filling.

You might find, like we do, that soups really suit you for breakfast. Batch cooking them once or twice a week, and making use of the freezer, frees up time in the evenings.

THE REBOOT PLAN

The following plan will feed **two people** for **seven days**, starting on Sunday. If you're doing a solo reboot, you could halve the quantities in the recipes or follow the recipes, which will make double what you need for the reboot week, and freeze the extras to use at a later date (we recommend the latter to get the most out of your time in the kitchen now).

ON SATURDAY: make sure that you've got all the ingredients you need by the end of today. See the next page for the full shopping list.

This shopping list is designed for two people cooking from scratch and includes all the ingredients you need to cook the reboot recipes, organised into groups as you would find them in the shops or at the market. You might already have many of the ingredients in this list ready to go. If so, use up what you have first then top up later in the week rather than doing one big shop, if you prefer.

THE SUNDAY COOK-OFF: the reboot is easy if you embrace the Sunday Cook-Off as follows (page 334).

After breakfast on Sunday (see table on page 23 and refrigerate your leftovers for Monday), make 1 quantity of Bone Broth (you'll need about 4 litres of broth so top with water if you're running a little low or don't get enough from your bones), prepare the quinoa flakes for Quinoa Kettle Porridge and make Tahini Applejacks.

After dinner on Sunday, whiz up Cream of Tomato Soup and Superbly Simple Broccoli Soup and all three toppings. Store everything in the fridge ready for the week.

IN THE WEEK: All you need to do now is cook up Minestrone 2 Ways on Monday evening, prepare Caroby Fruit and Nut Balls on Tuesday evening and make a double batch of Super-charged Store Cupboard Spinach Soup on Thursday evening. Breakfast can be made in minutes and all your snacks are ready to go.

Bone Broth is key to this reboot. Vegetarians, remember to add other sources of protein and fats to suit you (see page 17).

SHOPPING LIST

Fresh fruit/veg

1 small butternut
   squash (500g)
5 lemons
10 onions
4 bulbs garlic
4 limes
8 avocados
1 bag fresh spinach
5 large carrots
2 leeks
2 bunches celery
4 medium
   courgettes
4 heads broccoli
1 medium white
   /green cabbage
1 turnip/swede/
   celeriac
2 bunches
   spring onions
1 bag kale/cavolo
   nero (about 200g)
1 punnet
   blueberries
   (or 1 small bag
   of frozen
   blueberries)
5 apples
1 banana

Frozen veg

1 x 1kg bag frozen
   spinach
1 small bag
   frozen peas
   /broad beans

Fresh herbs/spices

1 large piece
   ginger
1 large bunch
   coriander
1 small bunch mint
1 small bunch
   rosemary
   (or use dried
   rosemary)
1 large bunch
   parsley
1 small bunch basil
1 small bunch
   thyme (or use
   dried thyme)
1 red chilli

Dairy/meat

1 small pot coconut
   yoghurt/full-fat
   probiotic yoghurt
1 small block
   mature
   Cheddar/feta
1 small block
   Parmesan
12 medium eggs
3kg beef/lamb
   bones/chicken
   carcass

Dried herbs/spices

1 pack bay leaves
1 jar each of: ground
   cinnamon;
   ground turmeric;
   cumin seeds;
   ground cumin;
   hot smoked
   paprika;
   chilli powder
   /cayenne pepper
sea salt
black pepper
   /peppercorns
1 bottle vanilla
   extract

Nuts/seeds
/dried fruit

ground almonds
   (100g)
whole almonds
   (100g)
unsalted
   whole peanuts
   /pecans (100g)
raisins/sultanas
   /dried
   cranberries
   (about 50g)
dried goji berries
   /mulberries
   (about 50g)
black sesame seeds
   (about 20g)
white sesame seeds
   (about 20g)

shelled hemp
   seeds (50g)
pumpkin seeds
   (40g)
sunflower seeds
   (100g)
chia seeds (50g)
flaxseeds (50g)
dessicated coconut
   (about 100g)

Bottles/jars
/packets/tins

350g coconut oil
   /butter/ghee
1 bottle each of
   maple syrup;
   ACV; tamari;
   EVOO; balsamic
   vinegar
1 jar almond
   butter
carob powder
   (about 60g)
quinoa flakes
   (120g)
1 jar raw honey
1 tube tomato
   puree
2 x 400g tins
   tomatoes
3 x 400g tins
   cannellini/
   butter beans
1 x 400g tin borlotti
   beans/chickpeas

3 x 400ml tins
   coconut milk
dried red lentils
   (500g)
1 jar light tahini
quality miso paste
   (1 tablespoon)
coconut flour
   (1 tablespoon)
buckwheat/soba
   noodles (85g)

To help you move on from the reboot,
we have also included two one-week
menu plans with shopping lists at the
back of the book (pages 334–337).

022   THE ONE-WEEK REBOOT

	BREAKFAST	11AM SNACK	LUNCH	4PM SNACK	DINNER
SUNDAY	Butternut and Almond Porridge (page 34)	Tahini Applejacks (1 each, page 124)	Big Green Frittata (page 48)	Avocado Boats with Olive Oil and Balsamic Vinegar (page 114)	Quick Coconut Dahl (page 78)
MONDAY	Leftover Butternut and Almond Porridge	Apple slices with nut butter	Cream of Tomato Soup (page 85)	Leftover Big Green Frittata (½ slice per person)	Minestrone (summer or winter, page 67)
TUESDAY	Quinoa Kettle Porridge (page 29)	Leftover Big Green Frittata (½ slice per person)	Superbly Simple Broccoli Soup 3 Ways (page 64)	Leftover Tahini Applejacks (1 each)	Leftover Quick Coconut Dahl
WEDNESDAY	Leftover Cream of Tomato Soup	Caroby Fruit and Nut Balls (page 305)	Leftover Superbly Simple Broccoli Soup 3 Ways	Avocado Boats with Lemon and Honey Drizzle (page 114)	Leftover Minestrone (summer or winter)
THURSDAY	Quinoa Kettle Porridge (page 29)	Leftover Tahini Applejacks (1 each)	Leftover Superbly Simple Broccoli Soup 3 Ways	Caroby Fruit and Nut Balls (page 305)	Super-charged Store Cupboard Spinach Soup (make 2 quantities) (page 83)
FRIDAY	Hemsley Green Machine Smoothie (make 2 quantities) (page 323)	Leftover Caroby Fruit and Nut Balls	Leftover Super-charged Store Cupboard Spinach Soup	Leftover Hemsley Green Machine Smoothie	Leftover Quick Coconut Dahl
SATURDAY	Sunshine Eggs with Turmeric and Lime (page 55)	Avocado Boats with Olive Oil and Balsamic Vinegar	Leftover Superbly Simple Broccoli Soup 3 Ways	Leftover Tahini Applejacks (1 each)	Leftover Super-charged Store Cupboard Spinach Soup

BREAKFAST

**FOR MORE BREAKFAST
IDEAS TRY:**

APPLE AND BACON MUFFINS
118

BERRY BRAIN BOOSTER
325

BLUEBERRY MUFFINS
308

BONE BROTH
63

CAROBY FRUIT AND NUT BALLS
305

EASY DROP EGG SOUP
86

GINGER ZINGER SMOOTHIE
324

HEMSLEY GREEN MACHINE
323

PLUM CLAFOUTIS
296

QUICK COCONUT DAHL
WITH ZINGY SLAW
78

TAHINI APPLEJACKS
124

SQUASH AND GINGER SOUP
WITH LEMONY CORIANDER OIL
82

We've heard it all before – breakfast is the most important meal of the day. But so often we run our bodies on empty. Processed cereals, refined breads laden with sugary jam, and convenience foods such as pastries and cereal bars (all of which lack essential vitamins and minerals or are made with synthetic versions of them) have become the everyday fare. It's time to move away from the sugar and caffeine rollercoasters and fuel your body with something to help it on its way, not something that will ultimately slow it down.

Breakfast doesn't have to be sweet – we say anything goes! While we love Butternut and Almond Butter Porridge (page 34), Chestnut Pancakes (page 30) or Quinoa Courgette Toast (page 32) topped with butter and our chocolate BBtella Spread (page 293), there's not a recipe in this book that we wouldn't also enjoy for breakfast, depending on our mood and the weather – this includes soups, stews and even curries! If something is delicious, nourishing and energising, we'll have it any time of day. Why not try a homemade smoothie, for instance, like the Hemsley Green Machine (page 323)? These blended beverages allow you to concoct a bespoke nutritional hit, which you can drink on the go. With the right ingredients, a smoothie will keep you sustained until lunchtime.

We're really into elevenses: eating a mid-morning snack made from real foods helps steer you safely towards lunch without fear of the vending machine getting in the way. We have a whole chapter dedicated to sides and snacks (pages 88–131), but even quicker and easier is the 'two-step' breakfast. The idea is to enjoy part of your breakfast first thing and then have the rest later at 11am(-ish) when you find yourself bored, cranky or hungry and reaching for the biscuit tin. It also stops you bolting a full meal as you rush out the door, and if you work out in the morning, then elevenses becomes your post-gym recovery snack. Slices of the Big Green Frittata (page 48) are easily transported. Try making an extra-large smoothie or soup, such as the Berry Brain Booster (page 325) or the Squash and Ginger Soup with Lemony Coriander Oil (page 82), which you can split, or munch on some fruit and nuts. A plate of eggs and greens, for instance, followed by one of our Caroby Fruit and Nut Balls (page 305) a few hours later, will keep you satisfied and your blood-sugar levels stable.

A lazy weekend brunch is one of our favourite ways to catch up with friends. We make lots of different things for brunch but, as always, ease and enjoyment are the name of the game, so it's served family-style – usually one big pan of something, with eggs.

Make a good breakfast your priority, so that however your day pans out, you'll have started well and can feel good about it.

TIPS AND TRICKS

DRINK FIRST First things first – have a drink of water. Your body has been resting and restoring itself all night, so the best thing you can do is hydrate it with room-temperature, filtered water. Make sure you take a glass of water to bed with you ready for when you wake up.

PRIORITISE BREAKFAST Don't skip it! A nourishing breakfast will fuel you through to dinner and help you make better food choices for the rest of the day. If you've got an early start, prepare something the night before.

MAKE TIME Don't gulp down food in a hurry. This might be your one and only chance to sit still and enjoy a meal all day, so chew it well and make it count.

BALANCE IT OUT Make your breakfast go further by ensuring it's not a big old sugar hit that will have your tummy rumbling by 10am. A balance of fat, protein and carbohydrates is key for keeping you satisfied and sustained until lunch. Think coconut oil and almonds in your smoothie (page 325), avocado on your Quinoa Courgette Toast (page 32), and keeping the yolk in your eggs. We always include the egg yolks in our cooking as they are a great source of saturated fat and incredibly nutritious.

ANYTHING GOES Rethink your breakfast. There's no shame in eating last night's leftovers for breakfast when it's a delicious vegetable stew, bone broth or frittata. Got any homemade dip left over? Spread it on a slice of Quinoa Courgette Toast (page 32) or a Flaxseed Bun (page 136) and you've got yourself a simple, tasty brekkie.

SPLIT IT We'll often drink half of our breakfast smoothie at home and save the rest to beat the mid-morning munchies. Pour half into a stainless-steel flask or glass jar to go, and enjoy slowly later.

Make up a batch of our protein-rich quinoa porridge mix for an instant wholefood breakfast. Perfect for a meal on the go – we even take it on flights! Quinoa flakes are key to this speedy porridge mix. We toast the flakes first to enhance their flavour, which also means that we don't have to cook the porridge on the hob in the usual way. Into the mix goes coconut oil, ground almonds, desiccated coconut, dried berries, cinnamon, flaxseeds and a little maple syrup to sweeten for a delicious crumble that's good as it is. Keep in a glass jar and take to work or on your travels, add hot water, stir and voilà! As an alternative to the almonds, try more desiccated coconut or sesame seeds. It also makes a delicious dessert, served with coconut yoghurt or probiotic yoghurt.

QUINOA KETTLE PORRIDGE

MAKES 4–5 SERVINGS

120g quinoa flakes
8 tablespoons (about 120g) coconut oil
100g ground almonds
50g dried goji berries, raisins or other dried berries (such as mulberries)
50g desiccated coconut
2 tablespoons ground cinnamon or 6 tablespoons lucuma powder
3 heaped tablespoons chia seeds
3 heaped tablespoons flaxseeds (whole or ground)

2–4 tablespoons maple syrup (to taste – optional)

TO SERVE
About 125ml boiling water (per serving)
1 teaspoon raw honey (per serving – optional)

TOPPING IDEAS
Grated apple, chopped banana or fresh/frozen berries
A dollop of coconut yoghurt or full-fat probiotic yoghurt
Toasted nuts or seeds

1   Preheat the oven to fan 180°C/Gas mark 6 and line a baking tray with baking parchment.

2   Spread the quinoa flakes on the prepared baking tray in a layer no more than 5mm thick and bake for 10 minutes.

3   Transfer to a bowl with the coconut oil – the oil will melt in the heat. Add the rest of the ingredients, with the maple syrup (if using), and mix together well. Allow to cool completely, then store in a glass jar somewhere cool (or in the fridge) for up to a month.

4   When you're ready to serve, measure half a mugful (about 7 heaped dessertspoons) into a mug or bowl. Pour over half a mugful (about 125ml) of boiling water, cover with a plate and leave to soak for a few minutes.

5   If you haven't added any maple syrup to the mix, stir in some raw honey to taste. Add any preferred toppings and enjoy!

A nutritious batter made from ground chestnuts, eggs, water – and that's it. Known as *necci* in Tuscany, these easy-cook pancakes are often filled with thick and creamy ricotta. As a refreshing alternative, we like vanilla-infused yoghurt, cinnamon-coated apple spirals and toasted almonds. This is just one of three delicious options, two sweet and one savoury, that we've included below for you to try. Once you've made these, why not team the pancakes with anything else you might fancy – from cheese, chutney and rocket to a simple lemon and honey combo? The possibilities are endless!

CHESTNUT PANCAKES 3 WAYS

MAKES ABOUT 10 PANCAKES

100g chestnut flour
3 eggs
250ml water
1 tablespoon butter,
    ghee or coconut
    oil, melted

1   Place the chestnut flour in a large bowl and make a well in the middle. Beat in the eggs, one at a time, and then gradually add the water, continuously whisking until you have a smooth batter. Leave to rest for 15 minutes.

2   Place a frying pan on a medium heat and brush with the melted butter, ghee or coconut oil. Whisk the batter again before ladling 3–4 tablespoons into the pan. Tilt the pan to coat the bottom thinly but evenly in the batter.

3   Cook for a minute or so until the pancake lifts easily from the pan and is golden brown underneath. Turn (or flip!) the pancake to cook the other side – don't overcook, keep it chewy rather than crisp. Repeat with the remaining batter, stacking pancakes on top of each other to keep them warm.

4   Add your choice of filling (see opposite) to each pancake and fold in half, or roll up, to serve.

TIP

+   For vegan/egg-free pancakes, leave out the eggs and double the quantity of chestnut flour. This will make a thicker batter that holds without eggs. To make larger chestnut wraps, double the amount of batter you ladle into the pan.

+ APPLE SPIRALS OR SLICES AND YOGHURT

Fill each pancake with a dollop of full-fat probiotic yoghurt (or coconut yoghurt), sweetened with raw honey and vanilla extract to taste, and a portion of apple spirals or slices with toasted almonds (page 304) on top. Fold each pancake in half, or roll up, and drizzle over more honey to finish.

+ BBTELLA, BANANA AND COCONUT YOGHURT

Fill each pancake with chopped banana and a spoonful of BBtella Spread (page 293) and serve with a dollop of coconut yoghurt.

+ CUCUMBER, AVOCADO AND CHICKPEA SALAD

Add another 100g chestnut flour to the pancake mix and fill each pancake with a handful of Cucumber, Avocado and Chickpea Salad (page 156), then roll up and serve as a savoury wrap.

Golden and crunchy at the edges, this bread is really filling with protein-packed quinoa and a whole courgette in the mix. This deliciously nutty bake makes really good toast. We love it for breakfast simply topped with butter or with one of our favourite toppings (see opposite). A great wholefood recipe, suitable for vegans and anyone wanting to avoid eggs, it's easy to make in a food processor too: just remember to soak the quinoa overnight and the chia and courgette while you're about it. The bread can be stored, well wrapped and ready-sliced, in the fridge for up to a week or frozen until needed. Just take a slice whenever you need one.

QUINOA COURGETTE TOAST 3 WAYS

MAKES 1 LOAF (ABOUT 10 SLICES)

300g quinoa
300g courgette
 (about 1 medium)
60g chia seeds
1 teaspoon caraway
 or fennel seeds
 (optional)
½ teaspoon
 bicarbonate
 of soda
½ teaspoon sea salt
60g butter or
 coconut oil,
 melted, plus
 extra to serve
2 tablespoons apple
 cider vinegar or
 lemon juice

1 Place the quinoa in a bowl, cover with double the volume of water and leave to soak overnight or for a minimum of 8 hours. Grate the courgette into a separate bowl and add the chia seeds. Stir together well, cover and leave to stand in the fridge for a few hours or overnight.

2 When you're ready to cook, preheat the oven to fan 160°C/Gas mark 4 and line a 12cm x 23cm (900g) loaf tin with baking parchment.

3 Rinse and drain the soaked quinoa and place in a food processor with the soaked courgette and chia seeds and all the remaining ingredients. Blend until really well combined – at least 2 minutes – then pour into the prepared tin and bake for 1½ hours or more until crunchy and golden on top and firm to the touch.

4 Remove from the oven and leave to cool in the tin for 30 minutes, then take out of the tin and leave to cool completely on a wire rack.

5 Slice into 1cm-thick slices and toast under the grill or in a toaster until crunchy and golden at the edges, spread with butter and serve in one of the following ways (see opposite).

+ **HONEY CINNAMON SPREAD**

Spread with butter then raw honey
and sprinkle with ground cinnamon
and bee pollen if desired.

+ **BBTELLA**

Top with butter and a thick layer
of BBtella Spread (page 293).

+ **AVO TOAST**

Slice or roughly mash the flesh
of a ripe avocado and use to top the
toast. Drizzle with extra-virgin olive
oil, season with sea salt and black
pepper and a sprinkle of cayenne
pepper if desired.

This quick and easy porridge makes a warming wholefood breakfast that's completely satisfying whatever the time of year, not to mention a really good stop-gap snack, according to our recipe-testing friends. Just add your favourite fruits, nuts or seeds. We include a few tablespoons of almond butter for a delicious nutty flavour, and a spoonful of butter or coconut oil for extra protein and fat, making the porridge rich and creamy. Play around with the flavours, adding vanilla extract or lemon juice, a burst of blueberries for a summer option, or grated apple in the winter months. Try ground cardamom or nutmeg in place of the cinnamon, or grate in some fresh ginger for a spice hit. You can also save leftovers for your supper later in the day – add to soups or serve as a mash on the side.

BUTTERNUT AND ALMOND BUTTER PORRIDGE

SERVES 4

500g cooked
    butternut squash
    (about 1 small
    squash – see tip
    for cooking)
125ml water
    (optional)
2–3 tablespoons
    almond butter
1½ teaspoons
    ground cinnamon,
    plus extra for
    sprinkling
A small pinch
    of sea salt
1–2 teaspoons
    vanilla extract
    or lemon juice
    (optional)
1–2 tablespoons
    butter or coconut
    oil, to serve

TOPPING IDEAS

1 handful of
    blueberries
Grated apple or
    apple spirals
    (page 304)
A dollop of coconut
    yoghurt or full-
    fat probiotic
    yoghurt

1   Place the cooked butternut squash in a small saucepan, turn the heat to medium and add the water if needed (see tip). Stir the squash, mashing it with a wooden spoon, until fully heated through.

2   Add the almond butter, cinnamon, salt and vanilla extract or lemon juice (if using) and stir until smooth.

3   Serve with a curl of butter or coconut oil per bowl, a sprinkle of cinnamon and any desired toppings.

TIP

+   To cook squash, roast it whole at fan 180°C/Gas mark 6 for 30–40 minutes until a knife slides in easily, then scoop out the flesh (discarding the seeds). Alternatively, steam peeled, deseeded and cubed squash for about 20 minutes until soft. (If steaming the squash, you'll need to add less water when making the porridge.)

Wholefood muffins for breakfast – delicious sliced in half and served with butter, grated cheese and jam, all washed down with a big pot of tea. We've made these using quinoa, ground flaxseeds, plenty of cinnamon and juicy raisins to sweeten. Unlike many non-grain, gluten-free baking recipes, this one is also nut-free. Make sure you remember to soak the quinoa overnight – not only does this make the whole seeds easier to digest and more nutritious, it also renders them the perfect consistency for baking. Even if you're not cooking for so many people, be sure to make the full batch and freeze leftovers for rainy-day breakfasts.

CINNAMON, RAISIN AND QUINOA BREAKFAST MUFFINS

MAKES 12 MUFFINS

300g quinoa
2 large or 3 medium bananas (190g peeled)
3 eggs, lightly beaten
60g butter, softened, or coconut oil, plus extra to serve
1 teaspoon bicarbonate of soda
¾ teaspoon sea salt
2 tablespoons lemon juice or apple cider vinegar
1 tablespoon vanilla extract
2½ tablespoons ground cinnamon
4 tablespoons maple syrup
8 tablespoons ground flaxseeds
160g raisins

TO SERVE
Sliced full-fat cheese (such as mild/medium Cheddar or Stilton)
Sugar-free jam (preferably homemade) or try our Spiced Winter Apple Chutney (page 281)

1 Place the quinoa in a bowl with double the volume of water and leave to soak overnight or for a minimum of 8 hours. After soaking, drain the quinoa, rinse well and drain again.

2 When you're ready to cook, preheat the oven to fan 180°C/Gas mark 6 and line a 12-hole muffin tin with baking parchment cases.

3 Peel and roughly chop the bananas and add to a food processor with the soaked quinoa and all the other ingredients except the raisins, then blend until smooth. Remove the processor blade and stir in the raisins by hand. Alternatively, mash the bananas and add to a bowl with the other ingredients. Mix by hand before stirring in the raisins.

4 Divide the batter between the paper cases, then bake for 30–35 minutes until firm to the touch and slightly crunchy on top. Remove from the oven and leave to cool for a few minutes, transferring to a wire rack when they are just cool enough to handle.

5 Serve warm or at room temperature, spread with butter and alongside some slices of cheese and jam or chutney. The muffins will keep in a sealed container in the fridge for up to a week.

TIP

+ For a vegan/egg-free version,
  substitute four 'flaxseed eggs' (see
  page 17) for the eggs. Cook for 35–40
  minutes at fan 180°C/Gas mark 6 and
  allow to cool completely before eating.

Chia puddings are a fantastic invention. Not only is chia packed with nutrients, but, left to soak, these little seeds thicken up, making them ideal for this dish – just remember to chew well to get the most from them. If you have a high-powered blender, you can whizz the puddings smooth before adding the toppings to make them super-creamy; a standard food processor won't be able to break down the tiny seeds. Try these puddings as a delicious start to the day when you fancy something slightly sweet and cooling for breakfast. Dollop on your favourite wholefood yoghurt so they're even more filling, and sprinkle with fresh berries or seeds to make them pretty enough to serve to guests.

CHIA PUDDINGS 2 WAYS

SERVES 2

2 large ripe bananas
3 tablespoons
    extra-virgin
    olive oil
3 tablespoons
    chia seeds
A pinch of sea salt
50g pumpkin seeds

TOPPING IDEAS
Ground cinnamon
Maca powder
Dried goji berries
Coconut yoghurt
    or full-fat
    probiotic yoghurt
Extra banana slices

BANANA, OLIVE OIL AND PUMPKIN SEED CHIA PUDDING

1 Peel the bananas and, using a fork, mash them until smooth with the EVOO, chia seeds and salt, or blend in a food processor or high-powered blender. Divide between two bowls or glasses and leave in the fridge overnight or for a few hours, if you can, to allow the puddings to thicken.

2 Toast the pumpkin seeds in a dry pan over a medium heat for 2–3 minutes and then sprinkle over to serve, along with your choice of toppings.

SERVES 4

1 x 400ml tin
    of full-fat
    coconut milk
250g fresh or
    frozen berries
6 tablespoons
    chia seeds
2 tablespoons
    vanilla extract
1½ tablespoons
    raw honey
A tiny pinch
    of sea salt

TOPPING IDEAS
Ground cinnamon
Maca powder
Coconut yoghurt
    or full-fat
    probiotic yoghurt
Berries (fresh,
    dried or frozen)
Toasted nuts
    or seeds
Coconut flakes

BERRY AND COCONUT CHIA PUDDING

1 Blend everything together in a food processor or high-powered blender, transfer to a bowl and leave overnight in the fridge to thicken.

2 Serve cold, or warmed through gently on the hob, with any desired toppings.

A guaranteed hunger-buster that can be easily doubled to serve a crowd – perfect for a weekend breakfast, brunch or hearty lunch. You could even throw in some eggs, sprinkle with grated Cheddar and get the kids involved in preparing this wholesome breakfast. Also delicious without the bacon – just add ¼ teaspoon more salt.

BEAN AND BACON HASH

SERVES 4

1–2 tablespoons
    butter or
    coconut oil
3–4 rashers of
    unsmoked
    bacon, chopped
1 large onion
    or leek, diced
¼ Savoy cabbage,
    leaves shredded
1 teaspoon
    ground cumin
2 teaspoons sweet
    smoked paprika
¼ teaspoon sea salt
¼ teaspoon white
    or black pepper

1 x 400g tin of
    cannellini or
    borlotti beans,
    drained and
    rinsed
100g fresh
    tomatoes, diced,
    or ½ x 400g tin
    of chopped
    tomatoes,
    drained

1 Melt ½ tablespoon of the butter or coconut oil in your largest frying pan and fry the bacon and onion or leek together over a medium heat for 3–4 minutes until the bacon is browned and the onion/leek softened.

2 Tip in the shredded cabbage and cook for a further 2–3 minutes until just tender. Remove everything from the pan and set to one side.

3 Melt the rest of the butter/coconut oil in the pan and briefly fry the spices and seasoning. Add the remaining ingredients and fry for a further 4–5 minutes, stirring continuously and roughly mashing the beans with the back of the spoon.

4 Fold in the cabbage and bacon mix and fry for another couple of minutes to heat through. Serve immediately.

Eggs provide an amazingly compact hit of protein – we love their versatility and how quick and easy they are to prepare. These three egg dishes make a great meal at any time of day – and you will pack in the greens! We also like to add a ripe avocado and a handful of watercress when serving. For perfect eggs, look to slightly underdo them, remembering that they continue cooking when they are off the heat. Make sure that you and your crew are ready to eat before you start cooking, to enjoy these dishes at their very best.

'GREEN EGGS' 3 WAYS

SERVES 2

150g spinach
    (preferably
    baby spinach)
1 garlic clove
4 eggs
1 handful of fresh
    herbs (such as
    basil or parsley)
    or 1 teaspoon
    dried mixed
    herbs, oregano,
    thyme or
    rosemary
½ small onion or
    2 spring onions,
    roughly chopped,
    or 1 handful of
    fresh chives
1 small handful
    of grated
    Parmesan or
    mature Cheddar
    (optional)

2 teaspoons
    coconut oil or
    ghee, for frying
Sea salt and
    black pepper

IRON-RICH SPINACH AND HERB OMELETTE

1 Place all the ingredients in a food processor, season with salt and pepper and blend on high until the spinach is broken down.

2 Add the coconut oil or ghee to a large frying pan over a medium heat. When the coconut oil/ghee is hot, pour in half your egg mixture. Use a spatula to pull the edges of the omelette in slightly from the sides so that more of the egg mixture has direct contact with the pan. When the mix is nearly cooked through, after 5 minutes, fold one side over and slip out of the pan onto a serving plate.

3 Repeat with the rest of the mixture to make the second omelette.

TIP

+ Stuff with sliced avocado, tomatoes and handfuls of watercress.

→ CONTINUED OVERLEAF

SERVES 2

2 teaspoons coconut
oil or ghee
½ small onion or
2 spring onions,
chopped
2 teaspoons diced
pickled green
jalapeños or
fresh red chilli
(to taste)
½ teaspoon
ground cumin or
smoked paprika
4 eggs

1 small handful
of crumbled feta
or grated cheese
(such as
Parmesan or
mature Cheddar)
1 large handful of
fresh coriander,
parsley, dill or
basil, leaves
and stalks finely
chopped
Sea salt and
black pepper

JALAPEÑO AND FETA SCRAMBLED EGGS

1   Melt the coconut oil or ghee in a medium frying pan over
a medium heat and fry the onion or spring onions with the
diced chillies and spice for 1 minute, then reduce the heat.

2   Crack the eggs straight into the pan, then lightly scramble
and cook over a low heat, stirring occasionally, for about
4 minutes until the eggs are thick and creamy and still
a little runny (they will keep cooking off the heat).

3   Season with salt and pepper to taste and sprinkle with
crumbled feta and chopped herbs to serve. (Remember
that feta is rich and salty, so you'll need less salt.)

SERVES 2

2 teaspoons coconut
oil or ghee
200g kale, stems
removed and
leaves finely
shredded
1 garlic clove, diced
A pinch of diced
fresh red chilli
4 eggs
1 handful of grated
mature Cheddar
or crumbled
goat's cheese
(optional)
Sea salt and
black pepper

GARLICKY SCRAMBLED EGGS WITH KALE

1   Melt the coconut oil or ghee in a medium frying pan over
a medium heat. Add the kale and cook for 3 minutes until
softened, adding a splash of water to stop it sticking to
the pan.

2   Add the garlic and chilli and cook for a further minute, then
lower the heat and push everything to one side of the pan.

3   Crack the eggs straight into the pan, then lightly scramble
and cook over a low heat, stirring occasionally, for about
4 minutes, until thick and creamy but still a little runny,
before combining with the kale. Season with salt and pepper
to taste and scatter the cheese over at the end.

TIP

+   Try swapping the kale with chard,
spring greens or your favourite
greens, or adding grated carrot
for sweetness.

This is the ultimate breakfast, though we'd happily eat it at any time of day. To keep your morning as chilled as possible, get your oven to do all the hard work for you. Place everything in your largest dish, bung in the oven – et voilà! In a matter of minutes (13, to be exact), a delicious meal awaits. For the avo fans among you, why not chop up some avocado and add on top when it's cooked, or serve with some buttered Flaxseed Buns (page 136) to mop up the juices? We like it best with Homemade Sriracha (page 279) or BBQ Ketchup (page 278) and, if you're going all out, how about some guacamole (page 50)?

ONE PAN FULL MONTY BREAKFAST

SERVES 2

1 tablespoon ghee
   or coconut oil
4 rashers of
   unsmoked bacon
2 handfuls of small
   mushrooms
   (such as button
   or chestnut)
1 handful of cherry
   tomatoes
1 handful of
   asparagus
   spears (woody
   ends snapped
   off) or purple-
   sprouting
   broccoli
   (optional)
2 large handfuls
   of baby spinach
2 eggs
Sea salt and
   black pepper

1 Preheat the oven to fan 200°C/Gas mark 7 and line your widest baking tray with baking parchment. Add half the ghee or coconut oil and let it melt in the oven for a few minutes.

2 Spread out all the ingredients in the lined and greased baking tray, excluding the eggs and spinach (don't worry – you will make space for them later). If using asparagus or broccoli, add these now as well.

3 After 10 minutes in the oven, take out the tray, flip over the bacon and mushrooms and push them to one side, then add the rest of the ghee/coconut oil. Throw in the spinach, make two indentations in it and carefully crack in the eggs.

4 Put the tray back in the oven for a further 4–5 minutes until the egg whites are set but the yolks are still runny. Remove from the oven, and give a good grind of salt and black pepper to serve.

VARIATIONS

+ Experiment with different types of
  vegetables and herbs for this dish –
  it's a great way to clear out the fridge.
  The worst that can happen is that
  your frittata loses its shape and turns
  into a scramble – it'll still be tasty!

+ Cook the mixture in a muffin tin lined
  with baking parchment cases to make
  miniature individual frittatas: stir the
  cheese into the egg mix then bake for
  about 14 minutes at fan 190°C/Gas mark
  6. Perfect for a picnic and for snacks.

This quick and easy vegetable frittata is great for a speedy family breakfast that can be enjoyed on the go. Cold leftovers make a delicious packed lunch; just wrap individual slices in baking parchment. The best thing about this dish is that we've saved time by skipping the step of frying the veg like you do in a traditional frittata. Instead, our frittata is made with 50 per cent egg and 50 per cent fresh, green vegetables. Avoid using too many watery vegetables, and source seasonal produce where possible: wild garlic in spring is heavenly. If we are having people round for lunch and are pressed for time, we find that this with a large slaw or salad and a drizzle of watercress salsa verde (page 194) does the trick.

BIG GREEN FRITTATA

SERVES 4

8 eggs
4 medium courgettes, roughly grated
1 bunch of spring onions, chopped, or 1 medium onion, diced or grated
2 garlic cloves, diced or grated, or 1 handful of wild garlic, chopped
1 big handful of frozen or fresh peas or broad beans
A pinch of cumin seeds or hot smoked paprika (optional)
2 handfuls of fresh basil or parsley, leaves and stalks roughly chopped

A pinch of dried oregano or thyme
A big pinch of sea salt and black pepper
1 tablespoon ghee, butter or coconut oil, for frying
1 handful of grated or crumbled cheese (such as Cheddar or feta – if using feta, you'll need less salt)

1 Whisk the eggs together in a large bowl, then mix in all the other ingredients except the fat for frying and the cheese.

2 Choose a medium frying pan (that is grill-friendly – no wooden handles!) and melt the ghee, butter or coconut oil over a high heat. Swirl the pan to ensure the bottom is entirely coated in the melted fat to prevent your frittata from burning.

3 When the fat is hot, pour in the frittata mixture and set your grill to high.

4 Pop a lid on the pan, turn the heat down to medium and cook for 5–8 minutes until the base of the frittata is cooked and solid. Use a wooden spatula or tip the pan from side to side to test if the base is cooked, turning the heat down if you're worried about it burning.

5 Take the lid off, scatter the cheese on top and pop under the grill until the top is golden brown – which takes about a minute. To check if it is done, give the pan a shake – the frittata should be just cooked in the middle.

6 Remove the pan from the grill and allow to cool for 5 minutes, then, using a spatula to help, carefully edge the frittata out of the pan onto a chopping board and slice into four wedges to serve.

There is nothing better than eggs for breakfast (perhaps even in bed!), especially when paired with a spicy tomato sauce to wake up your taste buds and warm your tummy. This dish says Feast! So if you're looking to impress, knock this out at any time of day. The guacamole makes for a cool and creamy contrast to the fiery tomato sauce. We like to serve it with a refreshing handful of watercress dressed with a squeeze of lemon juice and plenty of flaxseed or extra-virgin olive oil. If you enjoy this, then try our Big Green Frittata on page 49 – another quick and easy one-pan winner that packs in tons of veggies.

HUEVOS RANCHEROS WITH GUACAMOLE

SERVES 2

4 large handfuls of spinach, roughly chopped
4 eggs
1 large handful of fresh coriander, leaves and stalks roughly chopped
1 small handful of grated mature Cheddar

**FOR THE
TOMATO SAUCE**

1 large onion, diced
1 tablespoon ghee or coconut oil
2 garlic cloves, diced
2 red peppers, halved lengthways, deseeded and sliced into strips
2 bay leaves
1 teaspoon smoked paprika

A pinch of cayenne pepper or finely diced fresh red chilli, to taste
2 x 400g tins of tomatoes or 800g fresh tomatoes
200ml water (100ml if using fresh tomatoes)
Sea salt and black pepper

**FOR THE
GUACAMOLE**

1 large ripe avocado
1 tablespoon extra-virgin olive oil
Juice of ½–1 lime
2 spring onions or 1 small handful of fresh chives, chopped
1 handful of fresh coriander leaves, chopped

1 First make the tomato sauce. Fry the onion in the ghee or coconut oil over a medium heat for about 8 minutes, stirring occasionally, until softened.

2 Add the garlic, peppers, bay leaves and spices to the pan and cook for another 2 minutes.

3 Add the tomatoes and water, season generously with salt and pepper, then stir everything together and leave to simmer for 10 minutes until reduced to a thick, rich sauce.

4 Meanwhile, make the guacamole. Halve and stone the avocado, then scoop out the flesh and roughly chop. Place in a bowl and stir in all the remaining ingredients and some seasoning. Set aside.

5 Check the seasoning of the tomato sauce, adding extra salt, pepper and cayenne/chilli as needed, then stir through the spinach and cook for a few minutes until just wilted.

6 Use a spatula or spoon to make four wells in the tomato sauce mixture and crack an egg into each. The eggs will poach in the sauce and cook in about 4 minutes (lid on) for set whites and runny yolks.

7 Scatter over the coriander and cheese. Serve immediately (as the eggs will keep cooking) with big heaped spoonfuls of guacamole on top.

We love a fast, easy breakfast that can be rustled up from whatever's in the fridge in under 10 minutes, and that's where our breakfast in a bowl comes in. You could even prepare the bulk of this the night before; as you're making dinner, chop a few extra tomatoes and make sure you save a handful of spinach or other greens too. Place the dressing ingredients in a jam jar ready to shake the next morning and make extra so you have some for the rest of the week. Get into the habit of always having a jar of dressing or pesto in the fridge, where it will keep for a week. When we soft-boil eggs, we always make extra as they keep for three days and make the perfect travel snack. Our favourite combo is smoked fish and spicy watercress along with the eggs – just the ticket for a hunger-busting breakfast to wake you up, ready to conquer the day.

THE BREAKFAST BOWL

SERVES 1

1–2 eggs
½ ripe avocado, sliced
1 handful of cherry tomatoes, halved
100g smoked fish (such as salmon, mackerel or trout), chopped or flaked
1 large handful of spinach or watercress, snipped, or rocket
1 handful of fresh herbs (such as parsley, basil or chives), chopped
Sea salt and black pepper
Black sesame seeds, to serve

FOR THE DRESSING

2 tablespoons extra-virgin olive oil or flaxseed oil
2 teaspoons lemon juice or apple cider vinegar

1 Fill a pan with boiling water and carefully drop in the eggs. Simmer for 6 minutes (if the eggs were room temperature) or 7 minutes (if fridge cold) until they are soft-boiled (we like our yolks yolky!). Remove from the pan and rinse under cold running water for a minute before peeling.

2 While the eggs are cooking, place all the salad ingredients in a bowl, and mix the ingredients for the dressing by whisking in a separate small bowl or shaking in a jam jar with the lid on. Drizzle over the salad or toss together.

3 Peel the cooled eggs, then sprinkle with salt and pepper and roll in black sesame seeds, cut in half and add them to your breakfast bowl to serve, or leave whole and pack up for breakfast on the go.

TIP

+ If you usually keep your eggs in the fridge, leave them out at room temperature overnight before cooking them and you'll have perfect soft-yolk eggs.

VARIATIONS

+ Replace fish with pieces of freshly cooked crispy bacon.

+ Swap the spinach or watercress for any leftover salads (e.g. Sesame Kale Salad, page 163, or slaw, page 78) and make use of any leftover dressing (page 275) or pestos too.

This vibrant scramble gets its sunshine colour from the immune- and mood-boosting golden turmeric as well as the protein-packed eggs. We love eggs from pasture-reared hens and there's nothing quite like cracking into one to reveal its deep-yellow, flavoursome yolk. If you're short of time, leave out the onions and garlic and sprinkle with spring onions or chives instead. Serve with fresh tomatoes and a green salad dressed with flaxseed or extra-virgin olive oil.

SUNSHINE EGGS WITH TURMERIC AND LIME

SERVES 2

1 small onion,
   finely diced
2 teaspoons coconut
   oil or ghee
1 garlic clove, diced
1½ teaspoons
   ground turmeric
4 eggs
A pinch of diced
   fresh red chilli,
   chilli flakes
   /powder or
   cayenne pepper
   (optional)
1 lime, quartered
Sea salt and
   black pepper

1 In a frying pan, fry the onion in the coconut oil or ghee over a medium heat for 5 minutes until softened, stirring once in a while.

2 Add the garlic and turmeric to the onion and stir in, then crack the eggs straight into the pan.

3 Lightly scramble the eggs, stirring occasionally, for about 4 minutes, using a wooden spoon to scrape any bits from the bottom of the pan. Sprinkle over some salt and pepper and the chilli or cayenne pepper (if using).

4 Scrambled eggs will keep on cooking, so take off the heat when still a little runny. Serve immediately with lime juice squeezed over.

SOUPS AND STEWS

We love soups. Whether chunky, smooth, thick, thin, hot, cold, sweet, spicy, savoury, warming or refreshing, they are our soul food and go-to meals. Nothing sums up *Good + Simple* more than a bone-broth-based, veg-heavy, old-fashioned soup. Highly nourishing, these versatile dishes are eaten the world over and are one of the simplest and most economical ways to feed yourself, your family or even a crowd. They are easy to batch-cook, freeze, reheat, serve – and very hard to ruin. A big steaming pot of soup on the table is always a welcome sight.

Soups are where Bone Broth (page 63) comes into its own. Nutrient-rich and soothing on the digestion, we include this easy, inexpensive and energising 'liquid gold' in as many meals as we can. Plus of course it makes everything taste even better too – you can see why we love it so much! Soups and stews are a great way to enjoy plenty of bone broth on a daily basis, so that's why it's the first recipe you'll find in this chapter – with it, anything is possible.

With a nutritious and tasty base to build on, simply simmer up some roughly chopped veggies or grate them in for speed, add some seasoning, whisk in an egg and, hey presto, dinner is done – no need for a side of bread. With a base of broth you can throw in tinned beans, chopped tomatoes and some spices, or leftover cold cuts and roasted vegetables, and turn a hodgepodge of bits and bobs into a delicious meal. Add energising ingredients, such as ginger, garlic and cayenne pepper or lemon, for their flavour and health benefits, or our favourite superfoods: turmeric, watercress, spinach, broccoli, coconut oil.

A homemade soup is still a fantastic meal without the broth – you can use vegetable stock or water – though you might need to add some fat and protein, such as egg, cheese and/or pulses and oils to make it a complete, one-pot meal. And it's wonderfully reviving too. When you're not feeling your best, a well-cooked, vegetable-packed soup is the perfect dish to restore and soothe – being easily digestible, it allows your body to focus its energy where it's needed most. Try the quick and easy ones with immune-boosting ingredients like ginger and turmeric, such as Super-charged Store Cupboard Spinach Soup (page 83) or Squash and Ginger Soup with Lemony Coriander Oil (page 82).

In our recipes you'll also find ideas to adapt them throughout the year with seasonal produce, as well as tips to turn the leftovers from one recipe into another just by adding a dash of chilli, stirring in some miso paste or pesto or topping with fresh garlic, parsley or lemon zest. Mixing things up is what keeps old favourites from becoming boring. Use our soup recipes as inspiration and run wild with them!

TIPS AND TRICKS

OUT OF SORTS Nourishing soups form the basis of our One-Week Reboot – ideal for when you're feeling run down but still have to go to work and deal with family life. Turn to pages 21–23 for an at-home version that you can use to reset your taste buds whenever you fall off the wagon or just need a boost.

NOT JUST FOR WINTER Even in the summer, a bowl of hot, broth-based food always goes down well – try our Carrot Ramen Noodle and Miso Soup (page 70) or a chilled version of our Cream of Tomato Soup (page 85).

EASY ON THE DIGESTION For a hit of nutrition, cook up a soup with a bone broth (page 63), plenty of fresh veggies and a whole lot of love – a powerful combination that's easy on the system.

LATE NIGHTS When it comes to late-night suppers, soups are one of the best things to eat so that you can digest quickly and go to bed without feeling heavy.

YES, FOR BREAKFAST! We love nothing more than a piping-hot bowl of soup to start the day, whether it's Quick Coconut Dahl (without the zingy slaw) (page 78) or Easy Drop Egg Soup (page 86). Start with one of the sweeter ones, such as Cream of Tomato Soup (page 85) and Squash and Ginger Soup with Lemony Coriander Oil (page 82). Try it and see how good you feel for the rest of the day.

FRIENDS OVER Serve a soup supper straight from the pot with a crunchy, tangy salad (page 78) and some Quinoa Courgette Toast (page 32) – simple but special and stress-free.

LAST-MINUTE GUEST? Jazz up your soup with a drizzle of something ready made in your fridge, like a spoonful of Spinach and Butterbean Hummus (page 273) or pesto (pages 245 and 246), or sprinkle over crumbled cheese, butter-fried onions or grated courgette and toasted pumpkin seeds.

PORTABLE HOT LUNCH ON THE GO Invest in a flask for quick, portable lunches that stay hot for hours. Soups are so good you could eat them for breakfast, lunch and dinner. Or make up a noodle pot (pages 75–77) and just add hot water at lunchtime.

COULDN'T BE EASIER No fancy knife skills needed; just roughly chop and simmer – a hand-held stick or stand blender, or a food processor, come in handy too.

FREEZING Soups are ideal for freezing; always make double the quantity and portion them up in one, two or more servings – whatever you need to feed you or your family at once. We love building up a variety of flavours to have to hand in the freezer.

NO BONE BROTH? Add a cold-pressed oil such as flaxseed oil, extra-virgin olive oil or macadamia nut oil when the soup is cool enough to eat.

BOIL YOUR BONES!

This is your back-pocket recipe from which a whole host of delicious, everyday dishes begin. If you have our first book, *The Art of Eating Well*, you'll already be aware of how much we champion our highly nourishing, gut-healing, economical diet staple. We see it as an all-rounder, packed with protein, vitamins, minerals, collagen and keratin, making it amazing for skin, digestion and even the dreaded cellulite! We love its simplicity – just bones, water and a really long simmer. You can add aromatics like bay leaves, peppercorns and onions, if you like, but we usually save any vegetables for our actual soups and stews and use our broth as a way of using up veg scraps instead – you could store odds and ends in the freezer ready for when you next make a broth. Adding an acidic medium, such as lemon juice or apple cider vinegar (ACV), helps to further extract the minerals we're after.

Boil your bones (well, simmer them actually) during your Sunday Cook-Off (page 334) and store in the fridge (see tips) or freeze the broth in batches to use throughout the week. The remains of your Sunday roast becomes a pot of simmering goodness on Monday; blended into a vegetable soup, it provides Wednesday's fuss-free supper, and sipped from a mug with a splash of lemon juice and a pinch of sea salt, it's an antidote for Saturday's hangover. Add to everything – soups, stews, sauces, risottos, for cooking quinoa or vegetables, even add a dash to scrambled eggs as it makes everything taste better.

When making bone broth, we favour a slow cooker. Just leave it on overnight, or while you're out during the day, and it does the work for you. What's more, it uses much less energy than a conventional cooker. For those with a pressure cooker, your broth can be ready in just 3 hours. You can even make bone broth in the oven, by bringing it up to the boil on the stove, covering with a lid and transferring to the oven, preheated to around fan 100°C/Gas mark ½, or even lower, and then let it simmer away. (Make sure the lid is heatproof and tight-fitting so that the broth doesn't evaporate.)

Remember that provenance is key when it comes to making bone broth. A healthy animal is essential for the nutrients that it can provide, and for this reason we source only high-quality bones from grass-fed, naturally reared animals. If you'd like to learn more about why bone broth is at the heart of our philosophy, see page 10.

TIPS

+ To use it in the week, divide the broth between 2 glass or stainless-steel containers and refrigerate. A layer of fat will form on top. Use one container in the first half of the week and start the second halfway through or freeze it in batches, leaving room for expansion.

+ Beef bones produce a lot of nutritious fat. Skim some of it off the broth and save it in a jar in the fridge for cooking.

+ Fresh chicken carcasses from the butcher usually have a fair amount of meat on them. We tend to poach the carcasses for 20 minutes, then pull off the meat (and save it for another meal, such as a chicken salad or soup) before returning the carcasses to the pot and continuing to simmer to make broth. If you have meaty bones you can roast them first.

BONE BROTH

**MAKES 3.5 LITRES
(IN A 4-LITRE PAN)**

3kg beef or lamb
bones (usually
free from your
butcher) or
chicken
carcasses, or
use the bones
leftover from
a roast

**OPTIONAL
EXTRAS**
A generous
splash of apple
cider vinegar or
lemon juice
Onion, leek, carrot
or celery ends
1 tablespoon black
peppercorns
A few bay leaves

1　Place the bones and any optional ingredients in a large
stainless-steel or ceramic pot, slow cooker or pressure
cooker and cover with cold water. The water should cover
the bones by 5cm while still leaving room at the top of
the pan.

2　Cover with a lid and bring to the boil, then reduce the heat
and simmer, with the lid on, for at least 12 hours for beef or
lamb bones and 6 hours for chicken. If using a slow cooker,
cook on high for at least 12 hours. If using a pressure cooker,
cook at high pressure for at least 3 hours.

3　Strain the liquid, using a fine-mesh strainer for chicken.
Use immediately or leave to cool before storing. Bone broth
will keep in the fridge for several days or up to a week if you
leave it undisturbed, as a layer of fat will form on the surface
and keep it sealed from the air.

TIP

+　The longer the bones simmer, the more nutrients are
released; we like to boil the chicken carcass for up to 12
hours and we keep beef or lamb bones going for 24 hours.
Since these bigger bones have more nutrients to give, the
broth will be more concentrated. You can strain the beef
and lamb broth at half-time, refill the pot with fresh water
and cook the bones again to make a double batch of broth.

Our favourite way to experiment with flavours is to take a trusted recipe and choose one particular element to tweak. Here it's our simple broccoli soup jazzed up with various toppings – a perfect way to cook in bulk while enjoying three different versions of the same dish. Make a huge batch of soup (this one makes nine portions) along with our Quinoa Courgette Toast (page 32) as part of your Sunday Cook-Off (page 334), freeze in single portions and dip into your freezer over the coming weeks. Don't forget that you can also make your toppings in bulk and keep, covered with a layer of oil, in a sterilised jar, or even freeze.

SUPERBLY SIMPLE BROCCOLI SOUP 3 WAYS

MAKES ABOUT 4 LITRES
SERVES 9

4 large onions,
   roughly chopped
2 tablespoons ghee
   or coconut oil
4 heads of broccoli
   (about 350g each)
8 garlic cloves,
   roughly chopped
1 bunch of celery
   (about 6 sticks),
   roughly chopped
2 litres Bone
   Broth (page 63)
   or water
Juice of 1½ lemons
Sea salt and
   black pepper

1   In your biggest saucepan (4 litres minimum in capacity, or use your two biggest pans), fry the onions in ghee or coconut oil over a medium heat for 8 minutes until softened.

2   Meanwhile, prepare the broccoli: cut into equal-sized florets and roughly chop the stalks (after first slicing off the tough outer layer).

3   Add the garlic, celery and broccoli stalks to the pan and cook for a further 2 minutes, then add the broth or water, cover the pan with a lid and bring to a medium simmer.

4   Add the broccoli florets and a big pinch of salt and pepper, then allow to simmer until the broccoli is just tender – about 5 minutes. (It is important that the broccoli does not become overcooked; test it by piercing with a knife.)

5   While the soup is simmering away, prepare your choice of topping or toppings (see page 66). Once the soup is ready, blend the soup using a hand-held stick blender or whizz in batches in a food processor – add a little hot water if your soup is too thick. Season to taste with salt and pepper and add the lemon juice.

6   To serve, divide between bowls, swirling your choice of topping into the hot soup.

→   **CONTINUED OVERLEAF**

THREE MARVELLOUS TOPPINGS

EACH MAKES 3 SERVINGS

FOR THE CUMIN GREMOLATA

1 handful of fresh parsley, leaves and stalks finely chopped
1 garlic clove, diced
1 teaspoon ground cumin
1 tablespoon lemon juice or apple cider vinegar
3 tablespoons extra-virgin olive oil
Sea salt and black pepper

FOR THE THYME AND FETA PESTO

2 teaspoons fresh thyme leaves or ½ teaspoon dried (or try oregano or rosemary)
3 tablespoons crumbled feta
1 tablespoon lemon juice or apple cider vinegar
3 tablespoons extra-virgin olive oil
Sea salt and black pepper

FOR THE MISO AND CORIANDER

1 handful of fresh coriander, leaves and stalks finely chopped
1 tablespoon unpasteurised miso paste
1 tablespoon lemon juice or apple cider vinegar
3 tablespoons extra-virgin olive oil
1 tablespoon black sesame seeds
Sea salt and black pepper

1 Place the ingredients for your choice of topping in a mixing bowl and whisk together. Taste for seasoning, then swirl your topping over bowls of the hot soup (see page 64) to serve.

VARIATIONS

+ Replace the broccoli with carrot, squash or cauliflower and try other sauces to swirl through, such as Avocado and Ginger Sauce (page 268) or Homemade Sriracha (page 279). Also try it drizzled with flaxseed oil.

The word 'minestrone' derives from *ministrare*, meaning 'to dish up', and this chunky soup is perfect for a gathering, at any time of year. Here we've included both a summer and a winter version. Save any Parmesan rind to throw in at the beginning of the cooking to add depth of flavour to either soup – just remember to pick it out at the end. In contrast to our Winter Minestrone (page 69), the soup below takes advantage of the abundance of sun-ripened tomatoes available during the summer months for a rich red bowl of goodness. Make it lighter for a broth-like starter, or thick and hearty for a main meal. As tomatoes aren't a natural winter crop here in the UK, we combine hearty root veg and beans in colder months. Borlotti beans complement this soothing soup perfectly, but any beans will do. Leftover quinoa or cooked lentils would go nicely with this dish too.

MINESTRONE 2 WAYS

SERVES 4

1 tablespoon ghee or coconut oil
1 large onion, diced
3 garlic cloves, diced
1 celery stick, diced
1 large carrot, diced
12 large tomatoes, diced
1 medium aubergine, diced
2 medium courgettes, diced
1 large red pepper, deseeded and diced
1 tablespoon fresh oregano or thyme leaves or 1 teaspoon dried
1 bay leaf
1 teaspoon tomato purée or 4 chopped sundried tomatoes in oil, drained and chopped

800ml Bone Broth (page 63), vegetable stock or water
Parmesan rind (optional)
1 large handful of fresh or frozen peas or broad beans
2 big handfuls of grated Parmesan, to serve (optional)

FOR THE BASIL OIL

2 large handfuls of fresh basil (leaves and stalks)
6 tablespoons extra-virgin olive oil
1 tablespoon lemon juice or apple cider vinegar
Sea salt and black pepper

SUMMER MINESTRONE WITH A VIBRANT BASIL OIL

1   Melt the ghee or coconut oil in a large saucepan over a medium heat and fry the onion, garlic, celery and carrot for 8 minutes until softened.

2   Meanwhile, make the basil oil by finely chopping the basil and mixing with the EVOO, lemon juice or ACV and salt and pepper to taste – or you could use a blender. Set aside.

3   Add the tomatoes and diced vegetables to the pan with the oregano or thyme, bay leaf, tomato purée or chopped sundried tomatoes and a big pinch of salt and pepper. Pour in the broth, stock or water and add the Parmesan rind (if using). Bring to the boil, then reduce the heat, cover with a lid and cook at a medium simmer for 15–20 minutes until the vegetables are just tender.

4   Stir in the peas or broad beans to heat through for the last 2 minutes of cooking, and taste for seasoning.

5   Ladle the minestrone into bowls, scatter with the grated Parmesan (if using) and drizzle over the basil oil.

→   CONTINUED OVERLEAF

MINESTRONE 2 WAYS (CONTINUED)

SERVES 4

1 tablespoon ghee
  or coconut oil
1 large leek or
  onion, diced
3 garlic cloves, diced
1 tablespoon fresh
  thyme leaves or
  1 teaspoon dried
1 tablespoon
  roughly chopped
  fresh rosemary
  leaves or 1
  teaspoon dried
1 celery stick, diced
1 large carrot, diced
2 handfuls of diced
  turnip, swede
  or celeriac
A pinch of diced
  fresh red chilli
  (optional)
Parmesan rind
  (optional)
800ml Bone Broth
  (page 63) or
  vegetable stock
1 x 400g tin of
  borlotti beans
  or chickpeas,
  drained and
  rinsed
85g buckwheat pasta
  or buckwheat
  (soba) noodles,
  broken

4 handfuls of kale,
  cavolo nero,
  spinach or
  cabbage leaves,
  shredded
Sea salt and
  black pepper
2 big handfuls of
  grated Parmesan,
  pecorino or other
  hard cheese, to
  serve (optional)

FOR THE GARLIC HERB DRESSING

1 garlic clove
1 large handful of
  fresh parsley
  (leaves and
  stalks)
6 tablespoons
  extra-virgin
  olive oil
1 teaspoon grated
  lemon zest
1 tablespoon apple
  cider vinegar
Sea salt and
  black pepper

WARMING WINTER MINESTRONE WITH PUNCHY GARLIC DRESSING

1 Blend all the dressing ingredients in a food processor (or finely chop, and then mix), seasoning with salt and pepper, and set aside.

2 Melt the ghee or coconut oil in a large saucepan over a medium heat and fry the leek or onion with the garlic, herbs, celery, carrot, diced root vegetables and chilli (if using) for 8 minutes or until softened.

3 Season with salt and pepper and add the Parmesan rind (if using), pour in the broth, stock or water and drained beans and stir everything together. Bring to the boil, then reduce to a medium simmer and cook for around 15 minutes, lid on, or until the vegetables are tender.

4 Add the buckwheat pasta for the last 10 minutes of cooking; if using noodles, add these with the kale, cavolo nero or cabbage (if using) for the last 5 minutes of cooking.

5 When the vegetables are tender, stir through the spinach (if using) and taste for seasoning.

6 Serve each bowlful with a drizzle of the garlic herb dressing and, if you like, some grated Parmesan or pecorino.

Vegetable noodles are both colourful and nutritious, and the spiralizer makes quick work of them for this ramen-style dish. If you don't have a spiralizer, simply use a vegetable peeler to peel strips from the carrots. Revered for thousands of years in Chinese medicine and cooking, shiitake mushrooms are known for their immune-boosting and heart-healthy qualities, and loved for their meaty texture. They are a bit more expensive but well worth it as they have that wonderful umami flavour or 'savoury deliciousness'. If you prefer, though, you can mix it up with other mushrooms. If you feel you're wilting and need a boost of energy, this is the soup for you!

CARROT RAMEN NOODLE AND MISO SOUP

SERVES 2

6 spring onions, finely sliced, retaining the sliced green ends to garnish
2 tablespoons coconut oil
2cm piece of fresh root ginger (unpeeled if organic), diced
2 garlic cloves, diced
½–1 fresh red chilli, finely sliced (to taste), plus extra to serve
300g shiitake mushrooms, tops sliced and stems chopped
700ml Bone Broth (page 63), vegetable stock or water
2 large carrots

2–3 teaspoons quality miso paste (depending on its strength and saltiness)
1 teaspoon tamari or sea salt
Juice of 1 lime
2 handfuls of pak choi or any leafy greens (such as kale, cavolo nero or spinach), shredded
1 small handful of fresh coriander (leaves and stalks) and a few fresh mint leaves, finely chopped

1   In a large saucepan, fry the white parts of the spring onions in the coconut oil with the ginger, garlic and chilli over a medium heat for 2 minutes until softened. Stir in the mushrooms and fry for a further 2 few minutes.

2   Pour in the broth, stock or water and bring to the boil, then reduce the heat and simmer for 5 minutes.

3   Meanwhile, spiralize the carrots, snipping long strands into shorter lengths for easier eating. Alternatively, peel into strips with a julienne peeler or standard vegetable peeler, then slice in half lengthways.

4   Add any extras (if using) – such as prawns, shredded cooked chicken, halved boiled eggs or wakame – and warm through for 1 minute. Turn off the heat and stir through the miso paste, tamari or salt and the lime juice and then drop the carrot noodles and pak choi or leafy greens into the broth.

5   Serve topped with the chopped coriander and mint leaves and the reserved green parts of the spring onions. Add extra chilli, if you like, or a drizzle of Sriracha.

TIP

+   Try unpasteurised miso paste and add right at the end when cool enough to eat so as to preserve the probiotics/good bacteria.

1 large handful of
cooked prawns
or shredded
cooked chicken
or beef

Soft-boiled eggs,
cut in half
(or poach
in the broth)

1 tablespoon
dried seaweed
(such as wakame),
soaked according
to packet
instructions, then
drained, chopped
and added to
the soup

Homemade
Sriracha (page
279), to serve

VARIATIONS

+   Replace the carrots with an
    equivalent quantity of squash,
    celeriac or courgette noodles.

We created this recipe for a two-day retreat, where it acquired its name. With its medicinal spices and hearty flavours, this is one of those fail-safe recipes that will not only warm you on a cold winter's night, but is really simple to throw together using odds and ends from the fridge. We believe that stews should have no rules: play around with what is in season or readily available – swap the lentils or chickpeas for whatever tins you have hiding at the back of the cupboard, and use plenty of fresh greens and herbs at the end of cooking to brighten it up. We highly recommend our '4C' spice mix – cinnamon, cumin, coriander and chilli. Use it in any stews or soups, and mix it with some lemon juice and coconut oil as a rub for meat or fish.

MOROCCAN MEDITATION STEW

SERVES 4

2 large onions, finely diced
1½ tablespoons coconut oil or ghee
4 garlic cloves, diced
4 dried dates, pitted and chopped
2 large carrots, diced into 1cm chunks
4 large handfuls of mixed root vegetables (such as beetroot, swede, celeriac or squash), diced into 2cm chunks
2 x 400g tins of tomatoes
100g dried red lentils or 1 x 400g tin of chickpeas or beans, rinsed and drained

1 litre Bone Broth (page 63), vegetable stock or water, plus an extra 300ml if cooking lentils
1 large red pepper, roughly chopped
4 large handfuls of chopped greens (such as spinach or chard)
1 large handful of fresh parsley and/or coriander, leaves and stalks chopped
Grated zest and juice of 1 lemon
Sea salt and black pepper
Extra-virgin olive oil or flaxseed oil, for drizzling

1 Fry the onions in the coconut oil or ghee in a large saucepan over a medium heat for 8 minutes until soft and starting to caramelise.

2 Turn down the heat to low and stir in the 4C spices (see opposite) and garlic and cook for a further minute making sure the garlic and spices don't burn.

3 Add the chopped dates, carrots, root vegetables and tomatoes with the dried red lentils (if using) and season with salt and pepper.

4 Pour in the broth, stock or water, then bring to a medium simmer and cook for about 12 minutes until the vegetables are just tender.

5 Add the chopped red pepper with the greens and the chickpeas or beans (if using) and cook for a further 5 minutes. Turn off the heat and stir in half the herbs and all the lemon juice. Season with salt and pepper to taste.

6 Serve each bowl with a drizzle of EVOO or flaxseed oil, the lemon zest and remaining herbs.

**FOR THE 4C
SPICE MIX**

2 teaspoons
   ground cumin
1½ teaspoons
   ground cinnamon
1 teaspoon ground
   coriander
A pinch of chilli
   flakes /powder
   or finely diced
   fresh red chilli

VARIATION

+   In the summer, you can swap the
    root veg for fresh peas, green beans
    and courgettes for a light and vibrant
    evening meal. Just remember that
    they cook in one-third of the time,
    so add them at step 5.

A noodle pot is a simple and fun way to experiment with flavours and ingredients for a packed lunch. It's the ultimate ready meal: all you need is a large heatproof glass jar with a lid and access to a kettle. We've even taken these with us on long-haul flights – just ask a flight attendant to fill up the jar with hot water. Try the following three recipes, which are our absolute favourites, and then have a go at the DIY Noodle Pot on page 77.

THE REINVENTED NOODLE POT 3 WAYS

SERVES 1

1 handful of
    spiralized or
    grated butternut
    squash
1 handful of greens
    and/or cabbage
    (red or white)
1 or 2 spring onions,
    finely sliced
1 soft-boiled egg,
    peeled and halved
2 teaspoons
    garam masala
    or medium
    curry powder
1 small garlic clove,
    finely minced
A pinch of chilli
    flakes or
    cayenne pepper

2 tablespoons
    grated ginger
    squeezed to get
    1 tablespoon of
    ginger juice
1 tablespoon tamari
1 small handful
    coriander leaves
1 tablespoon
    coconut milk
1 tablespoon
    coconut oil
Sea salt and
    black pepper

CURRIED EGG NOODLE POT

1   Layer up the veg in a 1-litre heatproof jar and place the egg on top. Top with the garam masala or curry powder, the garlic, chilli flakes, ginger juice and tarmari, the coconut milk and coconut oil and then season. Top with the coriander leaves.

2   When you're ready to eat, add 200ml boiling water (or enough to fill the jar), mix together well and serve.

TIP

+   It's also great with courgette noodles (courgetti) in the summer.

→ CONTINUED OVERLEAF

SERVES 1

1 handful of
cooked quinoa
1 tablespoon tomato
sauce (page 50)
or passata
1 tablespoon
chopped fresh
basil or pesto
(page 245)
Sliced fresh
tomatoes
½ small onion, diced

½ teaspoon garlic
(powder or finely
chopped fresh)
1 small handful of
grated Parmesan
2 handfuls of grated
or spiralized
courgette (or
other seasonal
greens, such as
asparagus or
spinach)

ITALIAN QUINOA NOODLE POT

1   Place the quinoa in a 1-litre heatproof jar, followed
    by all the other ingredients.

2   When you're ready to eat, add 200ml boiling water
    (or enough to fill the jar), mix together well and serve.

SERVES 1

1 handful of shredded
roast chicken
½ teaspoon garlic
(powder or finely
chopped fresh)
1 teaspoon tamari
1 tablespoon
chopped fresh
coriander leaves
1 teaspoon finely
grated fresh root
ginger (unpeeled
if organic)

1 teaspoon toasted
sesame oil
2 handfuls of grated
or spiralized
carrots
1 handful of your
favourite veg/
salad (we used
sliced radish,
broccoli, green
beans)
1 wedge of lime

CHICKEN AND SESAME NOODLE POT

1   Place the chicken in a 1-litre heatproof jar, followed
    by all the other ingredients.

2   When you're ready to eat, add 200ml boiling water
    (or enough to fill the jar), mix together well and serve.

Pick your base, vegetables and flavourings, pop them all together and you're done. As a rule of thumb, you'll want two handfuls of vegetables and a handful of meat/egg/beans/lentils. It's also a great way to use up leftovers in the fridge, such as salads, quinoa, roast chicken, or dips and dressings such as pesto and barbecue ketchup.

DIY NOODLE POT

SERVES 1

PROTEIN BASE
1 handful of cooked quinoa
1 handful of cooked lentils
1 handful of cooked/tinned beans, drained and rinsed
1 handful of cooked buckwheat (soba) noodles or pasta spirals
1 handful of cooked and shredded roast chicken
1 soft-boiled egg, peeled

RAW VEGETABLES
Grated or spiralized root vegetables (such as carrot and/or beetroot)
Grated or spiralized butternut squash
Grated or spiralized courgettes
Chopped greens (such as pak choi, spinach or kale)
Shredded cabbage
Chopped red pepper (deseeded)
Sliced radishes
Fresh or frozen peas or broad beans

COOKED VEGETABLES
Leftover cooked greens (such as broccoli or kale) or cauliflower
Roasted vegetables (such as butternut squash or carrots)

FLAVOURINGS
Sea salt and black pepper
2 teaspoons miso paste
1 teaspoon tamarind paste
1 teaspoon tamari
A pinch of chilli flakes or cayenne pepper
½ teaspoon finely chopped fresh red chilli or
1 teaspoon finely chopped pickled jalapeños
1 teaspoon finely grated fresh root ginger
½ teaspoon garlic (powder or finely chopped fresh)
½ onion, diced, or 1 tablespoon chopped chives or spring onions
1 teaspoon ground spices (curry powder, garam masala, turmeric, Chinese five spice or harissa spice mix)
1 tablespoon chopped fresh herbs or 1 teaspoon dried
1 tablespoon coconut milk
1 teaspoon coconut oil
1 teaspoon toasted sesame oil
1 small handful of grated Parmesan
1 tablespoon Homemade Sriracha (page 279)
1 tablespoon pesto (pages 245–6)
1 tablespoon BBQ Ketchup (page 278)

1   Choose one protein base, add two handfuls of raw or cooked vegetables (whatever you have ready to go), then add your chosen flavourings, picking as many as you like from the list.

2   Place all the ingredients in a 1-litre heatproof jar, placing the delicate ingredients at the top so they don't get crushed.

3   When you're ready to eat, add about 200ml hot water – enough to fill the jar – and mix everything together well before digging in.

Soothing and aromatic, dahl is in our top five meals of all time – we love it served hot or cold at anytime, including breakfast. For a speedy dahl, red lentils are the best as they don't need pre-soaking and cook really quickly. A bowl of this with a big handful of zingy slaw on top is the ultimate comfort food. The recipe here makes six portions: enjoy any leftovers throughout the week or freeze to use another time.

QUICK COCONUT DAHL WITH ZINGY SLAW

SERVES 6

1 tablespoon coconut oil

2 medium onions, diced

4 garlic cloves, diced

2.5cm piece of fresh root ginger (unpeeled if organic), finely chopped

1 tablespoon ground turmeric

1 teaspoon chilli powder (or to taste)

500g dried red lentils, rinsed and drained

1 x 400ml tin of full-fat coconut milk

1 litre Bone Broth (page 63) or water

Juice of ½ lemon /lime or 2 tablespoons apple cider vinegar

2 teaspoons tamari

2 handfuls of fresh coriander, leaves and stalks chopped

1 tablespoon black sesame seeds

FOR THE SLAW

1 medium white or green cabbage, leaves shredded

1 handful of fresh coriander, leaves and stalks chopped

Juice of ½ lemon /lime or 2 tablespoons apple cider vinegar

2 tablespoons extra-virgin olive oil or flaxseed oil

Sea salt and black pepper

1 Melt the coconut oil in a large saucepan over a medium heat. Add the onions and fry, stirring now and then, for 8 minutes until softened.

2 Add the garlic to the pan with the ginger, turmeric and chilli powder. Fry for a further minute, stirring to prevent the mixture catching on the bottom of the pan.

3 Tip in the lentils and add the coconut milk and broth or water to the pan. Turn up the heat, then stir, cover with a lid and cook at a medium simmer for 20–25 minutes until the lentils are tender. Add a little more broth or water if you like a soupier dahl.

4 While the dahl is cooking, make the slaw. Toss the cabbage and herbs in the lemon/lime juice or ACV and EVOO or flaxseed oil and season with salt and pepper to taste.

5 Add the lemon/lime juice or ACV to the dahl, season with the tamari and salt and pepper to taste and sprinkle over the coriander and sesame seeds. Serve with the slaw, either on the side or spooned on top.

VARIATION

+ Instead of the slaw, try a big pile of
  peppery watercress served on top of
  the hot dahl with a squeeze of lemon.

This dish is inspired by everyone's favourite carrot and coriander soup, using squash instead. We make this with anti-inflammatory ginger for a perfect winter warmer. This soup is quick and easy, especially if you have already roasted a squash during your Sunday Cook-Off (page 334). We make this with bone broth for the protein and fats, so that it's a hearty one-pot meal – no need for a side of bread (recipe photo on page 80). If you don't have any broth, coconut milk and water make a good substitute. You could also make this with 1kg carrots, chopped and roasted for 30 minutes until tender. We use the whole lemon here: don't forget to zest it before you juice it – much easier!

SQUASH AND GINGER SOUP WITH LEMONY CORIANDER OIL

SERVES 4

1 large butternut
    squash
1 tablespoon ghee
    or coconut oil
2 medium onions,
    roughly chopped
3 garlic cloves,
    crushed
3cm piece of fresh
    root ginger
    (unpeeled if
    organic), grated
    or roughly
    chopped
3 celery sticks,
    roughly chopped
1.4 litres Bone
    Broth (page 63)
    or 1 x 400ml
    tin of full-fat
    coconut milk
    plus 1 litre water
Juice of 1 lemon
1 tablespoon tamari

**FOR THE
CORIANDER OIL**
2 handfuls of fresh
    coriander, leaves
    and stalks finely
    chopped
Zest of 1 lemon
1 garlic clove,
    finely chopped
6 tablespoons extra-
    virgin olive oil
Sea salt and
    black pepper

TIP

+   Keep a knob
    of fresh root
    ginger in the
    freezer to
    preserve it,
    and grate
    from frozen.

1   Preheat the oven to fan 220°C/Gas mark 9. Pop the whole butternut squash in the oven and roast for 40 minutes until a knife slides in easily.

2   Meanwhile, make the coriander oil. Mix the coriander in a small bowl with the lemon zest, garlic and EVOO (or blend everything in the small bowl of a food processor) and season with salt and pepper to taste. Set aside.

3   Melt the ghee or coconut oil in a large pan, add the onions and fry over a medium heat for 5 minutes until softened.

4   Add the garlic with the ginger and celery and cook for a further 2 minutes. Pour in the bone broth or coconut milk and water, bring to a medium simmer and cook for 5 minutes.

5   Halve the roasted squash, remove the seeds and discard, then scoop the flesh into the pan and add a big pinch of salt and pepper. Simmer for a final 5 minutes.

6   Add the lemon juice and tamari, then purée the soup until smooth with a hand-held stick blender or in batches in a food processor. Taste for seasoning, bearing in mind that tamari is salty so you'll need to add less salt.

7   Serve each bowl of soup with a drizzle of the coriander oil.

This is a quick and easy creamy spinach soup – perfect for fighting off a bug. The immune-boosting properties of ginger, garlic, turmeric and lemons, along with the nourishing broth, will pep you up in no time. From your store cupboard to a bowl of soup in front of the fire (we wish!) in 10 minutes – it's our secret weapon against the British weather (recipe photo on page 81).

SUPER-CHARGED STORE CUPBOARD SPINACH SOUP

SERVES 3

2 teaspoons
    coconut oil
2cm piece of fresh
    root ginger
    (unpeeled if
    organic)
2 garlic cloves
½ lemon or 1 lime
2 teaspoons ground
    turmeric
4 spring onions or
    ½ small onion,
    roughly chopped
1 x 400ml tin full-fat
    coconut milk
1 x 400g tin of
    cannellini or
    butter beans,
    drained and
    rinsed

450g spinach,
    fresh or frozen
2 teaspoons tamari
A pinch of chilli
    powder or
    cayenne pepper
    (optional)
Sea salt and
    black pepper

1 Gently melt the coconut oil in a saucepan and grate the ginger, garlic and lemon or lime zest straight into the pan. Add the turmeric and spring onions or onion and cook on a medium heat for 2 minutes.

2 Pour in the coconut milk and bring to a medium simmer. Add the drained beans and the spinach, place a lid on the pan and cook for 2 minutes.

3 Squeeze in the lemon/lime juice and add the tamari with a pinch of salt and pepper and chilli powder or cayenne pepper (if using).

4 Blend everything together using a hand-held stick blender or in a food processor and check the seasoning before serving up.

We've given this classic recipe a healthy Hemsley twist and added carrots, rather than sugar, for sweetness, and beans to make it creamy and more filling. Try adding Homemade Sriracha (page 279) drizzled over the top or a spoonful of pesto (pages 245–246), for a flavour punch. This soup is also delicious served chilled in the summer, using up the abundance of ripe fresh tomatoes – check out your farmers' markets at the end of a summer day for a bargain job lot. If you have any left over, simmer it down to reduce it and enjoy as an Italian-style tomato sauce for your courgetti. You can also make double quantities and freeze half. Great with Quinoa Courgette Toast (page 32).

CREAM OF TOMATO SOUP

SERVES 4

1 tablespoon ghee
    or coconut oil
1 large onion,
    roughly chopped
2 garlic cloves,
    roughly chopped
2 medium carrots,
    roughly chopped
1 tablespoon
    tomato purée
2 x 400g tins of
    tomatoes or 800g
    fresh tomatoes,
    chopped
1 x 400g tin of
    cannellini or
    butter beans,
    drained and
    rinsed
400ml Bone Broth
    (preferably
    chicken bones
    – page 63)
    or water

1 teaspoon
    maple syrup
    (optional)
Sea salt and
    black pepper

TO SERVE (OPTIONAL)
Extra-virgin olive
    oil, for drizzling
1 large handful
    of fresh basil
    leaves, chopped,
    or pesto
    (page 245)

1   Melt the ghee or coconut oil in a large saucepan, add the onion and fry on a medium heat for 8 minutes until softened.

2   Add the garlic, carrots, tomato purée and a big pinch of salt and pepper and cook for a further minute.

3   Tip in the tinned or fresh tomatoes and the drained beans, followed by the broth or water, turn up the heat, cover with a lid and cook at a medium simmer for 10 minutes until the carrots are tender. (Pierce a carrot chunk with a knife to check that it cuts through easily.)

4   Purée the soup until smooth in the pan using a hand-held stick blender, or in batches in a food processor, and then taste for seasoning, adding salt, pepper or maple syrup (if using) if needed. You can also add more broth or water to get to the consistency you want.

5   Ladle into bowls. Stir through the basil (if using) and serve with a drizzle of EVOO.

This light, brothy soup is our go-to supper whenever we come home late, tired, hungry and in need of something speedy and easy to digest to ensure a good night's sleep. Broth, ginger, eggs and greens provide a powerhouse combination that is surprisingly delicious for breakfast, too, and sets you up perfectly for the day ahead. For a heartier meal, double all of the ingredients except for the broth. You'll soon not need the recipe and you'll be using this as a base for a variety of veggie, bone broth drop-egg soups.

EASY DROP EGG SOUP

SERVES 4

1 litre Bone Broth (page 63)
½ teaspoon grated fresh root ginger (unpeeled if organic)
3 spring onions, chopped, plus extra (optional) to serve
1 big handful of favourite greens (such as spinach, pak choi, cabbage or chard), roughly chopped as needed
¼ teaspoon white pepper
1–2 tablespoons tamari, to taste

2 eggs
1 small handful of fresh coriander or chives, roughly chopped, to garnish (optional)

1 Pour the broth (see variation below) into a large saucepan, add the ginger and then the spring onions and greens. Bring to the boil, then reduce the heat and season with the white pepper and tamari.

2 Crack the eggs into a bowl and lightly beat. When the broth is gently simmering, slowly drizzle in the beaten eggs in a circular motion and stir, then turn off the heat, letting the eggs cook for about 1 minute. Alternatively, crack each egg whole into the broth and poach lightly for a few minutes.

3 Top with chopped coriander, chives or extra spring onions (if using) and serve immediately.

TIP

+ If using baby spinach, only add it in the last few minutes of cooking.

VARIATION

+ If you don't have any Bone Broth, use 1 litre of water instead and add 1–2 tablespoons of unpasteurised miso paste to the soup when it's off the heat, just after adding the eggs, and stir until thoroughly mixed.

SIDES AND SNACKS

So what is the 'right' snack, we hear you say. Well, to us it's something that provides sustained nourishment and energy with no down side. Snack foods labelled 'low fat' or 'diet' have no place in a real-food diet – they tend to be full of preservatives, additives and highly processed ingredients, as well as artificial sweeteners in order to keep them 'low cal'. By contrast, the 'smart' snacks in this chapter provide slow-burning fuel for your body while keeping the munchies at bay.

When eating real, well-balanced foods, those peaks and troughs that make you think that only another dose of sugar or caffeine can save the day will no longer be an issue. Eating a small serving of real food between meals, even if it's leftovers, helps quash those crazy cravings that can cause you to make poor choices or overeat at your next meal. A quick-and-easy example is half or a whole 'avo' – fresh and filling – we've shown you our favourite ways (page 114) to enjoy this nutritious bite. Getting into the habit of stocking up on delicious snacks for home and work helps, whether it's making a batch of Apple and Bacon Muffins (page 118) or Tahini Applejacks (page 124) during your Sunday Cook-Off (page 334), or enjoying our favourite quick fix: a mug of Bone Broth (page 63).

Now you are prepared, it's not just what you eat but *how* you eat it. Popping nuts and dried fruit all day at your desk, spooning out almond butter every time you get bored or absent-mindedly polishing off food while watching TV is not good, and it's easy to overdo. Take a break from what you're doing so that you can savour your snack properly. You don't have to leave your desk if you're busy (though stretching your legs and back regularly is always a good idea); just turn your attention to your snack, then get back to work. It makes all the difference to your digestion and energy levels and you'll feel satisfied with less than you'd expect.

If you feel as though you are having a craving, try having a drink first. Wait 20 minutes and then see what has happened to the craving. Eating well-balanced meals for breakfast, lunch and dinner will also lessen the need to graze throughout the day. Usually something sour, bitter or zingy on your taste buds does the trick to blow away sweet or salty snack attacks.

We've also included an array of side dishes to complement the veg and meat mains, from our Creamy Carrot Bake (page 93) to Celeriac and Blue Cheese Gratin (page 105), and quick and colourful veg mashes (pages 111–113). Add them to packed lunches or team them with anything from the salad section (pages 147–165) to make a smorgasbord-style feast. Last but not least, if you're looking for entertaining ideas, start a party off with our Sri Lankan Squash Croquettes (page 98), Cucumber and Smoked Salmon Canapés (page 116) and Broccomole (page 128) with crudités.

TIPS AND TRICKS

KEEPING FOOD HOT OR COLD For a hot meal on the go, keep your lunch hot by packing it into a flask (you can get small ones too); a flask will keep a cold dish or smoothie cool too.

FOURSIES The mid-afternoon version of elevenses! (For splitting breakfast into two, see page 26). Why not split your dinner in the same way? Enjoy half as a 4pm snack before your evening workout and finish the rest straight after, so that you don't end up eating a big meal too late in the evening.

POP VEGGIES Not usually found in a vending machine, vegetables might seem the most unlikely snack, but they are one of the best. Try our Coconut Roasted Sprout Pops with Gomashio (page 94) or Spicy Coconut Kale Crisps (page 121) – better than popcorn for a rumbling belly, we promise!

CRACKERS AND DIPS Our Multiseed Crackers (page 127) make the perfect dunkable snack and will satisfy cravings for crunchy foods. Teaming a tasty dip such as hummus with crudités is also a great way of getting in lots of raw veggies even if you're not usually a fan of them.

ON THE MOVE On short-haul flights, when it's usually just a sandwich and bag of salted nuts on offer, we always take our own food. A boiled egg, fresh fruit, avocado and some biltong (beef jerky) are easily portable. Make sure to bring a few of your favourite sweets too – like Tahini Applejacks (page 124) or Nicky's Chocolate Chip Cookies (page 302) – and always have a stash of non-perishables in your suitcase for emergencies and airport munchies (page 346).

MAKE USE OF LEFTOVERS Leftovers make the best snacks, so we'll often enjoy a bowl of our Moroccan Meditation Stew (page 72) or one of our soups (pages 56–87), even on the move – just don't forget your flask (see left).

SMOOTHIE TO GO A homemade green smoothie (page 324) is the best way to concentrate your greens in an easy-to-consume and portable way, especially when you're not sure when you'll get your next plate of veg.

ENJOY BONE BROTH It's the ultimate snack. Simply poured into a mug, this liquid gold (page 63) makes a wonderful snack at any time of day. Whisk in an egg towards the end of heating for added fats and protein and to make it super creamy.

MAKE IN BULK Most of the snacks in this chapter can be made in large quantities and frozen. So make use of your freezer and save yourself time in the long run.

FOOD COMBINING For optimal digestion, remember our simple food-combining rules (page 14) when choosing side dishes to accompany your main meal.

A light, fluffy carrot dish, this is perfect for serving with roast dinners as it soaks up gravy like standard mash but, being low in carbs, adheres to our food-combining rules, pairing with meat better than starchy potatoes. You can make this ahead and reheat it, and any leftovers can be turned into carrot croquettes (page 98) in place of the squash. Treat this like any other mash and throw in other ingredients to jazz it up – grated cheese, caramelised onions and mustard or any leftover roasted veggies. You can also serve this freshly blended instead of baked and adjust the liquid to whatever suits you.

CREAMY CARROT BAKE

SERVES 4 AS A SIDE

500g carrots,
    roughly chopped
5 tablespoons Bone
    Broth (chicken
    or beef bones
    – page 63) or
    vegetable stock
½ medium onion,
    roughly chopped
25g butter, at room
    temperature
¼ teaspoon ground
    cinnamon
¼–½ teaspoon
    freshly grated
    nutmeg
½ tablespoon
    coconut flour
1 egg
Sea salt and
    black pepper

1   Preheat the oven to fan 180°C/Gas mark 6.

2   Simmer the carrots in the broth for about 15 minutes until very tender. Place in a food processor with the onion, butter, spices and coconut flour. Season with a pinch of salt and some pepper and pulse until smooth.

3   Allow to cool a little and then pulse in the egg until well combined.

4   Pour into an ovenproof dish and bake for 35 minutes until firm in the middle and browning on top. Serve immediately.

We're pretty mad on sprouts! This underrated veg makes a star appearance at Christmas, often tarted up with cranberries, bacon and chestnuts, but they're equally delicious throughout their cool weather season simply roasted in a little coconut oil. The natural sweetness of the coconut counterbalances any bitterness in the sprouts, while the roasting process sweetens it further with some light caramelisation. This recipe is our savoury (and healthy!) answer to 'cake pops' – bursting with nutrients and quicker and easier to do. Just pop each roasted sprout on a cocktail stick and dip into our homemade gomashio – a Japanese condiment made from ground sesame seeds and salt. Once made, store the gomashio in a glass jar in the fridge and use for sprinkling over all sorts of things – just remember not to salt them first!

COCONUT ROASTED SPROUT POPS WITH GOMASHIO

SERVES 2–3 AS A SIDE OR SNACK

1 tablespoon
    coconut oil
500g Brussels
    sprouts

FOR THE GOMASHIO
100g white or black
    sesame seeds
1 tablespoon
    sea salt

1   Preheat the oven to fan 200°C/Gas mark 7, add the coconut oil to a large roasting tin and place in the oven to allow the oil to melt.

2   Slice off the ends of the sprouts and remove any brown or yellow leaves. Remove the roasting tin from the oven, add the sprouts and very carefully toss in the hot coconut oil.

3   Roast for 20 minutes, then remove any that are starting to caramelise. Stir the remainder and roast for a further 3–5 minutes until done.

4   Meanwhile, make the gomashio. Toast the sesame seeds in a dry pan on a medium-to-low heat for 2 minutes until popping and fragrant, taking care that they don't burn or you'll need to start over with a clean pan.

5   Grind the salt and sesame seeds together using a pestle and mortar or spice grinder or high-powered blender until roughly chopped or fairly fluffy.

6   Serve the roasted sprouts in a dish with a few cocktail sticks on the side and a small bowl of gomashio, or spear each sprout with a stick, dip in the gomashio and serve upside down in the hot roasting tin. They are also delicious cold.

TIPS

+ Take care when toasting black
  sesame seeds as it's harder to
  see if they're burning.

+ If using a high-powered blender, try
  not to overblend or you'll end up with
  tahini! Pulse and stir regularly.

VARIATIONS

+ Try mixing desiccated coconut
  with the salt instead, but don't
  put it through the grinder as it
  releases too many oils.

+ Dip into Parmesan or try with any
  of our dips and dressings (pages
  262–281).

Our top five favourite greens have to be spinach, parsley, watercress, cabbage and, of course, broccoli – our kind of superfoods. Dubbed 'gut brushes' by one of our friends due to their shape and their benefit to one's insides! As kids, we loved to prop broccoli 'trees' up in mash and have a gravy river running round them. Broccoli is standout with the right dressing – and here are two of our favourites. Remember that you can apply this cooking method and dressing to cauliflower florets too. The recipe below was inspired by a dish from the famous Café Habana in New York, and it's always on the menu at home if we've made a batch of our Quick-cooked Mayo (page 277).

BROCCOLI 2 WAYS

SERVES 2 AS A SIDE

300g broccoli
1½ tablespoons coconut oil
½ quantity of Quick-cooked Mayo (page 277)
¼ teaspoon cayenne pepper
Grated zest of ½ lime, juice of 1 lime
Sea salt and black pepper

1 tablespoon finely chopped fresh coriander, to serve
1 handful of finely grated Parmesan or other hard cheese (such as mature Cheddar), to serve

BROCCOLI WITH SPICY LIME MAYO

1 Prepare the broccoli by cutting into equal-sized florets and roughly chopping the stalks (after first slicing off the tough outer layer).

2 Melt the coconut oil in a large frying pan on a medium-high heat, add the broccoli and sauté for 4–5 minutes. Season with salt and pepper and set to one side in a serving bowl.

3 In a separate bowl, blend the mayonnaise with the cayenne pepper and lime zest and juice. Adjust the seasoning to your taste. Drizzle over the warm broccoli, or serve in a bowl alongside the broccoli as a dip. Sprinkle the coriander and cheese over the broccoli to serve.

TIP

+ The mayo can be substituted with full-fat probiotic yoghurt, or throw in some butter or coconut oil.

SERVES 2 AS A SIDE

1 teaspoon
  fennel seeds
300g broccoli
2 tablespoons
  butter
½–1 tablespoon
  mustard
  (to taste)
¼–1 teaspoon
  maple syrup
Sea salt and
  black pepper

MUSTARD MAPLE BROCCOLI

1 On a medium-high heat, toast the fennel seeds in a large, dry frying pan for about a minute or so until fragrant.

2 Prepare the broccoli by cutting into equal-sized florets and roughly chopping the stalks (after first slicing off the tough outer layer).

3 Add the butter to the fennel seeds in the pan, along with the broccoli, mustard and maple syrup and sauté for 6 minutes or more – adding a dash of water, if needed, to prevent burning – until the broccoli is tender. Season with salt and pepper. Serve hot or cold.

Sri Lankan food offers a wide array of different flavours. Often more heavily spiced than Indian dishes, it is renowned for its fiery curries, sweet onion relishes and sour lime pickles, not to mention all that lovely coconut. Inspired to make croquettes using leftover roasted butternut squash, we thought the natural sweetness would be ideal to carry all that heat and spice. We use toasted chickpea flour to bind the mixture (toasting reduces the bitterness of the flour, while making it easier to digest) and then rolled the croquettes in desiccated coconut to coat before baking in the oven. Absolutely moreish: once you pop, you just can't stop! Delicious with a yoghurt and lime dip or, as here, straight-up lime juice.

SRI LANKAN SQUASH CROQUETTES

MAKES 10–12 CROQUETTES

1 medium butternut squash (about 1kg – to make 300g roasted flesh)
60g chickpea flour
1 tablespoon coconut oil, ghee or butter
½ teaspoon grated fresh root ginger (unpeeled if organic)
1 garlic clove, diced
1 teaspoon fennel seeds
A pinch of cayenne pepper or chilli powder
20g spring onions, sliced
2 teaspoons grated lime zest

10g fresh coriander (leaves and stalks) or mint leaves, finely chopped
80g desiccated coconut
½ teaspoon sea salt
¼ teaspoon white or black pepper

FOR THE DIP
Juice of 3 limes
A pinch of sea salt

1   Preheat the oven to fan 180°C/Gas mark 6. Line a baking tray with baking parchment.

2   Roast the butternut squash whole for 30–40 minutes until a knife slides in easily, then slice in half to cool so that much of the moisture evaporates. Alternatively, slice the squash in half lengthways and roast cut side up to allow the moisture to evaporate during cooking. When it's cool enough to touch, discard the seeds and scoop the flesh out into a bowl to dry out further. Leave the oven on for the croquettes.

3   Meanwhile, place the chickpea flour in a dry pan and toast on a medium heat for 5 minutes until fragrant and golden brown, being careful not to let it burn, then add it to the bowl with the squash. Give the pan a quick wipe clean.

4   In the same pan, melt the coconut oil, ghee or butter and fry the ginger with the garlic, fennel seeds and cayenne pepper or chilli powder for 5 minutes, being careful not to let them burn, then add to the bowl. Mash everything together with a fork until well combined, then stir in the spring onions, lime zest and coriander or mint. Add 20g of the desiccated coconut and the salt and pepper.

5   Spread out the remaining desiccated coconut on a plate.
    Take roughly 2 tablespoons of the butternut mixture, shape
    into a croquette and roll in the desiccated coconut (use two
    metal spoons to help you do this) until completely covered,
    then place on the lined baking tray. If the mixture is quite
    moist, adding a bit more desiccated coconut and chilling
    in the fridge for 10 minutes will make it easier to roll.

6   Bake on the top shelf of the oven for about 20 minutes until
    golden brown all over. Mix the lime juice and salt for the dip
    in a bowl. Serve the croquettes warm with the dip.

Even if you're not that keen on parsnips, parsnip chips are guaranteed to win you over! Smoky and sweet from the paprika and coconut oil, they make an addictive accompaniment to any main dish, especially when served with one of our dips, such as Homemade Sriracha (page 279) or BBQ Ketchup (page 278), or something cool and creamy like Quick-cooked Mayo (page 277) or Creamy Cashew Ranch Dressing (page 276). They also pair wonderfully with Mushroom Lentil Burgers (page 258). For those times when parsnips are harder to track down, and for a low-carb option that's more easily digested with a protein-based main dish such as our onglet steak (page 219), we've included our equally tasty Carrot and Rosemary Chips. Both are delicious cold the next day – a good one for the lunch box.

VEGETABLE CHIPS 2 WAYS

SERVES 4 AS A SIDE

1 tablespoon
    coconut oil
500g parsnips
    (about 4 large),
    topped and tailed
1 tablespoon hot
    smoked paprika
    (or to taste)
Sea salt and
    black pepper

SMOKY PARSNIP CHIPS

1   Preheat the oven to fan 200°C/Gas mark 7. Line a baking tray with baking parchment, add the coconut oil and leave it in the oven for a few minutes until the oil has melted.

2   Meanwhile, scrub the parsnips until clean and then lightly peel them. (No need to peel them if yours are organic.) Slice into thin chips.

3   Remove the hot tray from the oven, add the parsnips with the other ingredients and, using tongs, toss in the oil until the chips are evenly coated. Spread out evenly on the tray, then bake for 35 minutes until golden brown. Flip the chips halfway through baking so they crisp up evenly.

4   Remove from the oven and serve immediately with an extra sprinkling of sea salt.

SERVES 4 AS A SIDE

1 tablespoon
   coconut oil
500g carrots (about
   5 large), topped
   and tailed
2 teaspoons
   roughly chopped
   fresh rosemary
   leaves or
   1 teaspoon dried
3 tablespoons finely
   grated Parmesan
   (optional)
Sea salt and
   black pepper

CARROT AND ROSEMARY CHIPS

1   Preheat the oven to fan 200°C/Gas mark 7. Line a baking
    tray with baking parchment, add the coconut oil and leave
    it in the oven for a few minutes until the oil has melted.

2   Meanwhile, scrub the carrots until clean and then lightly
    peel them. (No need to peel them if yours are organic.)
    Slice into thin chips about 1cm wide.

3   Remove the hot tray from the oven, add the carrots with
    the other ingredients (not too much salt if you're including
    Parmesan) and, using tongs or two spoons, toss in the oil
    until the chips are evenly coated. Spread out evenly on the
    tray, then bake for 30–35 minutes until golden brown. Flip
    the chips halfway through baking so they crisp up evenly.

4   Remove from the oven and serve immediately.

TIP

+   Use two baking trays, if needed,
    to allow plenty of space between
    the chips so that they bake rather
    than steam.

Quick and easy to prepare, this Indian-inspired dish can be on the table in fifteen minutes. It's even better served cold the next day, so make ahead or save any leftovers for a packed lunch. The flavours here go especially well with the tomato-based Slow-Cooked 'No Fry' Chicken Curry (page 197). Cook the cabbage according to your preference for crunch: for us this varies according to our mood, what we're serving it with or whether we are short of time! To make it more of a meal, combine with buckwheat noodles or quinoa, or serve quick-cooked and crunchy with two fried eggs. The spice mix here would be delicious with green beans, broccoli or any other green vegetables.

SPICED COCONUT CABBAGE

SERVES 4 AS A SIDE

1 tablespoon
   coconut oil
1 garlic clove, diced
4cm piece
   of fresh root
   ginger (unpeeled
   if organic),
   finely diced
1 large green or
   white cabbage,
   shredded
2 tablespoons
   desiccated
   coconut
Grated zest and
   juice of ½ lemon
   or 1 lime
Sea salt and
   black pepper

FOR THE SPICES
1 teaspoon
   cumin seeds
   or ½ teaspoon
   ground cumin
½ teaspoon ground
   turmeric
1 teaspoon
   mustard seeds

1 Toast the spices in a deep, wide frying pan on a medium heat for 30 seconds. Add the coconut oil with the garlic and ginger and fry for 1 minute.

2 Tip in the cabbage and desiccated coconut and cook for 10 minutes, covered, until softened and fragrant (or cook for 3 minutes if you want it crunchy – with the lid off).

3 Season with salt and pepper to taste and stir through the lemon or lime zest and juice.

Hot or cold, this immune-boosting side dish of greens goes with absolutely everything. Top cold leftovers with freshly fried eggs or stir it into cooked quinoa for a speedy lunch on the go. You could even add a spoonful to a bowl of steaming hot soup. Use rainbow chard when in season to give dinner-party finesse to a knockout dish of vibrant colours. Try making it with cavolo nero, spinach or kale, too – we love all these iron-rich super-greens.

GARLICKY CHILLI CHARD

SERVES 4 AS A SIDE

400g chard
    (preferably
    rainbow),
    spinach, cavolo
    nero or kale
1 tablespoon ghee
    or coconut oil
2 garlic cloves,
    diced or crushed
½–1 fresh red chilli
    (to taste), diced
4 tablespoons water
Juice of ½ lemon
    (to taste)
2 tablespoons
    extra-virgin olive
    oil, for drizzling
Sea salt and
    black pepper

1   Discard any particularly tough ends of the chard or other choice of greens (and discard the kale stems, if using), then slice the stalks into 1cm-wide pieces before shredding or roughly chopping the leaves.

2   Add half the ghee or coconut oil to a large pan and fry the stalks with the garlic and chilli over a medium heat for a minute until the garlic is softened but not browned.

3   Add the leaves and the water, put a lid on the pan and steam for a further 2–3 minutes until the stalks are tender, the leaves just cooked and the water fully absorbed.

4   Season with lemon juice, salt and pepper to taste and drizzle with the EVOO.

This simple one-pot dish always inspires much appreciation when it leaves the oven and lands in the centre of the table – earthy root vegetables baked in bone broth, topped with a crunchy layer of blue cheese and buckwheat groats. Our recipe is really versatile – swap grated turnip for the celeriac, top with roughly chopped hazelnuts or ground almonds, and substitute with any hard cheese, such as Cheddar. You can easily double the quantities, too. For a dairy-free dish, season the gratin with onion powder, herbs and extra sea salt, and dot with coconut oil, dripping or ghee (suitable for most people who are lactose intolerant).

CELERIAC AND BLUE CHEESE GRATIN

SERVES 4

3 tablespoons
    butter, plus extra
    for greasing
1 large celeriac
A pinch of freshly
    grated nutmeg
½ teaspoon dried
    thyme
5 tablespoons
    Bone Broth
    (page 63) or
    vegetable stock
100g buckwheat
    groats or ground
    almonds
200g blue cheese
    (such as Stilton),
    crumbled
Sea salt and
    black pepper

1   Preheat the oven to fan 180°C/Gas mark 6 and grease a 25cm x 18cm ovenproof dish with butter.

2   Peel and quarter the celeriac and grate by hand or in a food processor using the S-curved blade or grater attachment.

3   Toss in the prepared dish with the nutmeg, thyme, 2 big pinches of salt and some pepper, then pour over the broth or stock.

4   Sprinkle over the buckwheat groats or ground almonds, crumble over the blue cheese so that it's evenly spread, and dot with the butter.

5   Bake for 30 minutes, then raise the oven temperature to fan 200°C/Gas mark 7 and bake for an extra 10–15 minutes until crispy and golden on top.

Everyone loves a tomato sauce with garlic and onions. Throw in some green beans and you have the most delicious dish to go with meat or fish, or to accompany quinoa or butternut squash. Made with sliced runner or green beans, this has roots in Greek and Middle Eastern cooking. Traditionally, olive oil is used to cook the beans before adding the tomatoes; here we save the goodness of extra-virgin olive oil to finish the dish and use ghee or dripping instead to cook the beans. We've based this recipe on the Lebanese version recommended by our friend Miss Bibi, who emailed us specially to say that it's perfect for this book. It's a favourite of ours, too – not only because it can all be chucked into a pot and left to simmer, but because it uses ingredients from the store cupboard. We call it 'Lubee Beans'; the correct name is *loubieh bi' zayt*.

LUBEE BEANS
(LEBANESE GREEN BEANS IN TOMATO SAUCE)

SERVES 6 AS A SIDE

1 large onion,
   finely diced
1 tablespoon ghee
   or dripping
5 large garlic
   cloves, diced
1 x 400g tin of
   chopped
   tomatoes
1 tablespoon
   tomato purée
500g frozen
   green beans
   or trimmed
   fresh beans
¾ teaspoon sea salt
½ teaspoon
   black pepper
3 tablespoons extra-
   virgin olive oil,
   to serve

1 Sauté the onion in the ghee or dripping on a medium heat for 5 minutes until softened. Add the garlic and cook for an extra 3–4 minutes.

2 Add the rest of the ingredients except the EVOO and simmer, covered, on a low heat for 20 minutes. Remove the lid and continue to cook for a further 5–10 minutes, stirring frequently, until the sauce has thickened.

3 Allow to cool slightly and then stir in the EVOO to serve. Store any leftovers in the fridge and serve cold the next day.

VARIATIONS

+ You can use butter instead of the ghee or dripping, giving a creamier taste.

+ Replace the green beans with runner beans. Choose young ones so that you don't have to de-string them, and slice on the diagonal. They will need cooking for slightly longer.

+ We also make this with okra (super-nutritious!) and even Savoy cabbage and peas. Very British!

+ Delicious served with Kasha Buckwheat Burgers/Balls and Quick-cooked Mayo (pages 234 and 277).

We all know that carrots are great for the eyes. But did you know they are also good for the skin and the brain, as well as helping to reduce inflammation? This two-way Ayurvedic recipe was taught to us by our meditation teacher, Gary Gorrow, over in Sydney, Australia. Just grate the carrots and lightly stir-fry with mustard seeds, or mix the raw carrots with the toasted seeds, then enjoy on its own or serve as a side dish. This dish 'food combines' with everything: try it with our Kasha Buckwheat Burgers/Balls (page 234), Easy Cheesy Broccoli Risotto (page 248) or Spicy Miso Salmon with Broccoli Rice (page 170). Cooked carrots are sweet and nourishing, easy to digest yet contain plenty of fibre – perfect as part of your supper. Raw carrot, on the other hand, is said to be stimulating – excellent eaten earlier in the day or during hot weather.

AYURVEDIC CARROT STIR-FRY/SALAD

SERVES 2 AS A SIDE

1 tablespoon ghee
    or coconut oil
1 tablespoon black
    mustard seeds
2 large carrots,
    grated
Juice of ½ lemon
    or ½ lime
Sea salt and
    black pepper

1 **FOR THE STIR-FRY:** Heat the ghee or coconut oil in a small pan over a medium heat. Add the mustard seeds and cook until they begin to pop out of the pan (taking care not to let them burn and become bitter). Add the grated carrots and stir-fry for 5 minutes until just tender, then season with salt and pepper and toss with the lemon juice.

2 **FOR THE SALAD:** Place the grated carrots in a bowl, toast the seeds in the ghee or coconut oil as in step 1 and pour over the carrots, stirring to mix. Season with salt and pepper and toss with the lemon juice.

Our mash recipes call for nutrient-rich, lower-starch vegetables in place of standard potatoes, to help you feel satisfied for longer! We love to experiment with different root vegetables depending on the season. Here, we use beetroot, carrot or cauliflower as the base and flavour each one differently so that you have mash for any occasion. You can steam or roast your vegetables before mashing. Try the cauli mash with bangers and onion gravy or topped with a fried egg, and serve the carrot and mustard mash with roasted chicken and our Sensational Sprout Salad (page 148). For optimum food combining, serve beetroot mash with vegetable dishes, such as Kasha Buckwheat Burgers/Balls (page 234) or Mushroom Lentil Burgers (page 258). Any leftover mash can be reheated in a pan with a few tablespoons of bone broth or water, covered with a lid, until steaming hot.

VEG MASH 3 WAYS

SERVES 4 AS A SIDE

2 large cauliflowers,
    outer leaves
    removed
25g butter
4 tablespoons water
4 garlic cloves
Sea salt and
    black pepper

VARIATIONS

+   **CHEESY CAULIFLOWER MASH**
    Make the cauliflower mash in
    the same way, adding 2 handfuls
    of grated cheese in step 3 above.
    Use any cheese you have to hand,
    but for a nostalgic mash we prefer
    good old Cheddar.

+   **CAULIFLOWER MUSTARD MASH**
    Make the cauliflower mash in the
    same way, adding 1 tablespoon of
    mustard to the pan in step 1 above.

GARLICKY CAULIFLOWER MASH

1   Slice off the tough skin at the base of the stem, then roughly chop the cauliflower into 5cm chunks. Place the butter and water in a large pan and add the cauliflower and garlic.

2   Cover the pan with a lid and steam over a medium heat for around 8 minutes until the cauliflower is tender when tested with a knife. All the water should be absorbed, but add a splash more water during cooking if needed and allow any excess water to evaporate.

3   Add the cauliflower and garlic to a food processor – or leave in the pan and use a hand-held stick blender – and purée until smooth and creamy or roughly textured, as you wish. Season with salt and pepper to taste. Garnish with fresh herbs (such as chives) if you like.

TIP

+   If the cauliflower mash is too sloppy or wet, reheat in a pan, over a low heat, to allow some moisture to evaporate.

→   CONTINUED OVERLEAF

VEG MASH 3 WAYS (CONTINUED)

SERVES 4 AS A SIDE

2 tablespoons water
5 large carrots,
    roughly chopped
1 garlic clove
    (unpeeled)
1 tablespoon butter
2 teaspoons mustard
    (to taste)
Sea salt and
    black pepper

CARROT AND MUSTARD MASH

1   Put the water in a pan, along with a pinch of salt then add the carrots and garlic and steam over a medium heat, with the lid on, for 15 minutes until tender. Drain off any excess liquid, reserving some for thinning the mash if needed.

2   Slip the garlic from its skin using your thumb.

3   Add all the ingredients to a food processor and blend until smooth, seasoning with salt and pepper to taste.

VARIATION

+   We've also added leftover celeriac to this mash, and swede makes a good addition too.

SERVES 4 AS A SIDE

300ml water
4 large beetroots,
    scrubbed and
    quartered
    (roughly 500g)
2 tablespoons
    grated (peeled)
    fresh horseradish
    or creamed
    horseradish
1 tablespoon butter
Sea salt and
    black pepper

PINK BEETROOT MASH WITH HORSERADISH

1   Put the water in a pan, along with a pinch of salt then add the beetroot chunks. Cover and simmer for 30–40 minutes until tender.

2   Once cooked, drain the beetroots of any excess water, peel them and place in a food processor with the horseradish and butter. Blend until smooth and creamy, adding a little water if needed, and season with salt and pepper to taste.

TIP

+   Wasabi would make a quirky alternative to the horseradish.

The avocado boat marks a return of the delicious 1970s-style starter, which we like to eat as a snack. Rich in satiating fats, these make real hunger-busters, especially if filled with full-fat cottage cheese for added protein and topped with a little paprika. For something light and refreshing, a splash of olive oil and a dash of balsamic will do. This was the family favourite growing up. If your taste buds are calling for something sweet, then drizzle with raw honey and squeeze over some lemon juice. A touch of sea salt is a must to bring out the flavours, and some black pepper wouldn't go amiss either – even on the sweet version.

AVOCADO BOATS 3 WAYS

SERVES 1–2 AS A SNACK

1 ripe avocado
Sea salt and
    black pepper

1 Cut into the avocado lengthways, producing two long avocado halves that are still connected in the middle by the stone. Take hold of both halves and twist them in opposite directions until they naturally separate. The stone will remain in one half: remove the stone if serving the whole avocado or store the unused half (with the stone still in it) in the fridge in an airtight container, to stop it going brown.

2 Fill the hole of each avocado half with one of the following combinations, season with salt and pepper and serve immediately.

OLIVE OIL AND BALSAMIC VINEGAR

Fill with extra-virgin olive oil and a splash of balsamic vinegar.

LEMON AND HONEY DRIZZLE

Squeeze over some lemon juice and drizzle with raw honey. A tiny sprinkle of ground cinnamon is also a nice touch.

COTTAGE CHEESE AND PAPRIKA

Add a spoonful of full-fat cottage cheese, topped with a dusting of paprika. Chopped spring onions and a pinch of ground cumin are delicious too.

We love these fun bites – using the best bits of a smoked salmon and cucumber sandwich! Dinner parties and gatherings are for enjoying, rather than spending too much time in the kitchen, so this is the perfect canapé for such occasions because it allows you to do just that. The cucumber and horseradish cream can be prepared in advance then assembled just before your guests arrive. These also make a delicious starter, as well as a quick and easy mid-afternoon snack and are great for picnics too: just put out the sliced cucumber, smoked salmon, horseradish, lemon halves for squeezing and cream cheese and let everyone help themselves. No more fiddly canapés!

CUCUMBER AND SMOKED SALMON CANAPÉS

SERVES 4 AS A CANAPÉ

150g full-fat cream cheese or soft goat's cheese
1–2 teaspoons grated horseradish (peeled fresh root or a good-quality one from a jar), to taste
2 teaspoons chopped fresh dill, plus dill sprigs or chopped chives, to garnish
1 teaspoon lemon juice
1 large cucumber (the thinner the better for canapés)
100g smoked salmon
Sea salt and black pepper

1   Place the cream cheese or goat's cheese in a bowl with the horseradish, dill, lemon juice and a pinch of salt and pepper. Mix together and chill in the fridge for up to 1 hour, if you have time, to allow the flavours to develop. You can always add more horseradish later, if needed.

2   Cut the cucumber into 1cm-thick slices and carefully scoop out some of the seeds, making sure not to go through to the bottom.

3   Arrange the cucumber slices on a platter and distribute the cream cheese mixture evenly between them, neatly filling the centres.

4   Cut the smoked salmon into strips. Roll up and place one on top of each piece of filled cucumber. Garnish with dill sprigs or chopped chives and a sprinkling of black pepper.

VARIATIONS

+   This recipe works with any smoked fish: switch it up and use mackerel, herring or trout, or top with cooked crab, small prawns or crayfish.

+   If you don't have horseradish to hand, up the black pepper so that you still have a kick, or try wasabi to taste.

+   For a vegetarian version, simply swap the salmon with half a cherry tomato or a slice of radish.

Fantastic for breakfast too (especially breakfast on the move), these delicious savoury muffins contain all the favourites – bacon, apple, onion (and cheese if you like!). Whole strips of bacon line the muffin moulds, with no need to pre-cook the rashers. Coconut flour gives the muffins a crumb, the apple keeps them fresh and yoghurt makes them fluffy. We also sneak in a few greens to offset the salty bacon and cheese. Here we've used kale, but you could try spinach, rocket, spring greens or chard, or pack in some parsley. Experiment with flavours: try different spices (cumin and egg always go together) or swap the bacon and Cheddar for Stilton. You can leave out the yoghurt for a denser, more eggy muffin, and use a little ground cinnamon instead of Cheddar – a great match for the bacon and apple too.

APPLE AND BACON MUFFINS

MAKES 6 MUFFINS

Butter or coconut
    oil, for greasing
    (optional)
5 eggs
4 tablespoons
    coconut yoghurt
    or full-fat
    probiotic yoghurt
4 tablespoons
    coconut flour
2 apples, cored
    and finely diced
1 handful of kale,
    thick stems
    removed and
    leaves shredded
    (about 20g)
2 spring onions,
    finely sliced
40g mature
    Cheddar, grated,
    or ½ teaspoon
    ground cinnamon

¼ teaspoon
    bicarbonate
    of soda
¼ teaspoon sea salt
A big pinch of
    black pepper
1½ teaspoons apple
    cider vinegar
    or lemon juice
6 rashers of
    unsmoked bacon

1   Preheat the oven to fan 190°C/Gas mark 6½ and line a six-hole muffin tin with baking parchment cases. If you are using a stainless-steel tin, lightly grease with butter or coconut oil (no need to add paper cases).

2   Beat the eggs and the yoghurt together, then stir in the rest of the ingredients except the bacon.

3   Use a rasher of bacon to line each hole or paper case, so that the fat side comes above the edge of the hole/paper case. Divide the batter between the bacon-lined holes or paper cases.

4   Bake in the oven for about 25 minutes until the tops of the muffins are golden brown. Remove from the oven and allow to cool in the tin for a few minutes before serving, or transfer to a wire rack and leave to cool completely before storing in an airtight container in the fridge.

It took us a little while to find the perfect way to cook kale crisps. The trick, in our opinion, is to let them bake nice and slowly, as well as making sure they are well spaced out on the baking sheet so they roast rather than steam. In our quest for the perfect kale crisp, we tried many flavour combinations and this chilli-paprika blend came out as our favourite. Try it yourself: it's the perfect excuse to use up any spices gathering dust in your cupboard! Kale crisps make great nibbles if you're having people round for drinks, especially if served alongside our Salty Cajun-roasted Cauliflower (page 122).

SPICY COCONUT KALE CRISPS

MAKES 1 BIG TRAY

2 teaspoons
    coconut oil
200g kale, thick
    stems removed
A small pinch of
    chilli powder or
    cayenne pepper
1 teaspoon sweet
    smoked paprika
½ teaspoon sea salt

1   Preheat the oven to fan 150°C/Gas mark 3½. Line a large baking tray with baking parchment, add the coconut oil and place in the oven to allow the oil to melt.

2   Wash the kale, then pat it dry with a clean tea towel (the drier the kale, the crispier the chips will be).

3   Tear the kale leaves into pieces that are just larger than bite-sized.

4   Remove the hot tray from the oven, add the kale with all the remaining ingredients and, using tongs or two forks, toss together until the kale is evenly coated.

5   Spread the kale evenly over the tray, leaving a little space between the leaves (it's important you don't overlap the kale pieces), and return to the oven to bake for 25 minutes.

6   Watch the kale carefully and remove it from the oven as soon as the edges start to brown. If you can resist them, leave for 3 minutes to crisp up even more before serving.

This is the easiest snack to serve to peckish guests. Do all the prep before they arrive – use a quality ready-made Cajun/Creole spice mix if you're short of time – and then just chuck in the oven. They are always a crowd-pleaser and we love surprising people with yet another way to enjoy cauliflower. Serve with BBQ Ketchup (page 278), a drizzle of Homemade Sriracha (page 279), Creamy Cashew Ranch Dressing (page 276) our Quick-cooked Mayo (page 277) or any of our dips or dressings (pages 262–281) – they will all be delicious. Or just sprinkle over some chopped fresh herbs like chives. Pop any leftovers in a Power Salad in a Jar (page 160) for a packed lunch, whizz into a quick soup with some Bone Broth (page 63), or make into a frittata for your Sunday brunch.

SALTY CAJUN-ROASTED CAULIFLOWER

MAKES 1 BIG TRAY TO SERVE 4

1 tablespoon
    coconut oil
1 large cauliflower
    (outer leaves and
    stalk removed),
    chopped into
    equal-sized
    florets
1 handful of fresh
    chives, snipped,
    to serve (optional)

FOR THE CAJUN SPICE MIX

1 teaspoon sweet
    smoked paprika
1 teaspoon dried
    oregano or
    thyme
1/8 teaspoon
    cayenne pepper
    or chilli powder
1 teaspoon
    garlic powder
    (optional)
1/2 teaspoon
    onion powder
    (optional)
Sea salt and
    black pepper

1 Preheat the oven to fan 215°C/Gas mark 8½. Put the coconut oil in a large baking tray and leave in the oven for a few minutes until the oil has melted.

2 Meanwhile, mix together all the ingredients for the spice mix, seasoning with salt and pepper.

3 Remove the hot tray from the oven, add the cauliflower with the spice mix and, using tongs or two spoons, toss together until the florets are evenly coated. Spread them out on the tray, then roast for 30–40 minutes, tossing in the tray at regular intervals, until golden brown but still with a bit of bite.

4 Serve with an extra sprinkling of sea salt and eat as they are or serve with the snipped chives sprinkled over, if you wish.

Shop-bought flapjacks, trail mixes and granola may have a healthy image, but they can be loaded with a variety of sugars, processed vegetable oils and other undesirables. Try making your own seed bars – not too sweet, not too savoury – using only wholesome ingredients. Just stir the ingredients together and bake. The egg white in this recipe adds protein and gives the mixture a crispier texture, though you could leave it out for a more crumbly bar.

TAHINI APPLEJACKS

MAKES 9 BARS

6 tablespoons
    light tahini
1 tablespoon
    coconut flour
1 tablespoon
    raw honey
A pinch of sea salt
1 teaspoon vanilla
    extract
2 teaspoons ground
    cinnamon
1 egg white
1 apple, cored
    and grated
5 tablespoons
    shelled
    hemp seeds
5 tablespoons
    pumpkin seeds
5 tablespoons
    sunflower seeds

5 tablespoons
    desiccated
    coconut
Sesame seeds in
    different colours
    (black, white),
    to decorate
    (optional)

1   Preheat the oven to fan 180°C/Gas mark 6 and line a 20cm-square cake tin or ovenproof dish with baking parchment.

2   Mix the first seven ingredients together in a mixing bowl and then fold in the rest of the ingredients except the sesame seeds.

3   Pour the mixture into the prepared tin or dish. Flatten down evenly with the back of a spoon and sprinkle with the sesame seeds if desired.

4   Bake in the oven for 30–35 minutes until lightly golden at the edges. Remove from the oven, allow to cool completely in the tin/dish and then slice into bars. Store in the fridge or freezer.

TIP

+   Save the unused egg yolk for making Quick-cooked Mayo (page 277) or for adding to soups or Green Eggs 3 Ways (page 43).

These easy sweet and savoury crackers are crispy and nutritious. We use a mix of chickpea flour and buckwheat flour to make the base. Each of these has a distinctive flavour but, in an equal blend, one offsets the other, allowing the cinnamon and maple syrup for the sweet crackers and the spices for the savoury version sing through. Ground flaxseed binds them for an egg- and nut- free cracker that's also dairy-free if you use coconut oil instead of butter. These last well in the fridge and are also great for freezing, so make big batches of them for a regular supply. Dip them (try the Spicy Turmeric and Red Lentil Dip, page 269), smother in Broccomole (page 128), top with cheese or just slather with butter or coconut oil – yum!

MULTISEED CRACKERS

MAKES ABOUT 40 CRACKERS

6 tablespoons
  chickpea flour
6 tablespoons
  buckwheat flour
5 tablespoons
  ground flaxseed
  or 6 tablespoons
  (90g) whole
  flaxseeds
½ teaspoon sea salt
4 tablespoons water
2 tablespoons
  coconut oil or
  butter, melted
4 tablespoons
  sunflower seeds
4 tablespoons
  pumpkin seeds

FOR THE FLAVOURINGS

2 tablespoons
  ground
  cinnamon and
  2–3 tablespoons
  maple syrup (for
  sweet crackers)
½ teaspoon
  ground cumin,
  3 teaspoons
  garlic powder
  and a pinch
  more sea salt
  (for savoury
  crackers)

1 Preheat the oven to fan 150°C/Gas mark 3½. You'll need a 27cm x 39cm baking tray.

2 Combine the chickpea and buckwheat flours, flaxseed and salt in a bowl. Stir in the water and use your hands to mix together. Add the coconut oil or butter, seeds and your choice of flavourings. For the savoury you might need another ½ tablespoon of water to make the dough come together.

3 Use your hands to bring everything together into a dough and place on a piece of baking parchment the size of the tray. Cover with a second piece of baking parchment and, using a rolling pin, roll the dough as thin as possible between the sheets to the thickness of the pumpkin seeds.

4 Use the back of a knife to mark the cracker shapes through the paper into about 40 squares and then carefully peel back the top sheet of baking parchment and discard.

5 Put the crackers with the baking parchment onto the baking tray and bake in the oven for 25 minutes until deep golden brown and crisp. Remove from the oven and cool completely before snapping into pieces. Store in an airtight container in the fridge or freezer.

TIP

+ These freeze really well, so take advantage of the oven being on and make more than one batch.

VARIATION

+ You can split the dough into two and make one half savoury and the other sweet, remembering to halve the quantities of the flavourings for each half-batch.

A broccoli version of guacamole, this is an easy dip that goes with just about everything. Try it with Punchy Piri-piri Chicken Wings (page 192) or Mexican Beef and Carrot Burgers/Balls (page 214), or dunk your Smoky Parsnip Chips (page 100) or Multiseed Crackers (page 127) into it. For a little more punch, add a clove of garlic – either raw or steamed – with the broccoli or roasted during your Sunday Cook-Off (page 334). We've given the option of cashews or yoghurt to make it creamy, and even avocado for those who prefer it to be more like guacamole – so you can try a different version each time.

BROCCOMOLE

MAKES 660G

1 large head
    broccoli
    (about 300g)
1 garlic clove
    (optional)
4 tablespoons water
150g cashews
    (soaked in
    double the
    volume of water
    for 2–3 hours,
    then drained
    and rinsed),
    or 80g full-fat
    probiotic
    yoghurt, or
    1 medium-sized
    ripe avocado
4 slices of pickled
    jalapeño (or to
    taste) or a pinch
    of cayenne
    pepper
2 spring onions or
    ¼ small onion

Juice of 1 lime
4 tablespoons extra-
    virgin olive oil,
    plus extra for
    drizzling
¼ teaspoon sea salt
¼ teaspoon
    black pepper

1   Prepare the broccoli by cutting into equal-sized florets and roughly chopping the stalks (after first slicing off the tough outer layer).

2   Place the broccoli (and the garlic clove if desired) and water in a saucepan and steam, covered with a lid, on a medium heat for 5 minutes until tender, then transfer to a food processor along with 1–2 tablespoons of the remaining cooking water.

3   Add the remaining ingredients and blend until smooth. Taste and adjust the seasoning if needed. Drizzle with EVOO and serve warm or cold.

This delicious pink condiment not only adorns the plate with its rich colour and tantalises the taste buds with its garlicky, spicy-sour tang, but it's also a tasty source of probiotics on the cheap. Cabbage leaves have their own bacterial cultures, so by creating the right conditions for them to ferment, we end up with an even more nutritious food that keeps in the fridge for months and months! We've gone for red cabbage for its glorious colour, ranging from a pale pink to a deep purple, and added our favourite combo of garlic, ginger and jalapeño so that it not only does us good, but tastes good too. Great served with sausages and cauli mash (page 111) and other hearty flavours like steak and dahl (pages 219 and 78), it's also good added to leftovers and drizzled with olive oil for a quick meal.

PINK CHILLI KRAUT

MAKES A 1-LITRE JAR

1.5kg red cabbage
    (about 2 medium)
3 garlic cloves,
    diced
30g grated fresh
    root ginger
    (unpeeled
    if organic)
4 slices of pickled
    jalapeño
    (or to taste)
1 tablespoon
    sea salt

1   Remove the outer leaves of each cabbage and set aside. Quarter each cabbage, remove the core and shred the leaves by hand or in a food processor using the grater attachment.

2   Add to a large mixing bowl with the rest of the ingredients, pop on some rubber gloves and knead everything together for several minutes. Let the mixture stand for a few more minutes and knead again. By now, the cabbage juices and salt should have created a nice brine.

3   Layer the cabbage mixture in a sterilised 1-litre jar (see tip opposite), packing down regularly with your fist or the end of a rolling pin so that the mixture is submerged in the brine.

4   Roll up the reserved outer cabbage leaves and use to wedge the mixture down so that it is completely submerged in the brine by at least 2cm. If there is not enough brine, add 1–2 tablespoons of water and give a little shake to mix.

5   Seal the jar with its sterilised clip-top lid, or tightly cover with a muslin cloth fastened with an elastic band.

6   Stand the jar on a plate and leave at room temperature for a few days to ferment. (This will vary depending on the time of year – in warmer weather, it will ferment more quickly.)

7   After a few days, taste to see if it has fermented to the desired degree of sourness. Transfer the jar to the fridge, where it will keep for months. Use a clean spoon every time you dip into the jar to serve from it, then reseal it.

TIPS

+ If you can't find red cabbage, white cabbage will do just as well. But if you just have to have pink, then throw in some grated raw beetroot too!

+ Remember when introducing probiotics to your diet to build up slowly. Start with a teaspoon as a condiment and before you know it you'll be enjoying this dish as a side!

+ To sterilise your glass jar and lid, add boiling water and leave for 10 minutes then drain, or put through a hot dishwasher cycle.

SANDWICHES AND SALADS

We kick off with sandwiches: some tasty fillings (pages 138–140) and delicious recipes for open sandwiches or toasties (pages 141–145) made with our Quinoa Courgette Toast (page 32) or soft and doughy Flaxseed Buns (page 136). Both offer an easy and nutritious wholefood alternative to commercial breads. The buns can be knocked up so quickly: just mix together and bake – no need for any kind of proving and no baking skills required. The same with the quinoa bread – you just need a food processor and to remember to soak the ingredients overnight. With a good balance of protein, carbohydrates and fat to keep you fuller for longer, you will avoid the bloated sensation that often comes after eating many types breads. Freeze the flaxseed rolls and the quinoa bread in slices ready to throw together a portable meal at any time.

When it comes to packed lunches, our Power Salad in a Jar (page 160), for instance, is ideal for munching on when you're out and about. Simply throw in some dressing at the bottom to avoid 'soggy-salad syndrome' and layer up your ingredients, starting with a protein base – shredded chicken or beef strips, cooked lentils, beans or quinoa – followed by any veg you have to hand and top with a handful of fresh salad leaves. Seal tightly and you're good to go!

Even when the weather gets nippier, don't forget about these recipes – salads needn't be relegated to the summer months. Change things up as the seasons change: swap courgettes for root veg, for instance, and add peas, defrosted from frozen, and sundried tomatoes for that taste of summer in the winter. Mixing elements of both hot and cold warms up a salad – think hot dressing or sauce on some leftover veggies or hot quinoa tossed through green leaves.

If you're having people over, choose three of the salad recipes to group together. Make ahead, adding any delicate leaves and the dressing at the last minute, and serve them mezze-style. Try a spread of our Sesame Kale Salad (page 163), Chilli Kick Cucumber Snack (page 155), Mum's Aduki and Green Bean Salad (page 152) and Cucumber, Avocado and Chickpea and Tangle salads (pages 156 and 150) for a riot of colour, flavour and texture. You could add a warm side dish from one of the other chapters, such as our Salty Cajun-roasted Cauliflower (page 122) or Sri Lankan Squash Croquettes (page 98).

A great dressing can transform even the most basic salad, making the ingredients all the more mouth-watering. We always favour homemade dressings over store-bought options so each of the salads here is accompanied by its own delicious dressing. For lots more dressings ideas, see 'Dips, Dressings, Sauces and Spreads' (pages 262–281).

TIPS AND TRICKS

SERVE WITH A SOUP Warm up your salad by combining with soup. Try grating vegetables onto a bowl of soup or stew – the combination of hot and refreshingly cool, and smooth versus crunchy, is always a winner.

MIX IT UP How satisfying a meal is depends just as much on texture as flavour, and how you prepare your ingredients can make the difference. Spiralizing, slicing or dicing work wonderfully for raw summer vegetables, while in the colder months, when you may want something a little easier on digestion, a warm salad of roasted vegetables on a bed of leaves can be the answer. You can even gently warm your dressing before pouring it over the salad.

GET A SALAD SPINNER Whether the vegetables are organic or not, they need to be washed thoroughly. And drying the leaves afterwards is essential for the dressing to really stick to them and to avoid diluting its flavour. The quickest and easiest way to do this is in a salad spinner.

DON'T DRESS UNTIL THE LAST MINUTE No one likes a soggy salad, so keep those ingredients crunchy by dressing your salad just before serving, unless the ingredients are more robust and need marinating, like a kale or cabbage slaw.

LOVE YOUR LEFTOVERS Chicken or vegetables from your Sunday roast, cooked quinoa, herbs that didn't go into your pesto – all of these leftovers can be brought to life again by adding to your salads.

CREATE YOUR LEFTOVERS! Whenever you make a dressing, make a big jar for the fridge. Whenever you're roasting veg for soups, make extra for salads.

TRAVELLING WITH SALADS We love packed lunches when we're travelling, and bringing your own food is one way to avoid vending machines and spending your money on lifeless fare. Opt for thick dips and pestos to fold through your ingredients rather than dressings, which can get messy and are a big no-no if you're travelling by plane.

REMEMBER TO CHEW Salads, by definition, incorporate plenty of raw veg, so chewing well is a must to get the most out of these foods and avoid the bloat!

After making variants of flaxseed bread for years, we've now simplified it to a nut-free version using just butter, eggs and flaxseeds. Dare we say, this recipe is lighter and even *more* bread-like than those you have enjoyed before! You can bake this in a tray focaccia-style, but we've taken to making buns. The dough keeps really well, so just cover and store somewhere cool, such as in the fridge or even on your countertop, for up to a week. Make double batches and freeze (pre-sliced) for last-minute breakfasts and lunches – just defrost and go. Sprinkle the top with sesame seeds before baking, for a proper burger-style bun. Team with our Mushroom Lentil Burgers (page 258) and some BBQ Ketchup (page 278) or try a Chicken Kiev (page 186) for an out-of-this-world burger! See the recipes that follow for various filling options, or just try them spread with butter and raw honey to accompany a cuppa.

FLAXSEED BUNS

MAKES 6 BUNS

150g ground or whole flaxseeds
1 teaspoon bicarbonate of soda
Just under ½ teaspoon sea salt
A pinch of black pepper
3 eggs, beaten
½ tablespoon maple syrup
2 tablespoons lemon juice or apple cider vinegar
3 tablespoons butter or coconut oil, melted
3 tablespoons water

½ teaspoon dried herbs (such as thyme) or bruised fennel /caraway seeds (optional)
1 tablespoon white sesame seeds, for sprinkling (optional)

1 Preheat the oven to fan 180°C/Gas mark 6 and line a baking tray with baking parchment.

2 Mix the dry ingredients together in a bowl using a fork. Beat in the remaining ingredients (except the sesame seeds) and leave the batter to rest for 5 minutes to thicken up. If using whole flaxseeds, mix with just the water and beaten egg first then allow to stand and thicken for 30 minutes before mixing with the rest of the ingredients.

3 Take 4–5 tablespoons of batter and shape into a bun with your hands. Place on the prepared baking tray and use wet hands to shape/smooth the top and to press down lightly so that the bun is 5mm–1cm thick. Repeat with the rest of the batter, sprinkling the tops with the sesame seeds (if using) and gently pressing them in.

4 Bake in the oven for 20–22 minutes until the buns spring back to touch.

5 Remove from the oven, transfer to a wire rack to cool completely, then slice in half and fill.

TIPS

+ Don't mix this in a food processor!
  The batter thickens so much it's a
  pain to get it out.

+ Use an ice-cream scoop to make neat
  and easy flax bread soup rolls.

+ Be sure to keep ground flaxseed
  well sealed and store in the fridge
  to preserve its nutrients. If you have
  a high-powered blender, you can
  grind whole flaxseeds to make your
  own 'flax flour', which gives a much
  smoother texture, while keeping the
  flaxseeds whole gives a nuttier texture.

VARIATIONS

+ Try this with golden flaxseeds for a
  lighter colour and lighter bun, or the
  more common brown flaxseeds for
  a dark, rye-type heavier bread.

+ To make this focaccia-style, place the
  dough in a lined 20cm-square baking
  tin, using wet hands to smooth it out
  on top and into the corners of the tin,
  then bake as above before cutting
  into squares and slicing in half to
  create 2 slices.

The world's your oyster when it comes to a real-food sandwich. Here are some other classic fillings that we like to team with our deliciously wholesome, protein-rich Flaxseed Buns (page 136): Tuna and Fennel, Hummus and Grated Carrot, and a BLT. Straight from the store cupboard, tinned tuna makes a quick and protein-rich topping. Be sure to look for line-caught/ sustainable tuna, preserved in spring water or extra-virgin olive oil. The hummus and carrot mixture also 'food combines' (page 14) well with our Quinoa Courgette Toast (page 32). Try adding other dips, spreads and salads (pages 262–281 and 147–165) to make your own tasty combinations.

SANDWICH CLASSICS 3 WAYS

SERVES 4

Butter, at room
temperature,
for spreading
4 Flaxseed Buns
(page 136),
halved

FOR THE TOPPING

3 x 160g tins of tuna
in spring water
or extra-virgin
olive oil, drained
3 tablespoons
capers, roughly
chopped
1 fennel bulb,
trimmed, halved
lengthways and
thinly sliced
1 small bunch of
fresh flat-leaf
parsley, leaves
and stalks
roughly chopped
5 tablespoons
extra-virgin
olive oil
4 teaspoons apple
cider vinegar
or lemon juice
A pinch of sea salt
½ teaspoon
black pepper

TUNA AND FENNEL

1   Mix together all of the topping ingredients in a bowl.

2   Butter one half of each of the flaxseed buns. Top with the tuna mixture, place the other bun half on top and serve.

VARIATIONS

+   Instead of fennel try deseeded red pepper. Top with some finely sliced red onion. Add a couple of tablespoons of Quick-cooked Mayo (page 277) if you have any already made. This sandwich would also be yummy with a dollop of Herby Tahini or Creamy Cashew Ranch dressings (pages 275 and 276), Avocado and Ginger Sauce (page 268) or Spiced Winter Apple Chutney (page 281).

SERVES 4

2 medium carrots, grated
150g hummus (such as Spinach and Butterbean Hummus, page 273) or Spicy Turmeric and Red Lentil Dip (page 269)

Butter, at room temperature, for spreading
4 Flaxseed Buns (page 136), halved
Sea salt and black pepper

HUMMUS AND GRATED CARROT

1 Mix the grated carrots with the hummus or lentil dip in a bowl.

2 Butter one half of each of the flaxseed buns, top with the carrot and hummus/lentil dip mixture and season, then place the other bun half on top and serve.

SERVES 4

12 rashers of unsmoked bacon
Butter, at room temperature, for spreading
4 Flaxseed Buns (page 136), halved
2 tablespoons Quick-cooked Mayo (page 277) or BBQ Ketchup (page 278)

8 romaine or iceberg lettuce leaves
2 large tomatoes, sliced
Sea salt and black pepper

BLT

1 Preheat the grill to high and grill the bacon on both sides until crispy.

2 Meanwhile, butter one half of each of the flaxseed buns and then add ½ tablespoon of the mayo or ketchup, followed by a lettuce leaf and a couple of slices of tomato.

3 Arrange three rashers of bacon evenly on top of the tomato, breaking the rashers in half to fit, if needed. Season then top with another lettuce leaf and the remaining half of the bun, press down gently and slice in half to serve.

VARIATION

+ A sausage and caramelised onion sandwich always goes down well with friends at the weekend. Add some of our Pink Chilli Kraut (page 130) for a big taste and a dose of probiotics.

Our Quinoa Courgette Toast (page 32) or Flaxseed Buns (page 136) are both perfect for open sandwiches. Serve topped with Pink Chilli Kraut (page 130) or with a side salad for a lovely light lunch or supper – or the Ayurvedic Carrot Stir-fry (page 109) goes really well for a warm evening meal. The tasty and nourishing sardine and avocado topping below comes courtesy of one of Jasmine's best friends, Sjaniel. Eaten for breakfast, lunch or supper, or enjoyed as a snack, it never fails to satisfy. Sardines are a super-nutritious food: high in omega-3 oils, cheap and sustainable (choose wild rather than farmed). The cheesy mushroom feast on page 143 takes a little longer to prepare than the others, but it's well worth it. A mix of shiitake, chanterelle and porcini would be the posh way to make this. Serve with a simple green salad or our Chilli Kick Cucumber Snack (page 155).

OPEN SANDWICHES 3 WAYS

SERVES 2

1 x 120g tin of
    sardines in extra-
    virgin olive oil,
    drained (retaining
    the oil)
1 ripe avocado
A pinch of cayenne
    pepper (optional)
Butter, at room
    temperature,
    for spreading
2 Flaxseed Buns
    (page 136),
    halved, or
    4 slices of Quinoa
    Courgette bread
    (page 32), toasted
2 handfuls of
    watercress,
    snipped (optional)
Sea salt and
    black pepper

SARDINE AND AVO MASH OPEN SANDWICH

1   Place the sardines and avocado flesh in a bowl and mash together with a fork. Season with salt and pepper and a pinch of cayenne pepper if desired.

2   Butter each bun half or slice of quinoa courgette toast, spread with the mash then top with watercress (if using) and a drizzle of the EVOO reserved from the sardine tin. Serve.

→   CONTINUED OVERLEAF

OPEN SANDWICHES 3 WAYS (CONTINUED)

SERVES 4

4 eggs
Butter, at room
    temperature,
    for spreading
    and frying
4 Flaxseed Buns
    (page 136),
    halved or
    8 slices of Quinoa
    Courgette bread
    (page 32)
100g watercress,
    snipped
3 tablespoons
    Quick-cooked
    Mayo (page 277)
Sea salt and
    black pepper

EGG, MAYO AND WATERCRESS OPEN SANDWICH

1   Place the eggs in a saucepan and cover with cold water.
    Bring to the boil, switch off the heat, cover the pan with a lid
    and leave for 10 minutes. Drain the eggs and cool under cold
    running water for a minute, then peel and slice. Or for speed,
    fry the eggs, sunny side up, in a knob of butter on a medium
    heat, basting with butter, until cooked to your liking.

2   Spread butter onto the halved flaxseed buns.

3   Top each bun half with dressed watercress and top with egg
    slices and some Quick-cooked Mayo, season then serve.

VARIATION

+   Instead of mayo, try this with 3 tablespoons of Herby Tahini
    or Creamy Cashew Ranch dressings (pages 275 and 276) or
    Miso and Aubergine Dip (page 272).

SERVES 2

1½ tablespoons
    butter, for frying
    and spreading
2 small red onions,
    thinly sliced
200g mushrooms,
    sliced
1½ teaspoons
    balsamic vinegar
4–6 slices of Quinoa
    Courgette bread
    (page 32) or
    2 Flaxseed Buns
    (page 136)
1 large handful of
    baby spinach
    leaves

80–100g cheese
    (such as Gouda
    or mature
    Cheddar), sliced
Sea salt and
    black pepper

MUSHROOM, SPINACH AND SAUTÉED ONION OPEN SANDWICH

1   Melt 1 tablespoon of the butter in a large frying pan. Add the
    onions and mushrooms and sauté over a medium-high heat
    for 4 minutes until tender, stirring frequently to stop the
    mushrooms sticking and burning.

2   Lower the heat, stir in the vinegar, plus ¼ teaspoon of salt
    and ⅛ teaspoon of pepper, and cook for 5 minutes more.

3   Meanwhile, lightly toast both sides of the Quinoa Courgette
    bread under the grill. Spread each slice of toast or each bun
    with the remaining butter, arrange some spinach leaves on
    top and about 2 spoonfuls of the mushroom mixture. Top
    with a slice of cheese and then grill until melted and
    browning on top.

4   Serve immediately, with a good grind of black pepper.

There's nothing better than grilled cheese on toast. This classic comfort food makes a delicious hot snack or side with salad or a bowl of soup. Jasmine had never heard of or eaten Welsh rarebit until meeting her 'brother-in-law', Doo. Below is his version, using Stilton as well as Cheddar and throwing in some cherry tomatoes. He also makes it with whole eggs rather than just the yolks – not only because it's less messy, but it adds an extra protein boost. Try the tuna melt with a drizzle of Homemade Sriracha (page 279) or BBQ Ketchup (page 278) and serve it with a big side salad, such as the Tangle Salad (page 150), or with a bowl of our Broccomole (page 128) or Lubee Beans (page 106).

GRILLED TOASTIES 2 WAYS

SERVES 2

2 eggs
2 teaspoons
 mustard
1 tablespoon
 Worcestershire
 sauce (or to taste)
100g extra-mature
 Cheddar, grated
100g Stilton,
 crumbled

4 cherry tomatoes,
 halved
2 Flaxseed Buns
 (page 136),
 halved
Black pepper
1 small handful
 of watercress,
 stems snipped
 for easier eating,
 to serve

WELSH RAREBIT ON FLAX WITH WATERCRESS

1 Beat the eggs in a bowl, then add the mustard, Worcestershire sauce, Cheddar and Stilton and give it a good mix. Add the tomatoes to the bowl and set aside.

2 Toast the bun halves under a hot grill (keeping an eye on them to ensure they don't burn).

3 Spread the cheese mixture over the toast and heat under the grill until bubbling and golden. Season with black pepper, top with a few sprigs of watercress and serve immediately.

SERVES 2

2 Flaxseed Buns
 (page 136)
Butter, at room
 temperature,
 for spreading
1 large tomato,
 sliced
1 x 160g tin of tuna
 in spring water,
 drained
2 spring onions,
 finely sliced

2 tablespoons
 Spiced Winter
 Apple Chutney
 (page 281)
3 tablespoons
 Quick-cooked
 Mayo (page 277)
50g mature
 Cheddar, grated
Black pepper

TUNA MELT ON FLAX

1 Halve the flaxseed buns and spread each half with butter, then top with the tomato slices.

2 Mix together the tuna, spring onions, chutney and mayo and spread the mixture over the tomato-topped bun halves.

3 Sprinkle over the cheese and heat under the grill until the tuna mixture is warmed through and the cheese melted and golden. Season with black pepper and serve immediately.

TIP

+ To avoid getting melted cheese on the bottom of your oven, place the bun halves on a baking tray lined with baking parchment – rather than a wire rack – before toasting under the grill. Take care not to use too much mixture and don't spread it right to the edge of the buns – it will spread naturally when it melts.

This colourful, striking dish is a super-simple variation of our ever-popular Beetroot and Goat's Cheese Terrine from *The Art of Eating Well*, and one that we love to serve as a starter. The creamy, rich flavour of the goat's cheese and zesty lemon dressing provide the perfect complement to the sweet beets. You'll need a very sharp knife or mandolin and a little patience to get your beetroot circles as thin as possible, and safely – you can also use the ribbon blade on the spiralizer for easy thin slices! If you can't source the yellow and candy-striped beets, go with the usual red/purple ones.

RAW BEETROOT CARPACCIO WITH GOAT'S CHEESE AND HERBS

SERVES 4 AS A STARTER

2 medium yellow
beetroots
2 medium candy-
striped beetroots
2 medium purple
beetroots
200g soft goat's
cheese or curd
1 large handful of
fresh parsley
leaves, finely
chopped
1 tablespoon finely
chopped fresh
mint, basil or
dill leaves or
snipped chives

FOR THE DRESSING

120ml extra-virgin
olive oil
1 teaspoon grated
lemon zest
3 tablespoons
lemon juice
1 large garlic
clove, grated
or finely diced
Sea salt and
black pepper

1 Peel the beetroots, then slice into 2mm-thick rounds using a very sharp knife or mandolin. Slice the purple ones last as the juice will stain the yellow and candy-striped beets.

2 Whisk the dressing ingredients together in a bowl, or shake in a jam jar with a lid, seasoning with salt and pepper to taste.

3 Arrange the sliced beetroots on a large serving plate, then pour over the dressing and leave to marinate for 1 hour at room temperature, before topping with the goat's cheese or curd – adding small pieces with your fingers or a teaspoon – and the fresh herbs.

TIPS

+ If there are leaves attached to your beets, save them and add to stir-fries and stews at the last minute, as you would spinach.

+ Save the parsley stalks to add to smoothies, pestos and soups.

Another sprout-starring recipe. Sprouts are one of our favourite veggies which we like to think of as mini cabbages! Because these are served raw, make sure they're fresh and remove any old, tough-looking outer leaves. We've used goji berries but dried cranberries or fresh pomegranate seeds would work just as well – anything ruby red to add a contrasting colour. The dressing here makes a delicious basic dressing, so why not make a double quantity and store in the fridge to use on other salads? Add raw honey to taste, depending on how sweet the carrots are. This salad is delicious with a roast.

SENSATIONAL SPROUT SALAD

SERVES 4 AS A SIDE

400g Brussels sprouts, tough outer leaves removed
1 small handful of walnuts or pecans, soaked in double the volume of water overnight or for a minimum of 8 hours (see also page 341)
2 apples
1 small handful of dried goji berries or cranberries

FOR THE DRESSING
6 tablespoons extra-virgin olive oil
4 tablespoons lemon juice or apple cider vinegar
1 tablespoon mustard (or to taste)
2 teaspoons raw honey or maple syrup (optional)
Sea salt and black pepper

OPTIONAL EXTRAS (1 HANDFUL OF EACH)
Thinly sliced Parmesan shavings
Crumbled blue cheese
Crispy unsmoked bacon pieces

1 Shake the dressing ingredients together in a jam jar with a lid or whisk together in a small bowl.

2 Shred the sprouts using a mandolin or the thinnest blade of a food processor, and place in a serving bowl.

3 Toast the walnuts or pecans for 1 minute in a dry pan on a medium-to-low heat or for 2 minutes in a baking tray in the oven (preheated to fan 180°C/Gas mark 6). Once toasted, roughly chop.

4 Core the apples and dice them, then add to the serving bowl with the toasted nuts and goji berries or cranberries. Add any optional extras and pour over the dressing. Toss everything together and serve.

VARIATION

+ When the sprout season is over, try this salad with cabbage or kale.

This big boisterous tangle of a salad is a riot of colour – orange, green and purple – thanks to the mix of spiralized vegetables tossed with buckwheat noodles. The anchovy and ginger dressing gives it punch, while the mellow flavour of the soft-boiled eggs pulls it together. This salad is very filling and a fantastic meal for entertaining: it looks stunning when you bring it out on a platter and makes for fun eating. Get your guests involved with spiralizing the courgettes with you when they arrive.

TANGLE SALAD WITH GINGER ANCHOVETTE DRESSING

SERVES 4

1 small butternut
   squash
   (preferably one
   with a long neck
   for spiralizing)
1 medium beetroot
85g buckwheat
   (soba) noodles
   (usually ⅓ of
   a packet)
2 medium
   courgettes
4 eggs
1 small handful
   of black sesame
   seeds

**FOR THE
DRESSING**

5cm piece of fresh
   root ginger
   (unpeeled
   if organic),
   finely grated
12 anchovies or
   6 pitted olives in
   olive oil, drained
4 teaspoons
   mustard
1½ tablespoons
   apple cider
   vinegar or
   lemon juice
160ml extra-virgin
   olive oil, plus
   extra for the
   noodles
A pinch of sea salt
   and black pepper
   (to taste)

1 For the dressing, add the ginger to a blender or food processor with the anchovies or olives, mustard and ACV or lemon juice and blend until smooth. Drizzle in the EVOO while the motor is still running. Season with the salt and pepper and set aside. Alternatively, mash the anchovies as finely as possible using a fork or finely chop the olives, place in a jar with the rest of the ingredients, seal and shake.

2 Slice off the top of the squash and the bulbous part (with the seeds) so that the squash is in two pieces. Peel off the skin, remove the seeds then spiralize or grate each piece.

3 Scrub the beetroot well, top and tail and then spiralize or grate. Add to a bowl with the squash noodles and dressing. Toss to combine then leave to marinate.

4 Cook the buckwheat noodles according to the packet instructions. Rinse under cold running water until cool, drain well and toss with a little EVOO.

5 Spiralize the courgettes – or use a julienne peeler or standard vegetable peeler to peel into strips – and add to the bowl with the drained buckwheat noodles. Toss everything together to coat with dressing. Transfer to a serving platter.

6 Fill a pan with boiling water and carefully add the eggs. Simmer for 6 minutes (if the eggs were room temperature) or 7 minutes (if fridge cold) until they are soft-boiled. Remove from the pan and rinse under cold water for a minute before peeling. Halve the eggs and arrange on top of the salad, sprinkling with the black sesame seeds to serve.

TIPS

+ If you're gluten-intolerant, it's important to check the labels of buckwheat (soba) noodles before you buy, as some brands contain wheat.

+ If you don't have anchovies, swap them for sundried tomatoes. Start with six then add to taste.

+ Make a double quantity of dressing if your blender is standard-sized (a small amount of the dressing wouldn't get blended otherwise), saving half in the fridge for dressing another salad.

This is our mum's signature salad that she is always being asked to bring to gatherings. It uses aduki or 'adzuki' beans – small, dark red beans popular in Asian cooking, particularly sweet recipes. This is a refreshing feast in itself, though you could fold in some cooked quinoa for more of a hunger buster or serve in the hollow of roasted butternut squash. We make the dressing first, as it mellows the sharpness of the raw onion, then add it to the green beans when they are hot so they soak up all the flavour. Tuck in straight away if you fancy a warm salad, but it's delicious hot or cold.

MUM'S ADUKI AND GREEN BEAN SALAD

SERVES 4 AS A SIDE

200g green beans, tops trimmed
6 tablespoons water
1 x 400g tin of aduki beans, drained and rinsed
400g cherry tomatoes, halved

FOR THE DRESSING

1 small red onion, finely sliced
1 large garlic clove, diced or crushed
5 tablespoons extra-virgin olive oil
3 tablespoons lemon juice or apple cider vinegar
1 teaspoon raw honey (optional)
Sea salt and black pepper

1 Add the dressing ingredients to a large bowl, season with salt and pepper and whisk together with a fork.

2 Place the green beans in a saucepan with the water, put a lid on the pan and allow to steam for 5 minutes until they are just tender, then drain.

3 Add the hot green beans straight to the dressing before mixing in the aduki beans and tomatoes.

This crunchy, spicy slaw is a nutritional goldmine thanks to the phytonutrients in red cabbage that are responsible for that gorgeous purple colour. Add some lime juice and red onion and you have a good-looking slaw that can be used to tart up anything. It's especially delicious as a side with our Mexican Beef and Carrot Burgers/Balls (page 214) or Slow-cooked Chicken Pot Roast with Sweet Paprika and Cayenne (page 185). Dress your slaw early and allow it to marinate for a juicy bite, or dress just before serving for a full-on crunch. The beauty of a cabbage salad, as opposed to a leafy one, is that it retains its texture and still tastes great the next day, and the next – so when making slaw, go big!

SPICY RUBY SLAW

SERVES 8 AS A SIDE

1 large red cabbage
1 large red onion or
    1 bunch of spring
    onions, finely
    chopped
2 large handfuls of
    fresh coriander
    or parsley,
    leaves and stalks
    roughly chopped,
    reserving some
    to serve

**FOR THE
DRESSING**
1–2 fresh red
    chillies,
    deseeded
    and diced
½ teaspoon
    ground cumin
Grated zest and
    juice of 1 lime
    or ½ large lemon
4 tablespoons
    extra-virgin
    olive oil
Sea salt and
    black pepper

1   In a large mixing bowl, whisk together all the dressing ingredients with a fork, seasoning with salt and pepper to taste.

2   Halve the cabbage and cut away any tough white core, then chop by hand or in a food processor, shredding the leaves as roughly or finely as you like.

3   Add the shredded cabbage to the bowl with the other ingredients and mix together with your hands. Serve with the reserved chopped coriander or parsley scattered on top.

TIP

+   You can shred your cabbage with a spiralizer using the ribbon blade.

Eva, our wonderful friend and colleague, grew up with this simple cucumber salad from Sierra Leone. The slippery crunch and spicy tang perfectly complement grilled fish or barbecued meats and it can be enjoyed as a refreshing snack too. This packs a seriously flavoursome punch, so if you're serving to guests who aren't keen on spicy food, set aside their serving before adding the chilli. Make and eat this on the same day, or keep refrigerated in a sealed glass jar for a mildly pickled version.

CHILLI KICK CUCUMBER SNACK

SERVES 4 AS A SIDE

1 large cucumber, peeled (optional) and thinly sliced

FOR THE DRESSING
1 small red onion, finely diced
1 Scotch bonnet chilli (preferably red) or ordinary fresh red chilli (or to taste), deseeded and very finely diced
A pinch of grated lime zest and juice of 2 limes
½ teaspoon tamari
Sea salt

1 Make the dressing by mixing all the ingredients together in a bowl.

2 Add the sliced cucumber to the dressing and mix well. You can eat this immediately or let it marinate for a couple of hours in the fridge before serving.

This delicious salad is quick and easy – ready in just 5 minutes. We like to wrap it up to go in a chestnut pancake (page 30) or serve it as a fresh and crunchy side to our Kasha Buckwheat Burgers/Balls (page 234). When in season, radishes make a great addition for a splash of pink and extra crunch. This salad is very versatile: swap the chickpeas for any tinned beans in your cupboard, or leftover cooked lentils or quinoa. We're not sticklers for uniform chopping as a rule, but in this case we like to dice the cucumber and avocado to roughly the same size as the chickpeas – it just seems to taste better – while a generous pinch of sea salt is vital to bring the flavours of this salad to life.

CUCUMBER, AVOCADO AND CHICKPEA SALAD

SERVES 2

1 medium cucumber

1 large ripe avocado, peeled and stoned

1 x 400g tin of chickpeas, drained and rinsed

1 small handful of fresh coriander (leaves and stalks), parsley, dill or mint

A few radishes, thinly sliced (optional)

4 tablespoons extra-virgin olive oil

Juice of 1 lime or ½ lemon, or 2 tablespoons apple cider vinegar

Sea salt and black pepper

1 Dice the cucumber and avocado flesh to about the same size as a chickpea, then add to a bowl with the chickpeas.

2 Roughly chop the coriander, parsley, dill or mint and add to the bowl, along with the radishes (if using), gently mixing everything together. Dress with EVOO and lime/lemon juice or ACV, seasoning with salt and pepper.

The best packed lunches are those you can throw together from any leftovers in the fridge. During a Sunday Cook-Off (page 334), make batches of quinoa, lentils or other pulses, or set aside leftover chicken or other cold cuts from a roast, so you have a variety of protein-rich ingredients to choose from. We've compiled a list of our favourite components, so pick and choose to suit yourself. Keep a balance of fat, protein, vegetables and, of course, flavours. Vegetables can be raw – diced, grated or spiralized, as appropriate – or cooked leftovers. You can prepare your salad jar up to three days in advance; just top with any fresh salad leaves as you're heading out to work. Tip out onto a plate when ready to eat. Look for a 500ml glass jar and make sure it's heatproof so you can use it for Noodle Pots too (pages 75–77).

POWER SALAD IN A JAR

SERVES 1 (500ML JAR)

DRESSINGS
French dressing
(page 148)
Creamy Cashew
Ranch Dressing
(page 276)
Avocado and Ginger
Sauce (page 268)
Miso and Aubergine
Dip (page 272)
Spicy Turmeric and
Red Lentil Dip
(page 269)
Spinach and
Butterbean
Hummus
(page 273)

PROTEIN
Soft-boiled egg,
peeled and
sliced or
roughly chopped
Smoked mackerel,
salmon or trout,
flaked or sliced
Tinned sardines or
tuna, drained
and flaked
Good-quality
cooked ham or
turkey, chopped
Roast chicken, lamb
or beef, shredded
or thinly sliced
Cooked quinoa,
lentils or beans
(such as mung,
aduki or butter)
or chickpeas

TOPPINGS
Seeds (sunflower,
pumpkin or chia)
Nuts (walnuts,
pecans, almonds,
brazil nuts,
pistachios, pine
nuts), activated
(page 341)
Pesto (pages
245–246)
Cheese (goat's
cheese,
Parmesan
shavings,
crumbled blue
cheese or feta,
grated Cheddar)
Broccomole
(page 128)

VEGETABLES
RAW
Avocado
Radishes
Cucumber
Celery
COOKED
Broccoli
Cauliflower
Asparagus
Mushrooms
Sweet potato
Butternut squash
Green beans
RAW/COOKED
Beetroots
Tomatoes
Onions or
spring onions
Peppers
Cabbage
Kale
Fennel
Carrots
Courgettes

SALAD LEAVES
Lettuce leaves
(romaine, lamb's)
Chicory leaves
Rocket leaves
Spinach
Watercress
Fresh herbs
(coriander, basil,
parsley, dill, mint,
chives, tarragon),
roughly chopped

TIPS

+ Use a vacuum flask to keep your ingredients cool if you don't have a fridge at work or if you're on the go.

+ Transform a thick dip into a silky dressing by stirring through a few tablespoons of EVOO and a tablespoon of ACV or lemon juice to thin it out.

+ Include the leaves and stalks of fresh herbs, except for mint.

1 The key to a successful power salad in a jar lies in the layering. Spoon your choice of dressing into the jar for the first layer, selecting one from the list.

2 Add the protein layer, choosing one handful from the options opposite, to act as a barrier between the dressing and the more delicate components of your salad.

3 Sprinkle in a handful of seeds, nuts or cheese for the third layer – something to give your salad a little texture.

4 Top it off with two handfuls of one of the vegetables in the list, diced, grated or spiralized, followed by one handful of fresh salad leaves. Screw on the lid and you're good to go.

5 When you want to eat your power salad, just give the jar a shake, tip it upside down onto a plate and you have a perfectly dressed salad!

Raw kale is delicious, but needs tenderising first. Leaving the leaves to marinate in the dressing for a few hours will soften them, allowing the flavours to develop and aid digestion. This salad is the perfect prepare-ahead meal or packed lunch as it's even better two days later (just pop it in the fridge)! As the leaves tenderise, you'll end up with half the volume you started with. Turn it into more of a meal with the addition of cooked beans, roasted squash, soft-boiled eggs, cooked flaked fish or shredded chicken.

SESAME KALE SALAD

SERVES 4 AS A SIDE

250g kale, thick stems removed and leaves finely sliced

1 large red pepper, deseeded and diced

2 large carrots, spiralized, julienned or peeled into ribbons

4 spring onions or 1 small onion, finely sliced

1 handful of sesame (white or black), pumpkin, sunflower or chia seeds (optional)

1 large handful of fresh coriander (leaves and stalks) or coriander and mint leaves, chopped

FOR THE DRESSING

3cm piece of fresh root ginger (unpeeled if organic), finely grated

3 garlic cloves, finely grated

4 tablespoons lime or lemon juice or apple cider vinegar

6 tablespoons extra-virgin olive oil

2 tablespoons sesame oil (non-toasted)

4 teaspoons tamari

2 teaspoons raw honey or maple syrup

A pinch of finely diced fresh red chilli or chilli flakes/powder (to taste)

Black pepper (to taste)

1 Whisk all the dressing ingredients together in a bowl with a fork.

2 Add the kale and toss together using your hands before leaving to marinate, covered, for a few hours in the fridge. If you're making it in a rush, massage the leaves for 1 minute with the dressing as this will speed up the softening process.

3 When the kale has finished marinating, add the red pepper, carrots and spring onions or onion to the bowl.

4 Toast the seeds (if using) in a dry pan on a medium-to-low heat for 30 seconds. Serve the salad with the fresh herbs and the toasted seeds sprinkled on top.

TIPS

+ To remove kale stalks quickly and easily, just hold onto the stalk with one hand and strip off the leaves with the other. The quickest way to slice the kale is to stack the leaves together, roll them into a cylinder and slice into ribbons.

+ Double the dressing quantities and save in the fridge for another dish.

These delicious rainbow-coloured rolls are bursting with fresh ingredients. Play around with the combinations; we like to eat seasonally as everything tastes better when it's naturally blooming. These rolls are perfect for parties, present them as open lettuce boats, drizzled with the sauce for a mezze-style sharing starter. If you have a bit more time, wrap each one and tie with a strip of spring onion as we do for events – both eye-catching and easier for dipping. For packed lunches or picnics, present your dipping sauce in a small jam jar, and be sure to try the with all of the dipping sauce variations we've suggested below to find your favourite.

VIETNAMESE RAINBOW ROLLS

SERVES 4 (2 ROLLS EACH)

200g fresh vegetables (such as red cabbage, carrots, courgette, peppers, radishes or cucumber)

2 handfuls of fresh herbs (such as coriander, mint or basil), chopped

4 spring onions, finely sliced

1 fresh red chilli, deseeded and finely sliced

2 handfuls of cooked prawns or shredded roast chicken, duck, lamb, beef or pork (optional)

4 lettuces (such as Little Gem for serving open-style or butter lettuce for wrapping), leaves separated

FOR THE DIPPING SAUCE

4 tablespoons homemade dressing: Peanut Lime Sauce (page 173) Homemade Sriracha (page 279) or Avocado and Ginger Sauce (page 268)

4 tablespoons lime juice

4 tablespoons sesame oil

Sea salt and black pepper (to taste)

1 Place your choice of sauce in a bowl and mix in the lime juice and sesame oil to make it more of a dipping consistency, then taste for seasoning.

2 Prepare your choice of vegetables by slicing or spiralizing into small matchsticks, as appropriate.

3 Assemble by piling some of the vegetables, herbs, spring onions, chilli and prawns or meat (if using) onto each lettuce leaf, then wrap as you would a burrito, and serve with the dipping sauce, or serve open-style and drizzle over the sauce.

TIP

+ For an authentic Asian taste, try holy basil, which adds a slightly aniseed flavour to the mix.

FISH AND MEAT

SPICY MISO SALMON
WITH BROCCOLI RICE
170

PRAWN AND CARROT
NOODLE STIR-FRY WITH
PEANUT LIME SAUCE
173

CURRY NIGHT
FISH CURRY
174

FISH AMOK
CAMBODIAN CURRY
176

SUPER-SIMPLE FISH
FINGERS
178

LEMONY CHILLI
PRAWN COURGETTI
WITH GREENS
180

SMOKED MACKEREL
NIÇOISE
182

SLOW-COOKED
CHICKEN POT ROAST
WITH SWEET PAPRIKA
AND CAYENNE
185

CHICKEN KIEV WITH A
SIMPLE SPINACH SALAD
186

CHICKEN AND SEA
SPAGHETTI SALAD WITH
GINGER ALMOND
DRESSING
188

CHICKEN COMFORT PIE
191

PUNCHY PIRI-PIRI
CHICKEN WINGS WITH
CELERIAC SKINNY FRIES
192

SPICED ROAST
CHICKEN THIGHS
WITH WATERCRESS
SALSA VERDE
194

SLOW-COOKED 'NO
FRY' CHICKEN CURRY
197

QUICK SAUSAGE
RAGÙ WITH CELERIAC
SPAGHETTI
198

SPINACH AND BACON
TART WITH A NUTTY
ALMOND CRUST
200

LIVER/BANGERS
AND MASH WITH
ONION GRAVY
202

CELERIAC SPAGHETTI
AND KALE CARBONARA
204

SLOW-COOKED SMOKY
APPLE PULLED PORK
207

ASIAN SHORT
RIB STEW
208

BEEF AND
BACON STEW
211

CHINESE-STYLE BEEF
AND BROCCOLI
212

MEXICAN
BEEF AND CARROT
BURGERS/BALLS
214

MUM'S PHILIPPINE
BEEF SINIGANG
216

POWERHOUSE STEAK
AND KALE SALAD
219

SLOW-ROASTED
BREAST OF LAMB
220

FOR MORE MEAT AND FISH IDEAS TRY:

APPLE AND BACON MUFFINS
118

BEAN AND BACON HASH
40

BLT SANDWICH
140

BONE BROTH
63

ONE PAN FULL MONTY BREAKFAST
46

SARDINE AND AVO MASH
OPEN SANDWICH
141

While vegetables for us are the star of the show, with non-starchy veggies making up most of the meal, we also believe that meat and fish (as well as eggs and dairy) of good provenance – naturally reared or sustainably sourced – are essential to a healthy, balanced diet, providing a range of nutrients that are hard to obtain from plants alone. (See 'Principles for Eating Well', pages 10–15, especially pillars 2 and 6, for more about this.) We champion eating the whole animal, the natural fats, organ meats and bone broth of course.

In this chapter, you'll spot some classic British comfort foods like bangers and mash (page 202), fish fingers (page 178) and Chicken Kiev (page 186), along with our own versions of a few takeaway or restaurant favourites, such as the Curry Night Fish Curry (page 174), Mexican Beef and Carrot Burgers/Balls (page 214) or Slow-cooked Smoky Apple Pulled Pork (page 207). Cheaper than ordering in or eating out, these are far tastier and more nutritious. We love the ease of an all-in-one dish, such as our Chinese-style Beef and Broccoli (page 212) or our Spiced Roast Chicken Thighs with Watercress Salsa Verde (page 194), which needs just 5 minutes to put together and then takes care of itself.

Quick Sausage Ragù with Celeriac Spaghetti (page 198) is a big family favourite, and we're bringing back liver, onions and mash (page 202) because it's just so tasty and good for you. Asian Short Rib Stew (page 208) shows off the frugal side of eating meat, as does our Punchy Piri-piri Chicken Wings (page 192) and Slow-roasted Breast of Lamb (page 220) – a fraction of the price of lamb shoulder or leg and, dare we say, more flavoursome.

If you're new to cooking meat or a little nervous about getting it right, then start off with our chicken pot roast (page 185). Sit a whole chicken on a bed of roughly chopped vegetables, add a little water, sprinkle over some seasoning, set the slow cooker for 8 hours and, hey presto, succulent chicken that cooks and keeps – ready when you are. We'd also recommend one of the best steak salads we've ever had (page 219), made using onglet or hanger steak, a cheaper cut of beef that is deservedly getting wider recognition. Look for the cheaper, less fashionable cuts of meat from a good butcher and get yourself a bargain!

Even if you don't eat meat, you can still enjoy many of these recipes as they showcase some of our favourite vegetable sides, which can be paired with other dishes in the book. Look out for celeriac fries (page 192), broccoli rice (page 170), cauliflower and root veg mash (pages 111–113), courgetti (page 229), carrot noodles (page 173) and celeriac spaghetti (page 198). All of them provide a deliciously easy way to bump up your vegetable intake while cutting down on refined foods.

TIPS AND TRICKS

BOIL YOUR BONES We use delicious Bone Broth (page 63) in some form most days; even some of our vegetarian friends enjoy chicken broth as they feel the benefits. Remember to reserve some of the excess fat and store it in a sterilised jar in the fridge ready for use in stir-fries, roasts and baking. It's 'free' food, plus it makes everything taste better.

MAKE MEAT GO FURTHER In our Mexican-style burgers, which also make excellent meatball canapés (page 214), we grate in carrots for flavour, to get more vegetables in and to make the meat go further. In the Chicken Comfort Pie (page 191), we combine leftover chicken with lots of veg and top with creamy cauliflower mash. We make the fish and chicken curries deliciously rich with spices and coconut milk, so that a small serving does the trick when combined with our vegetable sides.

PROPORTION OF MEAT TO VEG Keep low-starch vegetables to two-thirds of your plate, whether you're eating in or out. At home, make vegetables the star of the show – spiralize a courgette, grate in a carrot, mash up some leftover cauliflower and serve with handfuls of peppery watercress. Vegetables needn't ever be boring or complicated.

BUY THE BEST QUALITY MEAT YOU CAN If you haven't got a good local butcher, find your nearest farmers' market or look online. You can order meat and bones direct from farms, which may offer cheaper deals or discounts. Use your freezer to keep well stocked.

COOK CHEAPER CUTS Cheaper cuts from a good butcher do not mean inferior-quality meat; they just tend to be less fashionable. We love liver (page 202) and bone marrow or short ribs and cuts like oxtail, beef shin and lamb neck, where simple slow cooking gets the best out of them. Talk to the butcher and farmer and quiz them on their favourite cuts – that's how we discovered breast of lamb (page 220)!

CHOOSE SUSTAINABLE FISH AND SEAFOOD Read labels on packaging, find a good and helpful fishmonger. Avoid fish that is not sustainably farmed and opt for wild varieties when they're in season, responsibly fished and plentiful. Check prices – fish in good supply usually costs less. We especially like fish rich in omega-3 oils – sardines, herrings, mackerel. Quality tinned fish are a good source – cheap and non-perishable too.

FOOD COMBINING For better digestion, meat and fish combines best with non-starchy veg, so eat them with plenty of greens. Try it with broccoli rice (page 170) or cauliflower mash (page 111) or enjoy your favourite Bolognese or pasta sauces with courgetti (page 229) or celeriac spaghetti (page 198). Nothing beats a crunchy slaw (pages 78 and 154) – cabbages are always easy to find and one of the cheaper vegetables, as well as delicious raw. After a quick chop and a simple dressing, they will make a great side to any dish. Have a few other side dishes up your sleeve too, such as Garlicky Chilli Chard (page 103), Spiced Coconut Cabbage (page 102), Broccoli 2 Ways (page 96), Lubee Beans (page 106) or Creamy Carrot Bake (page 93).

GIVE DIGESTION A HELPING HAND As always, chew well and try to eat meat-based meals at lunchtime or for an early supper as some meats can take longer to digest: you don't want to go to bed having just eaten a steak!

This flavoursome and satisfying dish can be made in one pan in just 10 minutes – ready in no time, in other words, and with washing-up kept to a minimum. Broccoli rice is the perfect texture for soaking up the wonderfully savoury sauce. Traditionally fermented miso is rich in antioxidants and if you are buying unpasteurised, then it's also full of friendly bacteria. We like to keep a selection in our fridge because there are so many different flavours and they keep for months. Here, because there's no need to cook the sauce, we've used an unpasteurised miso, to make the most of its beneficial probiotics. The sauce is also perfect for dressing vegetables and stir-fries. This recipe serves two, but you could easily double the quantities and save any leftovers in the fridge for a packed lunch the next day.

SPICY MISO SALMON WITH BROCCOLI RICE

SERVES 2

2 teaspoons
   coconut oil
2 x 300g wild
   salmon fillets
   (skin on)
Sea salt and
   black pepper

FOR THE
BROCCOLI RICE

1 large head
   of broccoli
   (about 350g)
2 tablespoons
   of water
2 spring onions,
   finely sliced,
   or 1 tablespoon
   snipped fresh
   chives

FOR THE SPICY
MISO SAUCE

1 tablespoons
   unpasteurised
   miso paste
   (to taste)
2 teaspoons
   maple syrup
4 tablespoons
   hot water
1 tablespoon
   lemon juice
A pinch of chilli
   powder or
   cayenne pepper
A pinch of sea
   salt or dash of
   tamari, to taste

1   For the broccoli rice, grate the broccoli – including the stalk – into rice-sized pieces, either by hand (using the coarse side of a grater) or in a food processor (using the S-curved blade or grater attachment). Set aside.

2   Melt the coconut oil in a wide frying pan on a medium heat, season the salmon with salt and pepper, then fry, skin side down, for 3 minutes until crispy. Carefully turn over and fry the flesh side for 1–2 minutes until just cooked through. Transfer from the pan onto individual warmed plates and keep warm.

3   Tip the grated broccoli straight into the same pan with the water, turn up the heat, cover with a lid and leave to steam for 3 minutes, stirring halfway through, until tender but still with a little bite. Season to taste with salt and pepper and then add the spring onions or chives.

4   While the broccoli rice is cooking, stir or whisk the miso sauce ingredients together in a bowl, or shake in a jam jar with the lid on. Divide the broccoli rice between the plates, pour the sauce over the fish and serve immediately.

VARIATIONS

+ We love to pair broccoli with salmon, rich in omega-3 oils, but feel free to swap with pollock, hake, coley or sea bream, which tend to be cheaper. Ask your fishmonger for advice or his 'catch of the day'.

+ Try steaming the broccoli rice with some finely grated garlic or fresh root ginger, using 2 tablespoons of coconut milk instead of water and seasoning to taste with ½ teaspoon tamari, instead of salt, or a few drops of toasted sesame oil.

+ If you don't have broccoli, make the 'rice' using cauliflower instead!

This rich, tangy sauce is destined to become one of your fridge favourites. Velvety and thick, it'll double up as a delicious dressing if you add more liquid. Swap almond butter for the peanut butter, if you prefer, although this sauce has been proven to convert many a peanut butter-phobe! If you can't find big prawns in their shells, use the smaller, peeled variety and cook until they are just pink. It's handy to keep a bag of prawns in the freezer for an impromptu supper. Make this salad with any leftover meat or fish too, or go meat-free and add avocado and chunks of aubergine fried in coconut oil.

PRAWN AND CARROT NOODLE STIR-FRY WITH PEANUT LIME SAUCE

SERVES 4

3 large carrots
2 large cucumbers
4 big pak choi or 1 medium cabbage (such as Chinese cabbage)
1 tablespoon coconut oil
16 large raw prawns (shell on)

FOR THE PEANUT LIME SAUCE

8 tablespoons peanut butter (100% roasted peanuts with only salt added) or nut butter of your choice
1 tablespoon raw honey or maple syrup
Juice of 2 limes or 1½ lemons
2 garlic cloves
1 tablespoon tamari

A pinch of sea salt (to taste)
100ml water

TO SERVE

1 fresh red chilli, deseeded and diced
2 large handfuls of fresh coriander or basil (leaves and stalks) or mint leaves, roughly chopped

1   Blend the ingredients for the peanut sauce together in a blender or the small bowl of a food processor. Or dice the garlic and whisk the ingredients together in a bowl by hand. Set aside.

2   Spiralize the carrots and cucumber, snipping long strands into shorter lengths for easier eating, or use a julienne peeler or standard vegetable peeler to peel them into strips before cutting in half lengthways. Slice off the ends of the pak choi and discard, then slice the stems and cut the leaves into strips lengthways or finely shred the cabbage leaves.

3   Melt half the coconut oil in a frying pan on a medium heat and fry the prawns on each side for 1–1½ minutes (depending on their size) until cooked through, then remove from the pan and set aside.

4   Add the carrot noodles to the pan to soften for 1 minute in the remaining coconut oil, then turn off the heat and add the pak choi or cabbage, tossing so it wilts slightly in the heat.

5   In a large serving dish, toss the carrot and cucumber noodles and pak choi together in a few tablespoons of the peanut lime sauce, then top with the cooked prawns and drizzle over the remaining sauce.

6   Add the chopped chilli and fresh herbs and serve immediately.

This recipe, created by our dear friend Liam, is so called because whenever we go to his house, we request Curry Night, and he whips this up, mostly with white fish, but sometimes with chicken thighs or prawns. We think his curry paste is perfect: you can make double the amount of paste and pop half in the freezer for your next curry. If you don't have a few of the spices or lemongrass, don't worry – it will still be delicious. We use any leftover sauce with tinned chickpeas or red lentils, which are so quick to cook. This is great served with cauliflower rice (page 240) or a fresh and crunchy slaw (pages 78 and 154).

CURRY NIGHT FISH CURRY

SERVES 4

1 tablespoon
    coconut oil
    or ghee
3 red peppers,
    deseeded and
    roughly chopped
1 x 400g tin of
    chopped
    tomatoes
25 cherry tomatoes,
    crushed (or an
    extra 400g tin
    of chopped
    tomatoes)
250ml water
    or Bone Broth
    (from chicken
    bones – page 63)
1 x 400ml tin
    of full-fat
    coconut milk
600g firm white
    fish fillets (such
    as pollock, coley,
    haddock, cod or
    sea bream)

400g spinach, big
    leaves chopped
2 big handfuls of
    fresh coriander,
    leaves and stalks
    separated and
    roughly chopped
1 lemon or 2 limes,
    halved, for
    squeezing
Sea salt

1   Place all the ingredients for the curry paste (see opposite) in the small bowl of a food processor and blend at high speed.

2   Melt the coconut oil or ghee in a large pan over a medium heat, add the curry paste and fry, stirring occasionally, for 2 minutes until fragrant.

3   Add the red peppers and all the tomatoes with a large pinch of salt and cook for 5 minutes until softened.

4   Top with the water or broth and coconut milk and cook at a medium simmer for 30 minutes until the sauce reduces and thickens a little.

5   Meanwhile, chop the fish into 2cm chunks. Add to the reduced sauce and gently simmer for about 5 minutes until cooked through – it should be white and just about to flake.

6   Three minutes before serving, gently stir in the spinach and chopped coriander stalks and squeeze in the lemon or lime juice. Taste for seasoning, then top with the chopped coriander leaves and serve.

FOR THE CURRY PASTE

6 garlic cloves

4 lemongrass stalks (tough ends cut off by 1cm), roughly chopped

2 medium onions, roughly chopped

4cm piece of fresh root ginger (unpeeled if organic)

1 tablespoon tomato purée

2 tablespoons ground turmeric

1 tablespoon ground coriander

1 tablespoon ground cumin

1 teaspoon ground cardamom

2 fresh red chillies, deseeded, or ½ teaspoon chilli powder

1 tablespoon mustard seeds (optional)

This recipe was inspired by our travels to Cambodia where fish amok is a national dish. We ate it many, many times in varying styles – wrapped in pandan leaves, steamed in a coconut shell, or as a soupy stew – with little twists that had been passed down through the generations. This is an easy, one-pot version that will fill your kitchen with the divine fragrance of Southeast Asia. The curry sauce is delicately spiced, without the chilli usually associated with curries (great for children), and works well with veggies, chicken or seafood. We always double the paste recipe and freeze some to use for another meal. If you like this recipe, try our Curry Night Fish Curry (page 174). We like to serve this with steamed greens or broccoli or cauliflower rice (pages 170 and 240).

FISH AMOK CAMBODIAN CURRY

SERVES 2

350g firm white fish fillets (such as pollock, coley, haddock, cod or sea bream)
1 tablespoon ghee or coconut oil
1 x 400ml tin of full-fat coconut milk
1 handful of fresh coriander or basil (leaves and stalks) or mint leaves, roughly chopped
Sea salt and black pepper

FOR THE YELLOW KROEUNG PASTE

4 lemongrass stalks – tough ends cut off by 1cm), roughly chopped
2 garlic cloves
1 medium onion, roughly chopped
2 kaffir lime leaves (or ½ teaspoon grated lime zest and 1 teaspoon lime juice)
¾ teaspoon sliced fresh root ginger (unpeeled if organic) or ½ teaspoon sliced fresh galangal root
½ teaspoon ground turmeric
1½ teaspoons fish sauce (nam pla)
1 teaspoon tamari
¼ teaspoon maple syrup
½ teaspoon chilli flakes or finely diced fresh red chilli (to taste – optional)

1   Place all the ingredients for the yellow kroeung paste in a food processor and blend on high until smooth.

2   Cut the fish into 3cm cubes and sprinkle with a little salt and pepper.

3   Melt the ghee or coconut oil in a medium saucepan, add the kroeung paste and cook on a medium heat for 30 seconds, stirring regularly to stop the ingredients catching on the bottom of the pan.

4   Pour in the coconut milk and bring to a medium simmer, leaving the sauce to cook for 10 minutes.

5   Add the fish to the sauce and gently simmer, with a lid on the pan, for about 5 minutes until cooked through – the fish should be white and flaky.

6   Sprinkle the bottom of two bowls with most of the herbs and then gently ladle over the fish amok. Garnish with the remaining herbs and serve with your favourite veg side.

Fish fingers are the ultimate childhood comfort food. We like to eat them in a Flaxseed Bun (page 136) with a dollop of Quick-cooked Mayo (page 277) or Homemade Sriracha (page 279) or both. If you want to add some brilliant sides and make this more of a spread for guests, serve with a crunchy slaw (pages 78 and 154) and Celeriac Skinny Fries (page 192) or a bowl of Broccomole (page 128) to up your veggie intake. We like to use a firm white fish and play with the flavours each time. Rosemary, dill and tarragon go supremely well with fish – use dried or chop up fresh and mix into the ground almond mix.

SUPER-SIMPLE FISH FINGERS

MAKES 12 FISH FINGERS, SERVES 4

500g skinless firm white fish fillets (such as coley, pollock, haddock, cod or sea bream)
1 egg
100g ground almonds
Grated zest of 1 lemon
2 garlic cloves, diced, or ½ teaspoon garlic powder

A pinch of diced fresh red chilli or cayenne pepper (optional)
Sea salt and black pepper
A squeeze of lemon juice, to serve

1   Preheat the oven to fan 200°C/Gas mark 7 and line a baking tray with baking parchment.

2   Slice the fish fillets into 12 'fish fingers', the size depending on how large your fillets are, and season with salt and pepper.

3   Whisk the egg in a bowl, then place the ground almonds in another bowl and season with the lemon zest, garlic and chilli (if using).

4   Dip each fish finger into the beaten egg and then into the ground almonds mix, so that they are fully coated, before placing on the prepared baking tray. Bake on the top shelf of the oven for 15 minutes until golden brown.

5   Serve with a squeeze of lemon and a sprinkling of salt.

VARIATIONS

+   For a nut-free coating, try ground sunflower seeds or desiccated coconut.

+   For an egg-free batter, make the 2-flaxseed-egg mix (page 17) and dip the fish fingers into this before coating in the ground almonds mix.

Ready in less than 10 minutes, courgetti (courgette spaghetti) is our favourite quick meal, especially as it gets our daily greens intake up at the same time. Here we've added chilli, garlic and lemon, which are, in our opinion, one of the best flavour combinations, not to mention antiviral and immune-boosting. This recipe is incredibly versatile: swap the prawns for any seafood you fancy – squid, scallops or crayfish – or use flaked fresh or smoked fish. Broccoli is a fridge staple in our house, but green beans or asparagus would be equally delicious. Try purple-sprouting broccoli when in season.

LEMONY CHILLI PRAWN COURGETTI WITH GREENS

SERVES 4

1 large head
    of broccoli
    (about 350g)
2 teaspoons ghee
2 garlic cloves, diced
1 fresh red chilli,
    deseeded
    and diced,
    or ½ teaspoon
    chilli flakes
500g raw prawns
    (shell on)
4 tablespoons water
4 large courgettes
A big pinch
    of sea salt
Grated zest and
    juice of 1 lemon
1 large handful
    of fresh herbs
    (such as basil or
    parsley), roughly
    chopped

TO SERVE
2 large handfuls
    of rocket
1 handful of finely
    grated Parmesan
Drizzle of extra-
    virgin olive oil

1 Cut the broccoli florets into small pieces and finely slice the stalks (after first slicing off the tough outer layer).

2 Melt the ghee in a large saucepan on a medium heat, add the garlic, chilli and prawns and gently fry, stirring halfway through, until cooked (about 3 minutes, depending on the size of prawns). Remove from the pan and set aside.

3 Add the broccoli and water to the pan, cover with a lid and steam the broccoli for 3–4 minutes until just tender.

4 Meanwhile, spiralize the courgettes, snipping long strands into shorter lengths for easier eating, or peel into strips using a julienne peeler or standard vegetable peeler and cut in half lengthways.

5 Once the broccoli is cooked, add the cooked prawns with the salt and lemon juice. Stir together in the pan and then remove from the heat.

6 Toss everything (except the lemon zest) together with the courgetti, then serve on a platter of rocket with the lemon zest and Parmesan scattered over, and drizzle with EVOO.

TIP

+ Broccoli stalk – it's delicious, so don't throw it away. We always slice it up so that it cooks for the same length of time as the florets.

Here we've taken that salad classic tuna Niçoise and given it a twist with smoked mackerel. You could use smoked salmon or tinned sardines too – all are rich in omega-3 fats. We love to take this for our packed lunch: check out pages 160–161 for tips on how to store salads in a jar for eating on the go. The quick version of this salad is given here, but if you've got a bit more time, try the celeriac variation below. Add radicchio or red chicory leaves for their colour and delicious bitterness, or grated carrot for extra crunch. In the winter, sundried tomatoes (from a jar) make a tasty alternative to the fresh ones. The French dressing is a great one to double up and keep in a jar in the fridge – brilliant with just a big bowl of lettuce.

SMOKED MACKEREL NIÇOISE

SERVES 2

250g green beans, ends trimmed
3 tablespoons water
3 eggs
1 handful of tomatoes, halved if cherry or quartered if large
½ small red onion, thinly sliced
1 small handful of pitted olives in oil, drained
1 tablespoon capers (optional)
200g smoked mackerel, skin removed and flesh broken into large flakes
1 small lettuce (such as butterhead), separated into leaves, spinach or watercress

2 heads of radicchio or red chicory, roughly chopped, or 1 large carrot, roughly grated

FOR THE FRENCH DRESSING

4 tablespoons extra-virgin olive oil
2 tablespoons lemon juice or apple cider vinegar
2 teaspoons mustard (or to taste)
1 teaspoon raw honey (optional)
Sea salt and black pepper (to taste)

1 Place the beans in a saucepan with the water, put a lid on the pan and allow to steam for 5 minutes until the beans are just tender, then drain and set aside.

2 Fill the same pan with boiling water and carefully drop in the eggs. Simmer for 6 minutes (if the eggs were room temperature) or 7 minutes (if fridge cold) until they are soft-boiled (we like our yolks yolky!). Remove from the pan and rinse under cold running water for a minute before peeling.

3 Meanwhile, prepare the dressing by whisking all the ingredients together in a bowl or shaking together in a jam jar with the lid on.

4 Add the cooked beans to a bowl with the tomatoes, onion, olives and capers (if using), pour over half the dressing and toss together.

5 Halve the eggs and add to the salad with the fish, salad leaves and radicchio/chicory or carrot, and drizzle over the remaining dressing.

VARIATION

+ Instead of the potatoes traditionally
  used in a Niçoise salad, you can add
  small chunks of roasted celeriac.
  Peel 1 small celeriac and chop into
  bite-sized chunks, then toss in a
  tablespoon of melted ghee, coconut
  oil or dripping and roast in the oven
  (preheated to fan 180°C/Gas mark 6)
  for 30 minutes until tender. Add with
  the other salad ingredients in step 4.

There are so many plus points to this tasty, slow-cooked dish. A roast chicken usually takes 1½–2 hours in the oven and you have to calculate the number of minutes per kilo. With a slow cooker there is much more room for manoeuvre time-wise and the chicken will always be succulent, no basting needed. Pop it on before work and come home to a delicious hot supper. This dish is a one-pot wonder, meat, veggies and a delicious gravy all cooked at the same time, so all you have to do is steam a few greens or make a quick salad of watercress or grated courgette to serve alongside. Any leftover meat can be used cold in salads and sandwiches. If you don't have a slow cooker (we highly recommend getting one!), then use an ovenproof dish with a tightly-fitting lid and pop it in the oven on low.

SLOW-COOKED CHICKEN POT ROAST WITH SWEET PAPRIKA AND CAYENNE

SERVES 4

4 large carrots, roughly chopped
2 large onions, roughly chopped
3 large celery sticks, roughly chopped
1 celeriac or 2 small turnips or swedes, roughly chopped
4 garlic cloves, halved
100ml water
1 handful of fresh rosemary, parsley, basil or thyme or 1 tablespoon dried
1 x 1.8kg chicken

FOR THE STUFFING

1 lemon, halved
4 garlic cloves
1 medium onion, roughly chopped

FOR THE SPICE RUB

4 teaspoons sea salt
1½ teaspoons black pepper
1½ teaspoons cayenne pepper
1½ teaspoons sweet smoked paprika
1½ teaspoons dried thyme

1   Place the chopped vegetables in a slow cooker with the garlic, water and herbs.

2   Stuff the chicken with the lemon halves, garlic and onion and place on top of the chopped vegetables.

3   Rub the top of the chicken with the salt, spices and thyme. Put the lid on the slow cooker and set to low for 8 hours. Alternatively, place in an ovenproof casserole with a tight-fitting lid and cook in the oven (preheated to fan 140°C/Gas mark 3) for 4 hours. We like to serve this with Celeriac and Blue Cheese Gratin (page 105), Creamy Carrot Bake (page 93) and/or a simple watercress salad.

TIP

+   When you've served the chicken, throw the bones back into the pot to make chicken broth (page 63).

We rarely choose breast over the succulent and tasty dark meat of a chicken leg, but for this old-school classic we make an exception. Coated in a simple mix of ground almonds and eggs and filled with a parsley-garlic butter, feel free to make it your own with a twist of blue cheese and a coating of spices. If you can get the breasts with the skin on, even better – it keeps them super moist and helps flavour the crispy coating. These Kievs are simple to prep in advance for midweek meals. Make a big batch of them: no need to buy the pre-packaged kind when you can rustle up a load of these and pop in the freezer. Great with Carrot and Rosemary Chips (page 101) or slaw (pages 78 and 154) and some BBQ Ketchup (page 278) or our Homemade Sriracha (page 279).

CHICKEN KIEV WITH A SIMPLE SPINACH SALAD

SERVES 2

100g ground
   almonds
½ teaspoon cayenne
   pepper or sweet
   smoked paprika
   (optional)
1 egg
2 boneless chicken
   breasts (about
   350g in total),
   preferably with
   skin on

**FOR THE
GARLIC BUTTER**

3 garlic cloves,
   crushed or diced
50g butter, at room
   temperature
1 handful of fresh
   parsley, leaves
   and stalks finely
   chopped
1 teaspoon
   lemon juice
Sea salt and
   black pepper

**FOR THE
SPINACH SALAD**

250g baby spinach
2 tablespoons
   extra-virgin
   olive oil
Juice of ½ lemon
Sea salt and
   black pepper

1   Mix all the ingredients for the garlic butter together using a fork, season with salt and pepper to taste and roll in baking parchment into a sausage shape about 2cm in diameter. Leave in the freezer for 30 minutes until set.

2   Meanwhile, preheat the oven to fan 200°C/Gas mark 7 and line a baking tray with baking parchment.

3   Pour the ground almonds into a bowl and stir in some salt and pepper and the cayenne pepper or paprika (if using). Beat the egg in a separate bowl

4   Insert a sharp knife into the fat end of each chicken breast, pushing into the meat by about two-thirds to create a pocket. Halve the garlic butter and place one portion inside each breast before sealing the pocket closed with your hands.

5   Season the chicken pieces all over with the salt and pepper. Dip each first in the egg, then roll in the ground almonds until completely covered, and pat down, then place on the prepared baking tray.

6   Bake in the oven for 25–30 minutes until cooked through and golden brown.

7   Meanwhile, divide the spinach leaves between two plates, season with salt and pepper and dress with the EVOO and lemon juice. Add the chicken kievs, pouring over any garlic butter that's leaked out onto the tray during cooking.

TIP

+ We usually make a whole pack of garlic butter at a time, roll it into a sausage shape and keep it in the freezer so we can always slice off a chunk when we need it to make this dish. It's also delicious with roast chicken or fish, to top steaks or cooked vegetables, or to make garlic bread with Flaxseed Buns (page 136) or Quinoa Courgette Toast (page 32).

This salad is a great way to use up leftover chicken, though it is equally satisfying without. Sea spaghetti is a type of sea vegetable, aka seaweed – another superfood favourite which we like to call the sea's spinach! Rich in iodine, iron, magnesium and calcium, it contains almost all the nutrients found in the ocean and comes in a wide and wonderful array of textures and flavours, from mild and sweet to rich and smoky. If you're new to cooking with seaweed, start with wakame or sea spaghetti, which are milder tasting. Bear in mind that dried seaweed expands by about ten times in volume, so you only need a small amount if you buy the dried stuff. For speed, use a mandolin, spiralizer or food processor, if you have one, to shred your cabbages.

CHICKEN AND SEA SPAGHETTI SALAD WITH GINGER ALMOND DRESSING

SERVES 4

25g dried sea spaghetti or other seaweed (such as wakame)
1 small red cabbage, core removed and leaves shredded or spiralized
1 small green cabbage (such as pointed or sweetheart cabbage), core removed and leaves shredded or spiralized
2 large carrots, roughly grated or spiralized
1 handful of fresh chives or spring onions (about 20g), finely chopped
2 large handfuls of fresh coriander, leaves and stalks roughly chopped, plus extra to garnish
500g roast chicken, shredded
2 tablespoons black sesame seeds, to serve

1 Soak the sea spaghetti or other seaweed in water according to the packet instructions (usually for 8 minutes), then drain and rinse.

2 Blitz all the dressing ingredients together in the small bowl of a food processor, or grate the ginger and finely dice the garlic and whisk with the other ingredients in a bowl by hand.

3 Add all the prepared vegetables to a large bowl with the chives or spring onions and coriander. Pour over half the dressing and mix well to coat evenly.

4 Arrange the salad on a platter and scatter over the chicken. Garnish with the extra coriander and serve with the rest of the dressing drizzled on top and the sesame seeds sprinkled over.

VARIATIONS

+ If you have no leftover chicken, season 4 large chicken thighs (skin on) with salt and pepper and roast in the oven (preheated to fan 200°/Gas mark 7) for 25–30 minutes until cooked through, then shred with two forks to cool the meat quickly. The skins can be returned to the oven to crisp up before breaking into pieces and scattering on top of the salad for a crunchy, salty addition.

+ In cooler months, you could gently stir-fry everything for a warm salad.

**FOR THE
GINGER ALMOND
DRESSING**

2cm piece of fresh
    root ginger
    (unpeeled if
    organic)
2 garlic cloves
5 tablespoons
    almond butter
    or nut butter
    of your choice
Juice of 1½ lemons
    or 3 tablespoons
    apple cider
    vinegar
1½ tablespoons
    tamari
2 teaspoons
    raw honey or
    maple syrup
A pinch of black
    pepper or a little
    chilli powder
100ml water

This is real comfort food that, instead of leaving you feeling heavy and bloated like a sack of potatoes, fills you up with energy and goodness. Popular with everyone, make two at a time and pop one straight in the freezer, ready to whip out and bake whenever it's needed. We tend to make this pie as part of a Sunday Cook-Off (page 334) after roasting a chicken or two so that we have plenty of leftover chicken. Serve with a crisp green salad.

CHICKEN COMFORT PIE

SERVES 4

2 tablespoons butter or ghee
2 medium onions, diced
4 garlic cloves, diced
2 celery sticks, diced
4 medium carrots, diced
250g mushrooms (such as chestnut or Portobello), sliced
1 bay leaf
500ml Bone Broth (page 63)
1 tablespoon fresh thyme leaves or 1 teaspoon dried (rosemary would work well too)
500g roast chicken (preferably the juicy thigh meat), shredded
2 handfuls of frozen peas

1 large handful of chopped fresh parsley
1 quantity of Garlicky Cauliflower Mash (page 111)
Sea salt and black pepper

1 Preheat the oven to fan 200°C/Gas mark 7.

2 Melt half the butter or ghee in a frying pan over a medium heat. Add the onions and fry for 4 minutes until softened but not browned. Add the garlic, celery, carrots, mushrooms and bay leaf, increase the heat to high and fry for 1–2 minutes.

3 Pour the broth into the pan, add the thyme, bring to the boil, then lower the heat and simmer for about 12 minutes until the vegetables are tender and the sauce has reduced and thickened.

4 Remove the bay leaf and add the chicken, peas and parsley to the pan. Season with salt and pepper. Stir well, then transfer the mixture to a 25cm-diameter ovenproof dish with 5cm-high sides.

5 Spoon the cauliflower mash over the filling and spread into an even layer, then swirl it into peaks, if you like. Dot the top of the pie with the remaining butter/ghee, then bake for 25–30 minutes until the filling is bubbling and the topping is golden brown.

VARIATION

+ For a vegetarian option, swap the chicken with four large handfuls of cooked Puy lentils.

This delicious recipe was taught to us by our Portuguese friend Alexandra – or 'Al Shandra, Queen of Herbs', as we like to call her. We always make double quantities of the piri-piri paste and use the rest with prawns, fish or roast vegetables later in the week. We find using a mixture of fresh and dried chilli, here, gives a more complex flavour.These punchy little chicken wings make the perfect packed lunch as they taste just as fabulous cold. Serve with a salad of rocket and finely shredded white cabbage dressed in lime juice, plus some Homemade Sriracha (page 279) for extra spice.

PUNCHY PIRI-PIRI CHICKEN WINGS WITH CELERIAC SKINNY FRIES

SERVES 4

1 tablespoon
　　coconut oil
　　or ghee
1 large celeriac
　　(about 600g)
16 chicken wings
Sea salt and
　　black pepper

FOR THE PIRI-PIRI PASTE
6 tablespoons
　　(about 90g)
　　coconut oil
　　or ghee
4 fresh red chillies,
　　deseeded and
　　finely diced
2 teaspoons
　　chilli flakes
6 teaspoons
　　sweet paprika
　　(not smoked)
1½ teaspoons
　　sea salt

Juice of 2 lemons
2 bay leaves
2 large handfuls
　　of fresh parsley,
　　leaves and stalks
　　finely chopped
　　(retaining a little
　　to garnish)
6 garlic cloves,
　　finely chopped

1　Preheat the oven to fan 200°C/Gas mark 7 and line 2 large baking trays with baking parchment.

2　To make the piri-piri paste, melt the coconut oil or ghee in a small frying pan, add all the other ingredients except the garlic and fry over a medium heat for 2 minutes. Add the garlic and cook for a further minute until the mixture becomes a darker red colour. Allow to cool slightly.

3　Marinate the chicken wings in the paste for 30 minutes. Arrange the marinated chicken on one lined baking tray.

4　Add the coconut oil or ghee to the other lined tray, for the fries, and place in the oven to melt. Slice off the top and bottom of the celeriac and peel. Cut the flesh into thumb-thick slices and then into thin chip shapes.

5　Remove the tray of melted coconut oil/ghee from the oven, toss the fries in the hot fat and season with salt and pepper.

6　Place both trays in the oven and roast for 20 minutes. Baste the wings with the reserved paste and use two spatulas or forks to turn the fries. Return the trays to the oven and roast for another 10–15 minutes then serve immediately.

VARIATIONS

+ This is also delicious made with chicken thighs or drumsticks, or a whole roast chicken, adjusting cooking times accordingly.

This one-pan roast is perfect for a lazy weeknight supper, as well as providing you with leftovers for lunch the next day. Serve with sliced avocado and plenty of baby spinach or rocket. We look for any excuse to include antioxidant-rich turmeric and watercress in our dishes, both for their flavour and wealth of health benefits. This spice mix is delicious on lamb chops, too, or big chunks of roasted squash. The punchy watercress salsa verde makes double the quantity you'll need: so store it in the fridge and use the extra to toss through cooked quinoa or lentils after a Sunday Cook-Off (page 334).

SPICED ROAST CHICKEN THIGHS WITH WATERCRESS SALSA VERDE

SERVES 4

2 red peppers, deseeded and roughly chopped

1 large cauliflower (about 350g), cut into equal-sized florets and stem chopped (after first slicing off the tough outer layer)

2 medium fennel bulbs or 3 large carrots, roughly chopped

2 teaspoons ground cumin

2 teaspoons ground turmeric

A pinch of cayenne pepper or chilli powder (optional)

1 tablespoon ghee or coconut oil

4 large chicken thighs (skin on and bone in)

Sea salt and black pepper

1 Preheat the oven to fan 200°C/Gas mark 7 and line a large baking tray with baking parchment.

2 Spread the prepared vegetables on the baking tray and season with salt and pepper.

3 Mix the ground spices in a bowl with the ghee or coconut oil and a big pinch of salt and pepper and rub into the chicken thighs. Place the thighs on the prepared baking tray in-between the vegetables, or on top if space is tight. (Wash your hands afterwards as turmeric stains!)

4 Roast in the oven for 25–30 minutes until the chicken is golden and cooked through – the juices running clear when pierced with a knife. Halfway through cooking, toss everything together. Raise the oven temperature to fan 220°C/Gas mark 9 for the last 5 minutes to crisp up the skin of the chicken, then remove from the oven and leave to rest for 5 minutes.

5 Meanwhile, prepare the watercress salsa verde. Blend all the ingredients together in the small bowl of a food processor until chunky or smooth (whichever you prefer), seasoning to taste with salt and pepper. Alternatively, finely chop the first six ingredients, place in a bowl and stir through the lemon juice, mustard and EVOO, seasoning to taste.

6 Plate up the chicken and vegetables and spoon over a generous amount of the watercress salsa verde to serve.

80g watercress
   (including
   the stalks)
30g fresh parsley
   leaves
30g fresh mint leaves
2 garlic cloves
2 tablespoons capers
4 anchovies or a
   handful of pitted
   black olives in
   oil, drained
3 tablespoons
   lemon juice or
   2 tablespoons
   apple cider
   vinegar
1 teaspoon strong
   mustard
300ml extra-virgin
   olive oil

TIP

+ For those who love to cook, add an extra layer of flavour by caramelising the onions in ghee or coconut oil first, then add the garlic, ginger and spices and cook for a further 2 minutes before adding to the slow cooker with the rest of the ingredients. This takes a little more time and more washing up – you won't catch us doing it!

VARIATION

+ If any of the delicious sauce is left over, heat in a pan with a handful of greens, then make two holes in the sauce and crack an egg into each for an Indian take on shakshuka eggs. Simply cook the eggs to your liking.

This is the perfect curry if you are in a hurry. Yes, the words 'slow-cooked' and 'hurry' work together in this recipe! Five minutes of prep, pop everything in the slow cooker before work and you'll come home to a deliciously tender chicken curry. If you don't have a slow cooker, or to cook the chicken more quickly, you can cook the curry in the oven or on the hob instead. This curry pairs perfectly with broccoli or cauliflower rice (pages 170 and 240) or a crunchy slaw (pages 78 and 154).

SLOW-COOKED 'NO FRY' CHICKEN CURRY

SERVES 4

1.2kg chicken thighs
    (8 small thighs,
    skin on and
    bone in)
2 large onions, diced
6 garlic cloves, diced
6cm piece of fresh
    root ginger
    (unpeeled if
    organic), grated
2 tablespoons
    tomato purée
2½ tablespoons
    garam masala
2 teaspoons sweet
    smoked paprika
½ teaspoon chilli
    powder (to taste)
1 teaspoon tamari
    (optional)
1 x 400g tin
    of chopped
    tomatoes
1 x 400ml tin
    of full-fat
    coconut milk

2 handfuls of fresh
    coriander, stems
    finely chopped,
    leaves reserved
    to serve
Sea salt and
    black pepper
Juice of 1–2 lemons
    or 2 limes, to
    serve

1   Put everything except the coriander leaves and lemon juice in a slow cooker (the liquid should just cover everything), season, stir, cover with the lid and set to low to cook for 6 hours or high to cook for 3 hours.

2   If cooking on the hob, place all the ingredients except the coriander leaves and lemon juice, in a heavy-based pan with a tight-fitting lid (so that the liquid doesn't evaporate) and cook on the lowest heat for 1–1½ hours, stirring halfway through. If cooking in the oven, preheat the oven to fan 180°C/ Gas mark 6, then place the ingredients in an ovenproof dish with a tight-fitting lid and cook for 2 hours.

3   If you prefer a thicker sauce, remove the lid from the slow cooker – or pan on the hob or dish in the oven – and cook uncovered for the last 20–30 minutes so the liquid reduces down.

4   At the end of cooking, squeeze in the lemon juice and taste for seasoning, adding more salt or an extra dash of tamari (to give greater depth of flavour). Scatter over the coriander leaves to serve.

This is a super-speedy ragù. Using sausage meat means you can quickly chuck this on and, within half an hour, have a rich, delicious sauce to be enjoyed with a multitude of vegetable bases. Because it's so fast and simple, we always make double the amount and have it again a few days later (when it'll taste even better) or freeze half for another day. In the winter we like to serve this with celeriac spaghetti or cauliflower mash (page 111) and in the summer we go for courgetti (page 229) or cauliflower rice (page 240). We love chicken livers. They are incredibly nutritious – a good source of iron and vitamin A – and inexpensive too. We hide them in sauces like this ragù so that children (or even apprehensive adults) can enjoy them too.

QUICK SAUSAGE RAGÙ WITH CELERIAC SPAGHETTI

SERVES 4

2 medium celeriacs (about 600g each)

FOR THE RAGÙ

2 medium onions, finely diced
1 tablespoon ghee
4 garlic cloves, finely diced
1 fresh red chilli, deseeded and diced, or 1 teaspoon chilli flakes (to taste)
1 medium fennel bulb, finely diced, or 1 teaspoon fennel seeds
1 tablespoon fresh oregano leaves or 2 teaspoons dried
1 handful of chicken livers, finely diced (optional)

8 medium sausages (at least 97% meat content)
1 tablespoon tomato purée
1 x 400g tin of chopped tomatoes
1 large red pepper, deseeded and chopped
400ml Bone Broth (page 63) or water
Sea salt and black pepper

TO SERVE

2 handfuls of fresh parsley, leaves and stalks roughly chopped
1 large handful of finely grated Parmesan (about 60g)
Extra-virgin olive oil, for drizzling

1 First make the ragù. Fry the onions in the ghee in a frying pan on a medium heat for 8 minutes, stirring occasionally, until softened but not browned. Add the garlic, chilli, fennel, oregano and chicken livers, if using, and fry for a further minute.

2 Using a sharp knife, slice down the length of each sausage skin and empty the meat into the pan. Use a spatula or wooden spoon to break up the sausage meat into smaller chunks – we like to keep it quite rustic and chunky. Stir in the tomato purée and fry for 2 minutes.

3 Add the tomatoes, red pepper and broth or water and raise the heat to bring to a medium simmer.

4 Simmer for 20 minutes with the lid on, or longer if possible, for an even thicker, richer ragù. Season to taste.

5 About 10 minutes before the ragù is ready, prepare the celeriac spaghetti by first slicing off all the knobbly bits. If using a spiralizer, slot the celeriac lengthways into the spiralizer to make the noodles. If using a julienne or vegetable peeler, first cut the celeriac into a few long slices about 15mm thick and peel (using more pressure than if you were peeling other vegetables) thin noodle shapes 8–10cm long from the longest edge of each slice.

6 Simmer the celeriac spaghetti in a little salted water over a medium heat for 3 minutes until tender, then drain and serve immediately with a big ladleful of ragù, topped with chopped parsley and grated Parmesan and a drizzle of EVOO.

+ If you want to prepare the celeriac spaghetti ahead, keep it covered in cold water with a squeeze of lemon juice to prevent browning.

VARIATIONS

+ For a summer version of this dish, serve with raw courgetti.

+ Replace the sausages with 500g minced pork and the oregano with fresh or dried thyme, or use beef mince and allow the sauce to simmer for 1 hour or longer to tenderise.

Made with our nutty and crunchy almond pastry, this tart is filled to the brim with a quiche Lorraine-style filling, which we've jazzed up with caramelised onions and sweet cherry tomatoes. If you fancy a meat-free version, swap the bacon for earthy wild mushrooms. We like to serve it warm alongside a huge pile of dressed watercress. Enjoy it al fresco on a crisp spring day or for a summer picnic, and it makes a great packed lunch. It also keeps very well in the fridge and should still be good 3 days later!

SPINACH AND BACON TART
WITH A NUTTY ALMOND CRUST

SERVES 6

**FOR THE
PASTRY CASE**

375g ground
 almonds
2 teaspoons sea salt
½ teaspoon
 bicarbonate
 of soda
30g butter, at room
 temperature
2 eggs

**FOR THE
FILLING**

250g bacon
 or pancetta,
 chopped
1 large onion,
 halved and finely
 sliced
2 garlic cloves,
 finely diced
180g fresh spinach
 (preferably baby
 spinach),
 chopped
5 eggs
250ml full-fat
 coconut milk
80g cherry
 tomatoes, halved
1 handful of fresh
 parsley, leaves
 and stalks finely
 chopped
1 tablespoon fresh
 thyme leaves or
 1 teaspoon dried
Sea salt and
 black pepper

1 Mix the pastry ingredients by hand to form a dough and then roll into a 3mm-thick disc between two sheets of baking parchment. Line a 24cm-diameter ceramic flan dish or loose-bottomed tart tin with the almond pastry, trimming away the excess. Line the pastry case with greaseproof paper, fill with baking beans and chill in the fridge for 20 minutes.

2 Preheat the oven to fan 180°C/Gas mark 6.

3 Put the bean-filled, chilled tart case in the oven to bake for 10 minutes, then remove the baking beans and paper and bake for a further 10 minutes until lightly browned. Set aside and reduce the oven temperature to fan 170°C/Gas mark 5.

4 Meanwhile, for the filling, fry the bacon or pancetta in a large dry frying pan over a medium heat for 4 minutes until crispy. Remove from the pan and set aside.

5 Cook the onion in the bacon fat, over a low heat, for about 12 minutes until caramelised, adding a touch of ghee, if needed. Make sure not to overcrowd the pan as it will prevent the onion from caramelising. Add the garlic to cook for the final few minutes.

6 Tip in the spinach and allow it to cook down until any excess liquid has evaporated. Remove from the heat.

TIP

+ Save the remaining coconut milk from your 400ml tin for making smoothies or adding to soup or porridge.

VARIATIONS

+ Swap parsley and thyme for basil and oregano and add a handful of grated Parmesan or Cheddar.

7   In a large bowl, whisk together the eggs and coconut milk. Add the cooked bacon bits with the onion and spinach mixture, then season with salt and pepper.

8   Pour the egg mixture into your pre-baked tart case. Top with the halved cherry tomatoes, cut side up, and push them down slightly. Bake for 35 minutes until golden brown on top and just set in the middle – you want it to be slightly jiggly but not too runny. Remove from the oven.

9   Allow to cool for 15 minutes. Serve warm, sprinkled with chopped parsley and thyme leaves or wrap cold individual pieces in baking parchment for packed lunches or a picnic.

We love honest, home-cooked food that is easy on the bank balance, and this dish ticks all those boxes. Why not try liver for a change? Packed with vitamins A, D, E and K and all the B vitamins, especially the vital B12, it's a nutritional goldmine, as well as being relatively inexpensive to buy organic. We try to put it on the menu at least once a week. The onion gravy is rich and flavoursome, pairing wonderfully with the creamy cauli mustard mash. Of course it's a great recipe for bangers too (no need for the bacon) and if cooking for children, feel free to leave out the mustard. Serve with a plate of buttered greens, such as our Garlicky Chilli Chard (page 103), or simply steamed seasonal greens in the winter months, and a green salad or our Spicy Ruby Slaw (page 154) in the summer.

LIVER/BANGERS AND MASH WITH ONION GRAVY

SERVES 4

400g sliced liver
  (lamb's or calf's)
  and 3 rashers
  of unsmoked
  bacon, chopped
  OR
8 medium sausages
  (at least 97%
  meat content)

FOR THE GRAVY
2 tablespoons
  butter
1 large onion,
  finely sliced
250ml Bone
  Broth (preferably
  from beef bones
  – page 63)
1 teaspoon
  balsamic vinegar
Splash of double
  cream or crème
  fraîche (optional)
Sea salt and
  black pepper

TO SERVE
1 quantity of
  Cauliflower
  Mustard Mash
  (page 111),
  to serve

1 **FOR THE LIVER:** Wash the liver and pat dry with kitchen paper, then season with a generous amount of salt and pepper.

2 Melt half the butter in a frying pan and cook the liver on each side over a medium heat for 1½–2 minutes until browned but still a little pink in the middle. Transfer to a plate and set aside. Don't cook the liver for too long or it can become tough.

3 Reduce the heat and add the remaining butter to the pan (don't wash it out as you want to keep the cooking juices), followed by the onion and bacon. Cook for another 5 minutes or until the onions are soft and beginning to caramelise.

4 Pour in the bone broth and balsamic vinegar and give the mixture a good stir as you bring it to a simmer, then leave to cook for 7–8 minutes.

5 Once the mixture has reduced a little and started to thicken, return the liver to the pan and heat through for 2 minutes, then stir in the cream or crème fraîche (if using).

6 **FOR THE BANGERS:** Cook the sausages, butter and onion together (no need for the bacon) and when they are browned and are nearly cooked, add the bone broth and balsamic vinegar and reduce the heat to a simmer, until you reach the desired gravy consistency. Stir in the cream or crème fraîche (if using).

7 Serve the liver or bangers immediately with big spoonfuls of cauliflower mash (page 111).

TIP

+   Scrape up the bits on the bottom
    of the pan with a wooden spoon
    when stirring the gravy to get that
    rich flavour.

This is practically the real deal. We've been making this sublime dish for years and still remember the gasp from everyone trying it that it could actually work so well. Let's face it, anything covered in a carbonara sauce is going to hit the spot, but when we replace that white, refined spaghetti with celeriac noodles the whole recipe is still spot on. To add some colour to this otherwise super-pale dish, and to up the goodness factor, we've thrown in some kale but you can hide any greens in that delicious buttery, creamy, bacon sauce. On a summer's day, try trusted courgetti (page 229) with this dish – just toss it raw through the sauce – or lightly steamed ribbons of Savoy cabbage.

CELERIAC SPAGHETTI AND KALE CARBONARA

SERVES 2 WITH LEFTOVERS

3 eggs
100g Parmesan,
    grated
100g unsmoked
    bacon or
    pancetta,
    chopped
1 garlic clove,
    squashed
    with the back
    of a knife
25–50g butter (use
    less if you are
    using pancetta)
1 large celeriac
    (about 600g)
150g kale leaves
    (stripped from
    their stalks)
Sea salt and
    black pepper

1 Beat the eggs in a medium bowl, mix in the grated Parmesan, reserving a small handful to serve, and season with a little pepper before setting aside.

2 Add the bacon or pancetta to a large pan with the garlic and butter, and fry on a medium heat for about 5 minutes, stirring frequently, until the bacon/pancetta is crisp and golden at the edges. Remove the garlic.

3 Peel the celeriac and slice off the knobbly bits. Slot the celeriac lengthways into a spiralizer, using the small noodle blade to make 'spaghetti'; snip long strands into shorter lengths for easier eating. If using a julienne peeler or standard vegetable peeler, first cut the celeriac into a few long slices about 15mm thick and peel (using more pressure than if you were peeling other vegetables) into strips 8–10cm long, starting from the longest edge of each slice. Cut the strips in half lengthways.

4 Add the celeriac spaghetti to the pan with the bacon/pancetta and cover, cooking on a medium heat for 10 minutes or until al dente and removing the lid to toss it occasionally.

5 Add the kale and leave to cook for another 2–3 minutes, with the lid on, until just tender.

VARIATION

+ You can swap the bacon for sliced mushrooms or pieces of purple dulse. This dried seaweed has a smoky flavour that makes a great substitute for bacon in this dish. Just fry in butter as you would the bacon – no need to soak the dulse first.

6   Take the pan off the heat and quickly pour in the eggs and cheese. Use tongs or two forks to toss everything in the egg mixture, which will thicken from the residual heat without scrambling. Season with a little salt, if needed.

7   Use a long-pronged fork to twist the spaghetti onto a serving plate or into a bowl. Serve immediately with a little sprinkling of the remaining cheese and a grind of black pepper.

Sweet and smoky shreds of pork – delicious served in our Flaxseed Buns (page 136) with lettuce and gherkins and a side of slaw (pages 78 and 154), or atop a scoop of our Broccomole (page 128). Fresh apples add sweetness and reduce down to make an easy sauce. Let the slow cooker create a barbecue-style pulled-pork feast without any of the hard work, or pop it in the oven on low. Prep this in the morning and by the evening you'll have a meltingly tender dish – perfect for a supper party at home.

SLOW-COOKED SMOKY APPLE PULLED PORK

SERVES 6

1kg boneless pork shoulder (skin on), thick cut
2 bay leaves
4 tablespoons apple cider vinegar or lemon juice
400g apples (about 3 medium/large apples), cored and chopped into chunks

peppercorns or ground black pepper
½ tablespoon fennel seeds or ground fennel
1 tablespoon sweet smoked paprika
½ tablespoon ground cumin
2 teaspoons ground cinnamon
2 teaspoons chilli flakes, or 1 teaspoon chilli powder
1 tablespoon sea salt

FOR THE SPICE RUB

3 garlic cloves, crushed
½ tablespoon whole black

TIP

+ Remember not to lift the lid of the slow cooker to check on the pork. You can adjust the flavour after 8 hours, but every time you lift the lid you add on 20 minutes of cooking time!

1 Grind all the ingredients for the spice rub together using a pestle and mortar, or choose ground black pepper, crush the fennel seeds with the back of a knife to bruise them (or use ground fennel) and mix all the ground spices together in a bowl/jar. With a sharp knife, score the pork all over and then rub the spice mixture well into the meat.

2 Put the remaining ingredients in a slow cooker, give them a mix and place the meat, skin side up, on top. Cover with the lid and cook on low for 8 hours (or on high for 4 hours if you don't have the time). Alternatively, place in an ovenproof casserole with a tight-fitting lid and cook in the oven (preheated to fan 140°C/Gas mark 3) for 6–8 hours.

3 At the end of the cooking time, take out the pork and remove the top layer of skin and fat (set aside), place the meat in a dish and use two forks to shred it. Remove the bay leaves. Place the pulled pork back into the slow cooker or casserole and toss in the smoky apple sauce. Switch to 'warm' (or turn the oven temperature down lower) and keep covered until ready to serve.

4 Just before serving, we like to roast the reserved skin and fat in the oven (preheated to fan 200°C/Gas mark 7) on a baking tray for about 20 minutes until bubbling and crisp. Cool for 5 minutes, then cut the crackling into pieces to serve alongside the pulled pork, or keep in the fridge ready to roast for another meal (it's delicious with a salad).

This one-pot, brothy stew with hints of Asian spices, ginger and lemon relies on the salty tang of fish sauce to take it to the next level. If you can't find a sugar- and additive-free brand, then we've given a substitute using anchovies (see tip below). Chinese five-spice powder is a blend of star anise, cloves, cinnamon, Sichuan pepper and fennel seeds. The strength of the powder, as with any spices, will depend on its freshness and quality, so you may need to adjust the quantity. This succulent and soothing stew is easily prepared and a warming supper to come home to, so make double the quantity and freeze half for another day. It is delicious served straight up, with double the greens or paired with cauliflower rice (page 240), or spiralized courgette noodles (courgetti) stirred through at the end (page 229).

ASIAN SHORT RIB STEW

SERVES 4

2 tablespoons coconut oil
2.25kg English-cut short ribs
1 large red onion, finely diced
3 garlic cloves, finely diced
7cm piece of fresh root ginger (unpeeled if organic), finely diced
1½ teaspoons Chinese five-spice powder
3 whole star anise pods
1 fresh red chilli, deseeded and diced, or 1 teaspoon chilli flakes (optional)
4 large carrots, roughly chopped

2 celery sticks, diced
3 tablespoons fish sauce (nam pla)
2 x 400g tins of chopped tomatoes
500ml Bone Broth (page 63)
1 large handful of fresh coriander, leaves and stalks separated and roughly chopped
400g spinach or greens
Juice of ½ lemon or 1 lime, or 1 tablespoon apple cider vinegar
Sea salt and black pepper

1 Melt the coconut oil in a large flameproof casserole over a medium-high heat.

2 Season the ribs with salt and pepper and add to the casserole in two batches. Brown one batch for 4–5 minutes, transfer to a large plate and repeat with the remaining ribs.

3 Add the onion, garlic and ginger to the casserole and cook for 3 minutes until softened. Stir in the spices, chilli (if using), carrots, celery and fish sauce and cook, stirring, for 1 minute.

4 Return the ribs to the casserole with the tomatoes, broth and coriander stalks and bring to a simmer. Cover with a lid and cook over a low heat for 2½ hours, remembering to turn the ribs every hour or so. Alternatively, place in the oven (preheated to fan 180°C/Gas mark 6) for the same length of time.

5 Remove the star anise, add the spinach or greens (or serve lightly cooked on the side) along with the lemon or lime juice or ACV and taste for seasoning.

6 Serve as it is and allow people to help themselves, or divide between soup bowls and garnish with the coriander leaves.

TIP

+ If you can't find good-quality
  fish sauce (nam pla) for this dish,
  you can substitute with a blend
  of 3 tablespoons of tamari and
  3 anchovies in oil (drained).

Inspired by two classic campfire dishes – Boston baked beans and beef stew – this rich, smoky dish is sure to warm you up. Simply leave to bubble gently on the hob or in the oven, or throw it all into a slow cooker with half the amount of water and set to low for 8 hours. Serve with big handfuls of watercress and spinach, or throw in some greens during the last 10 minutes of cooking to keep this an easy one-pot dish. For a dinner party, add some cauliflower mash (page 111) or slaw (pages 78 or 154) or serve with buttered Flaxseed Buns (page 136). It's a great dish to make and freeze. Don't be put off by the long list of ingredients: you need this for the unique flavour each ingredient imparts to the mix.

BEEF AND BACON STEW

SERVES 6

200g unsmoked bacon or pancetta, chopped

1 tablespoon ghee or coconut oil

2 large onions, finely diced

1kg minced beef (minimum 20% fat)

4 garlic cloves, diced

2 teaspoons hot smoked paprika

1 tablespoon fresh thyme/oregano leaves or 2 teaspoons dried

2 tablespoons maple syrup

2 tablespoons apple cider vinegar or juice of 1 lemon

1 tablespoon tomato purée

2 x 400g tins of chopped tomatoes

4 medium carrots, roughly chopped

1 celeriac (about 400g), peeled and roughly chopped

2 large handfuls of fresh parsley, leaves and stalks separated and chopped

2 tablespoons mustard

400ml Bone Broth (page 63) or water

Sea salt and black pepper

1   In a large, heavy-based saucepan, cook the bacon or pancetta on a medium heat for 5 minutes until crispy.

2   Add the ghee or coconut oil and onions, stirring for 8 minutes until softened and caramelised, then tip in the minced beef with the garlic, paprika and thyme/oregano, and stir for another minute.

3   Add the maple syrup, ACV and tomato purée, season with salt and pepper and fry for a minute, stirring continuously.

4   Tip in the tomatoes, carrots, celeriac and parsley stalks, then add the mustard and broth or water. Bring to a simmer, cover with a lid and cook over a low heat for 2 hours, stirring occasionally. Alternatively, cook in an ovenproof casserole in the oven (preheated to 180°C/Gas mark 6) for 2½ hours. If there is excess liquid, remove the lid from the pan or casserole and cook uncovered during the final 15 minutes to let the sauce reduce.

5   Taste for seasoning and top with the parsley leaves to garnish.

Food is emotional, and this one tugs at our heartstrings – a trip to the local takeaway was so much fun when we were kids! We love the cuisines of different cultures and here is a quick and easy one-pan dish with a nod to our travels in the Far East. Since we've played about with it anyway, feel free to use minced lamb instead. No need for any 'rice' here; the meal works on its own, pan to plate, though a dash of Homemade Sriracha (page 279) would go nicely. A wok would be perfect, if you have one, but a large frying pan will do otherwise.

CHINESE-STYLE BEEF AND BROCCOLI

SERVES 4

2 tablespoons black sesame seeds
2 tablespoons coconut oil
500g minced beef (minimum 20% fat)
1 medium onion, sliced
2 medium carrots, cut into matchsticks or grated
1 red pepper, deseeded and sliced
1 tablespoon grated fresh root ginger (unpeeled if organic)
4 garlic cloves, finely diced
3 tablespoons tamari
1½ tablespoons fish sauce (nam pla)

1 teaspoon Chinese five-spice powder (optional)
Juice of ½ lemon, or 2 tablespoons apple cider vinegar
125ml Bone Broth (page 63)
1 large head of broccoli, cut into small florets and stalks sliced (after first cutting off the tough outer layer)
2 spring onions, finely chopped
1 tablespoon coconut flour, for thickening the sauce (optional)
Sea salt and white pepper

1   In a wok or large pan, lightly toast the black sesame seeds on a medium heat for a minute until fragrant, then remove from the pan and set aside.

2   Add the coconut oil to the pan, followed by the minced beef and onion, and fry until the meat begins to brown. Add the carrots and red pepper with the ginger, garlic, tamari, fish sauce, Chinese five-spice powder (if using) and the lemon juice or ACV. Season with salt and ¼ teaspoon of white pepper and continue to fry for 3–4 minutes, stirring continuously.

3   Add the broth, broccoli and spring onions and simmer for a further 4–5 minutes until the broccoli is tender but still has some bite and the sauce has reduced. If looking to thicken the sauce, add the coconut flour at the same time as the broth.

4   Sprinkle with the toasted sesame seeds and serve immediately, in individual bowls.

This makes a seriously spicy and juicy burger or meatballs; grated carrot makes the meat go further as well as adding moisture and sweetness. We like to double the recipe and freeze half of the raw patties for a quick and easy meal later in the month. Made into burgers this is delicious with our homemade BBQ Ketchup (page 278) and slaw (pages 78 and 154), or get some big crunchy lettuce leaves and make a lettuce burger wrap. For parties we make the mix into meatballs and serve with a little pot of guacamole (page 50) or Creamy Cashew Ranch Dressing (page 276) on the side. Enjoy any leftover balls with courgetti (page 229) for a Mexican-inspired take on spaghetti and meatballs. Feel free to swap the beef in this recipe for minced lamb – it's just as tasty.

MEXICAN BEEF AND CARROT BURGERS/BALLS

MAKES 8 BURGERS OR 20 MEATBALLS

500g minced
    beef (minimum
    20% fat)
2 large carrots,
    grated
1 large onion,
    finely diced
3 garlic cloves,
    finely diced
1 large handful of
    fresh coriander
    or parsley,
    leaves and stalks
    finely chopped
1½ teaspoons
    ground cumin
2 teaspoons sweet
    smoked paprika
2 tablespoons
    chopped pickled
    jalapeños,
    1 fresh red chilli,
    deseeded and
    diced, or
    ¼ teaspoon
    chilli powder

1 teaspoon dried
    thyme or
    oregano
1 egg, lightly beaten
Sea salt and
    black pepper

1   Preheat the oven to fan 200°C/Gas mark 7 and line a baking tray with baking parchment.

2   Place all the ingredients in a large bowl and mix together with your hands, seasoning with salt and pepper. Fry a small piece of the raw mixture until cooked to taste for seasoning, adding more salt and pepper or spices to the rest of the mixture as needed.

3   Take large handfuls of the mixture and shape into patties or roll into meatballs.

4   Place on the prepared baking tray, spaced apart, and bake in the oven for 30 minutes (for the patties) or 20 minutes (for the meatballs) until cooked through. Serve.

Our Filipina mum brought us up on traditional Philippine homemade food. One such dish is sinigang, a hearty and stew-like soup containing large chunks of meat or seafood and any seasonal vegetables. This slow-cooked dish is characterised by its sour and savoury taste, which comes from the inclusion of tamarind – a tart and tangy fruit synonymous with Asian cuisine – and ginger. We prefer it quite sour with a touch of sweetness from tomatoes, and slightly spicy from the addition of two whole red finger chillies at the end – removed just when they have released their fragrance. Delicious served as a one-pot dish, it also goes well with cauliflower rice (page 240) or with courgetti (courgette noodles – page 229) dropped in for the last few minutes of cooking. Try swapping the beef for chicken, pork or fish.

MUM'S PHILIPPINE BEEF SINIGANG

SERVES 4

700g rib-eye steak
1.2 litres water
   or Bone Broth
   (page 63)
2 medium onions,
   diced
6 garlic cloves,
   diced
5cm piece of fresh
   root ginger
   (unpeeled if
   organic), thinly
   sliced
20 cherry tomatoes,
   halved
3 tablespoons
   tamarind paste
   (or to taste)
A big pinch of black
   or white pepper
3–4 tablespoons
   fish sauce
   (nam pla)
400g green beans,
   tops trimmed

400g pak choi,
   leaves and stalks
   roughly chopped
2 whole fresh red
   chillies
400g spinach

1   Cut the meat into 3cm cubes, retaining the fat as it will flavour the stew. Place in a large saucepan and pour in the water or broth. Bring to the boil, then cover and quickly reduce the heat and cook at a medium-to-low simmer for 20 minutes.

2   Add the onions, garlic, ginger and tomatoes with the tamarind paste, pepper and fish sauce. Bring back up to a simmer and cook, covered, for a further 15 minutes. Taste for seasoning, adding more tamarind paste for a sourer flavour, if desired. Remember, fish sauce is salty and brands vary in strength.

3   Tip in the beans, pak choi and whole chillies, then bring back up to a simmer and cook, covered, for 5 more minutes.

4   Add the spinach and remove the pan from the heat, leaving the lid on the pan to allow the spinach to wilt in the residual heat. Remove the chillies and serve immediately.

Onglet or hanger steak is a cheap and tasty cut. Historically, it was the cut the butcher would take home for his own supper and therefore rarely made it onto the shop's counter. Popular in France, and deservedly so, it's being championed increasingly in restaurants over here and we love cooking it at home. If you cook it for too long though, the fibres of the meat will toughen to an extent that the steak will be inedible, so it should be cooked rare to retain its tenderness. This quick dish, with the iron-rich steak and vitamin-laden kale and avocado, is a nutritional powerhouse; best made for lunch or an early supper so that it can be digested more easily. We love it with a dollop of our Homemade Sriracha (page 279) or watercress salsa verde (pages 194–195).

POWERHOUSE STEAK AND KALE SALAD

SERVES 2

1 tablespoon ghee
250g onglet steak,
    at room
    temperature
1 tablespoon capers

FOR THE SALAD
1 big bunch of kale
    (about 300g),
    stems removed
    and leaves finely
    shredded
1 large ripe avocado
1 big bunch of
    watercress
    (about 250g),
    rocket or
    romaine or
    lamb's lettuce

FOR THE DRESSING
2 tablespoons
    fresh thyme
    /rosemary
    /oregano leaves
    or 2 teaspoons
    dried
1½ teaspoons chilli
    flakes, or a pinch
    of cayenne pepper
Grated zest
    and juice of
    1½ lemons or
    6 tablespoons
    apple cider
    vinegar
3 garlic cloves,
    crushed
150ml extra-virgin
    olive oil
Sea salt and
    black pepper

1 Start by making the kale salad so the raw leaves have time to soften. Whisk together (or shake in a jam jar with the lid on) the ingredients for the dressing, seasoning to taste with salt and pepper. Using your hands, toss the finely shredded kale in most of the dressing in a bowl, massaging it for a minute, and set aside.

2 Melt the ghee in a frying pan on a very high heat.

3 Season the steak all over with salt and pepper, then fry for 1½ minutes (for rare) and for a further minute on the second side. Remove to a board to rest for 5 minutes before cutting the steak into thin slices across the grain.

4 Meanwhile, fry up the capers for a minute in the steak pan – they will soak up the juices.

5 Slice the avocado, or cut into cubes, and snip the watercress stalks for easier eating or shred the romaine lettuce leaves, then arrange with the kale salad. Serve the steak on top with the hot fried capers spooned over and a drizzle of the remaining dressing, if you like.

Fatty and full of flavour, this forgotten cut of meat is the lamb equivalent of pork belly. You can roast it on the bone – just make sure it fits inside your dish, or for ease, we ask our butcher to bone and roll it, saving the bones to make broth (page 63). If you're buying it at the supermarket, you'll usually find it boned, rolled and ready to go. This cut works best cooked slowly for melt-in-the-mouth meat, with the juices from the bed of onions and celeriac combining with the fat to create a wonderfully rich, sweet gravy. Serve with a large helping of seasonal greens tossed in a zesty dressing (page 182).

SLOW-ROASTED BREAST OF LAMB

SERVES 4

4 large onions, sliced
1 large celeriac, peeled and cut into 5mm-thick slices
100ml water
600g lamb breast, boned and rolled
4 bay leaves
2 tablespoons apple cider vinegar
4 anchovies or 10 pitted olives in oil, drained (optional)
A large sprig of fresh rosemary or 1½ tablespoons dried

Sea salt and black pepper
1 small handful of fresh parsley, leaves and stalks chopped, to serve

1   Preheat the oven to fan 160°C/Gas mark 4.

2   Place the sliced onions and celeriac, and the water, in an ovenproof dish with a tight-fitting lid to make a bed for the lamb breast to sit on.

3   Generously season the lamb with salt and pepper and place, skin side up, on top of the onions. Add the bay leaves, ACV and anchovies or olives (if using) and then place or sprinkle the rosemary on top of the lamb.

4   Put the lid on the dish and cook in the oven for 3½–4 hours.

5   After around 3½ hours of cooking, check to see how tender the lamb is – there should be little resistance. If tender and falling apart, take off the lid and turn the oven temperature up to fan 200°C/Gas mark 7 to roast for a further 20 minutes to crisp up the fat and skin and brown the onions and celeriac. If it still needs more cooking, keep it a little longer in the covered dish at the lower temperature – there's no real danger of overcooking here – before crisping up the fat and skin.

6   Remove from the oven, cut off the string tying the meat together, if needed, and thickly slice the lamb or slice in portions. Serve immediately, piling the onions and celeriac alongside, spooning over some of the gravy and scattering with chopped parsley.

VARIATIONS

+ This is a super-fatty cut, so not for the faint-hearted if you're just starting to introduce real fat back into your diet. Since the fat melts into the gravy and veggies underneath, you can always eat them separately from the meat and serve with any of our vegetable sides and salads (pages 93–131 and 147–165) to make another meal.

+ You can also cook this in a slow cooker: cook for 8 hours on a low setting and then place under a hot grill to crisp up the skin, if you like.

VEGETABLE MAINS

COURGETTE AND
CANNELLINI BEAN
LASAGNE
226

COURGETTI WITH
QUICK CHICKPEA
TOMATO SAUCE
229

LENTIL BAKE
230

CAULIRONI
CHEESE
232

KASHA
BUCKWHEAT
BURGERS/BALLS
234

BEETROOT
FETA CAKE
237

MARINATED
BUTTERBEAN
GREEK SALAD
238

CAULIFLOWER RICE
3 WAYS
240

COURGETTI
PESTO 3 WAYS
245

EASY CHEESY
BROCCOLI RISOTTO
248

GREEN GODDESS
NOODLE SALAD
250

QUINOA 3 WAYS
253

SIMPLE AND
SPICED MUNG
BEAN SALAD
256

MUSHROOM LENTIL
BURGERS
258

TERIYAKI NOODLE
STIR-FRY
261

In almost every recipe in this book, and certainly every chapter, vegetables play the hero – from breakfast through to desserts – but this is the section that truly celebrates the plant kingdom. Here we've created hearty main courses where a piece of meat or fish won't be missed, thanks to innovative, satisfying dishes in which we team our favourite pulses, pseudocereals and starchy roots with a rainbow array of veg. We prefer less meat in the evenings as we find we digest it better earlier in the day, so these dishes make great suppers. You'll find bone broth and butter in among the ingredients, but you can easily swap them to suit vegetarian and vegan lifestyles (for more on this, see page 17).

As in recipes throughout the book, we replace grains, white potatoes and refined baking flours with less starchy, more nutrient-dense alternatives. Try our 'lasagne' (page 226) made from thinly sliced courgettes layered with a cannellini bean tomato sauce and a ricotta 'béchamel' – no pre-cooking needed! Check out our cauli rice (pages 240–243), we've pimped up this side dish to serve it as a main in three deliciously different ways, or Easy Cheesy Broccoli Risotto (page 248), with quinoa replacing standard Arborio. These wholefood alternatives are far more nourishing and will leave you feeling invigorated and pleasantly satisfied rather than bloated and uncomfortably full.

We're big fans of simple food combining, where we avoid mixing too much protein with starch in the same meal (such as chicken with quinoa) to improve digestion and also strive to ensure that two-thirds of our plate are made up of vegetables to enhance overall well-being. Think of vegetables in two main camps: the starchier roots and the low-starch varieties such as leafy greens. It's about teaming those leafy greens with either protein or starchy foods, as well as good fats such as olive oil or butter. When meat is off the menu, use a base of pulses, pseudocereals or starchy veg as the main part of your meal, along with nutritious fats. Bulk it out with green veggies, serve it with more veggies and slip veggies in wherever possible!

A spiralizer is perfect for transforming vegetables into noodles to use in place of starchy pasta – cutting out refined carbohydrates in one fell swoop while upping your veg quota in a tasty way. If you don't have a spiralizer, just use a julienne peeler or standard vegetable peeler. You'll see that we've put the spiralizer to good use in this chapter with our Courgetti with Quick Chickpea Tomato Sauce (page 229) or courgetti tossed in your choice of delicious pesto (pages 245–246). Our Beetroot Feta Cake (page 237) shows how imaginatively noodles can be incorporated into different dishes. Serve any of these with a salad – full of iron-rich greens like spinach and watercress – and you'll be able to enjoy your five a day with ease!

TIPS AND TRICKS

SOUP, STEW, SPIRALIZE For those who struggle with eating enough vegetables, we say follow the three 'S's – soup, stew and spiralize! These have been our secret weapons in making sure that we get plenty of nutrient-dense and refreshing veggies into our meals.

STICK WITH THE SEASONS Eat seasonal vegetables where possible. In general terms, food tastes better in season and is cheaper to buy.

MORE GREENS As well as avoiding protein and starch within the same meal, we concentrate on getting our greens or other low-starch veg to make up two-thirds of our plate. Avoid a meal of bean stew on quinoa with a side of squash equals (starch overload!).

VARIETY IS THE SPICE OF LIFE Liven up your food with a variety of veggies and cooking methods. Steam, fry, roast, grill, spiralize, grate and mash, mix cooked veg with raw – and add spices!

GET ACTIVATING Get into the habit of soaking nuts, lentils and pseudocereals to make the most of them – our recipes indicate where this is necessary. (See also page 341 for more information.)

SUNDAY COOK-OFF Save time by cooking up a few batches of lentils, quinoa or buckwheat noodles on a Sunday (page 334) so you can easily whip up a meal by adding veggies and a dressing.

NO TEETH IN YOUR TUMMY Remember to chew – especially raw food and tiny grains of quinoa... and even tinier chia seeds!

EMBRACE FAT Make sure you cook vegetables in fat or dress them with butter or an oil-based dressing – fat enhances flavour and your enjoyment of a dish, as well as helping you absorb the fat-soluble vitamins in your vegetables.

This delicious take on classic lasagne is not far off the real thing, in our opinion! It's tasty, slices well and is also delicious cold. The pasta sheets are replaced by fine layers of courgettes then, to make this dish more substantial and add a contrast in texture, we use a blend of cannellini beans, sundried tomatoes and tomato purée. There's no need to cook a béchamel sauce either – just whizz up the cheese and egg mix below. All you need is your food processor and a lasagne dish to layer everything up before baking. Simple!

COURGETTE AND CANNELLINI BEAN LASAGNE

SERVES 4

3 large courgettes

FOR THE 'BÉCHAMEL' SAUCE
250g ricotta
80g Parmesan or pecorino, finely grated, plus extra for sprinkling
1 egg

FOR THE TOMATO SAUCE
1 x 400g tin of cannellini beans, drained and rinsed
2 garlic cloves
120g sundried tomatoes (about 20 pieces) in oil, drained
3 tablespoons tomato purée
A pinch of sea salt
¼ teaspoon black pepper

1 Add the ingredients for the 'béchamel' sauce to a food processor and blend until smooth. Transfer to a bowl and set aside.

2 Add the ingredients for the tomato sauce to the food processor (no need to clean out the bowl) and blend until smooth.

3 Using a mandolin or very sharp knife, finely slice the courgettes lengthways into 3mm-thick pieces.

4 Preheat the oven to fan 180°C/Gas mark 6. Spread about half the tomato sauce over the bottom of a 16cm x 22cm ovenproof dish which is at least 8cm deep, as a thin layer. Top with about a third of the courgette slices in an even layer. Cover the courgettes with about half the 'béchamel' sauce, then top with half the remaining courgettes in an even layer.

5 Repeat the layering with the remaining tomato sauce, courgettes and 'béchamel', then sprinkle over a final layer of Parmesan to finish.

6 Bake for 45 minutes until golden brown on top. Remove from the oven and leave to stand for 5–10 minutes before serving.

VARIATIONS

+ Feel free to substitute the cannellini beans for chickpeas, aduki beans or butter beans.

+ The egg can be left out for a slightly sloppy lasagne – still tasty!

+ For a dairy-free lasagne, leave out the Parmesan and replace the 'béchamel' sauce with Minty Broad Bean Dip (page 270), leaving out the mint.

A quick store cupboard sauce: no need to bubble away on the stove – just blend and serve! This recipe makes plenty of sauce, which you can save for the next day. On a cold day, gently heat it through and fold through the courgetti for a more warming dish. Delicious just as it is, feel free to add your own spin with spices and herbs. We also like to sauté onions in ghee, add a couple of handfuls of frozen green beans and then pour in the sauce and warm through for another easy supper.

COURGETTI WITH QUICK CHICKPEA TOMATO SAUCE

SERVES 2 WITH LEFTOVER SAUCE

2 large courgettes

FOR THE SAUCE
1 x 400g tin
    of chopped
    tomatoes
1 x 400g tin of
    chickpeas or
    beans, drained
    and rinsed
2 garlic cloves
4 tablespoons
    tomato purée
    or 5 sundried
    tomatoes in
    oil, drained
2 tablespoons
    extra-virgin olive
    oil, plus extra
    for drizzling
6 anchovies or
    8 large pitted
    olives in oil,
    drained
Sea salt and
    black pepper

OPTIONAL EXTRAS
1 teaspoon dried
    oregano, basil
    or thyme
A sprinkle of
    cayenne pepper
    or chilli flakes
1 handful of finely
    grated Parmesan

1 Pour about 4 tablespoons of the tomato juice out of the tin of tomatoes into a bowl and set aside.

2 Place the rest of the ingredients for the sauce in a food processor and blend until smooth, adding some of the reserved juice, if needed, to blend to the desired consistency, along with the oregano, basil or thyme and cayenne pepper or chilli flakes (if using). Season with salt and pepper to taste.

3 Spiralize the courgettes, snipping long strands into shorter lengths for easier eating, or use a julienne or standard vegetable peeler to peel the courgettes into strips before cutting in half lengthways.

4 Toss the courgetti in half the sauce, adding more if needed, and arrange on a platter, or plate up one portion of courgetti per person and top with 4 tablespoons of sauce. Serve with a grind of black pepper or a sprinkle of Parmesan, if you wish, and drizzle with plenty of EVOO.

TIP

+ You can use other tinned beans, too, such as aduki, haricot or cannellini.

Comfort food at its best, this bake is an absolute winner! Red lentils, nutty buckwheat, sweet chestnuts and plenty of veg topped with cheese, plus smoked paprika and cayenne in the mix, it's a real winter-warmer. Replacing the spices with herbs makes for a tasty summer dish. You can leave the cheese and eggs out to make this vegan - without eggs the mixture will be a little runnier. Feel free to halve the recipe or go for double if you have a big family – you'll appreciate the leftovers and you might as well use up a whole packet of lentils in one go! This dish is also delicious served cold. For a packed lunch, line the dish first before baking so that you can lift out the bake once it's cooled and chill it before slicing into squares. Serve with our Broccoli 2 Ways (page 96) or Sensational Sprout Salad (page 148).

LENTIL BAKE

SERVES 6

4 tablespoons butter, ghee or coconut oil, plus extra for greasing
2 onions, diced
3 garlic cloves, crushed
2 celery sticks, finely sliced
1 tablespoon sweet smoked paprika
2 teaspoons ground cumin
A pinch of cayenne pepper (to taste) or black pepper
250g dried red lentils, rinsed and drained
500–600ml Bone Broth (page 63) or water
4 tablespoons tamari
2 carrots, grated

1 medium courgette, diced
200g mature Cheddar, grated
40g buckwheat flour
40g chestnut flour
2 eggs, beaten (optional)
2 tomatoes or 1 red onion, sliced into rounds, to garnish

1 Preheat the oven to fan 180°C/Gas mark 6 and grease a 17cm x 24cm ovenproof dish.

2 Melt the butter, ghee or coconut oil in a large pan and gently fry the onions over a medium heat for 5 minutes to soften. Add the garlic, celery and spices and continue to fry for a further 2 minutes.

3 Stir in the red lentils, bone broth or water and the tamari, bring up to a simmer and cook for at least 5 minutes, with a lid on the pan, until the lentils are just tender.

4 Stir in the carrots, courgette and three-quarters of the cheese. Add the buckwheat and chestnut flours and stir in the beaten eggs (if using). Transfer the mixture to the prepared dish, spreading it evenly.

5 Sprinkle over the remaining cheese and garnish with the tomato or onion slices. Bake in the oven for 50–60 minutes until bubbling and browned on top.

VARIATION

+ For a summer version of this dish, replace the spices with 4 teaspoons of dried mixed herbs, such as rosemary, parsley and thyme.

Sticky, stodgy and cheesy... Sold! We've combined two school-dinner favourites: macaroni cheese and cauliflower cheese. If you have a wide, flat cast-iron dish or ovenproof pan, you can take this straight from the stove to the oven and then over to the table. The tiny seeds of amaranth replace the macaroni with plenty of texture and bite, allowing you to savour a dish that you might otherwise polish off too quickly. The trick here is to have a super-strong Cheddar – use extra-mature or combine your usual Cheddar with some Parmesan and crumble in any leftover blue cheese, for added oomph. Nutmeg is a must for this dish, as is plenty of ground pepper – black or white (we love white for that nostalgic flavour). Serve with a big colourful salad, such as our Spicy Ruby Slaw (page 154) or Ayurvedic Carrot Stir-Fry/Salad (page 109).

CAULIRONI CHEESE

SERVES 6

250g amaranth (see variation opposite)
1 tablespoon butter, plus extra for greasing
2 celery sticks, finely sliced
1 medium onion, diced
250ml Bone Broth (page 63) or vegetable stock
1 very large cauliflower (about 750g)
250g extra-mature Cheddar, finely chopped or grated
½ teaspoon freshly grated nutmeg, plus extra for sprinkling
Sea salt
½–1 teaspoon white or black pepper

1   Soak the amaranth in double the volume of water overnight or for a minimum of 8 hours (page 341), then rinse and drain.

2   Place the drained amaranth in a large saucepan with the butter, celery, onion and ¼ teaspoon of salt. Pour in the broth or stock, then bring to a simmer and cook, covered with a lid, for 15 minutes until tender and most of the liquid has been absorbed. If it hasn't, simmer a little longer for a thick porridge, stirring every now and then to prevent the mixture from sticking to the bottom of the pan.

3   Meanwhile, preheat the oven to fan 180°C/Gas mark 6 and butter an 18cm x 25cm ovenproof dish.

4   Prepare the cauliflower by cutting into equal-sized florets and roughly chopping the stems (after first slicing off the tough outer layer). Add to the pan and simmer, with the lid on, for another 5 minutes – the cauliflower will continue to cook during baking.

5   Remove from the heat and stir in two-thirds of the Cheddar, half the nutmeg and 3 large pinches of pepper, then check for seasoning, adding more salt, pepper, nutmeg and/or cheese if needed.

6   Pour into the prepared dish, sprinkle over the remaining cheese and nutmeg, plus an extra grind of pepper, and bake on the top shelf of the oven for 20 minutes until golden brown. Serve immediately.

VARIATION

+ If you can't find amaranth, use quinoa instead (pre-soaked for the same length of time), which works just as well.

These deliciously meaty but meat-free burgers/balls taste a bit like sausage stuffing! It's important to use roasted buckwheat groats for this dish, for the flavour, or roast your own. Reddish brown in colour and generally known as 'kasha', roasted buckwheat has been used in eastern European cooking for thousands of years in porridge, pilafs, soups and casseroles. Much like quinoa, buckwheat is one of the best sources of protein in the plant kingdom. Slow roasting brings out its wonderful, earthy flavour while at the same time breaks down the phytates (page 341), avoiding the need to pre-soak. Make burgers and serve in our Flaxseed Buns (page 136) with a dollop of BBQ Ketchup (page 278) or Pink Chilli Kraut (page 130) and Quick-cooked Mayo (page 277) and a lettuce leaf and slice of tomato. If you make balls, serve with Lubee Beans (page 106) or make your own tomato sauce (page 50) and serve with a big green salad or steamed seasonal veg.

KASHA BUCKWHEAT BURGERS/BALLS

**MAKES 10 BURGERS OR
ABOUT 40 BALLS**

3 tablespoons ghee
    or coconut oil
3 medium red
    onions, diced
5 garlic cloves,
    finely diced
250g roasted
    buckwheat
    groats (kasha)
700–800ml water
1 egg
12 anchovies or
    12 pitted olives
    in oil, drained
    and chopped
4 tablespoons
    capers, chopped
1 large handful
    of fresh parsley
    (about 50g),
    leaves and
    stalks chopped

Grated zest
    of 2 lemons
½ teaspoon cayenne
    pepper or finely
    diced fresh red
    chilli (optional)
A large pinch of
    black pepper

1   Melt 1 tablespoon of the ghee or coconut oil in a large pan and sauté the onions over a medium heat for 5 minutes until translucent. Add the garlic and sauté for another minute.

2   Add the buckwheat groats and water to the pan, bring to a simmer, then cover with a lid and steam over a medium heat for about 5 minutes, stirring from time to time to prevent the buckwheat from sticking. Remove from the heat, take the lid off the pan and leave to cool while you prepare the rest of the dish.

3   Preheat the oven to fan 180°C/Gas mark 6, then line a baking tray (you may need more than one) with baking parchment, add the remaining ghee/coconut oil to the tray and leave in the oven for the fat to melt.

4   Meanwhile, beat the egg in a large bowl, then add the rest of the ingredients and mix well. Stir in the cooled buckwheat mix and taste for seasoning, adding more black pepper, if needed.

5   Take 4 heaped tablespoons of the mixture and shape into a burger-shaped patty, repeating with the rest of the mixture to make 10 large patties. Alternatively, take a heaped tablespoon of the buckwheat mixture, gently roll into a ball and place on a large plate. Repeat with the rest of the mixture to make about 40 balls.

TIPS

+ This recipe makes plenty, so freeze some before cooking.

+ Reserve the EVOO, if you like, from the drained anchovies for adding to salad dressings.

+ Chopped fresh rosemary is delicious in this dish too.

6 Remove the baking tray from the oven and add the patties /balls, basting the patties with a spoon or rolling the balls around the tray to coat in the melted fat, then roast for 45 minutes until golden and crunchy at the edges.

7 Alternatively, fry in batches in a frying pan in ghee or coconut oil over a medium-high heat for 2 minutes on each side for patties, or 4–5 minutes all over for balls, to let them get a nice crust.

Noodles are not just for slurping! Try this beetroot cake scented with rosemary and salted with feta. This was a nuts experiment for a leftover lunch that became an 'OMG!' moment. Beetroot noodles are so delicious, we urge you to have a go, though you'll definitely need a spiralizer for this dish: grating will make it too soggy and finely dicing takes forever, and both will make the cake too dense. Fresh rosemary really makes this dish, though mint is delicious too. Serve with our Chilli Kick Cucumber Snack (page 155), if you fancy a meal with real oomph, or with a simple green salad so that the rosemary sings through. You can also cook the noodles in individual ring moulds, if you have them, and eat like a burger in our Flaxseed Buns (page 136).

BEETROOT FETA CAKE

SERVES 2

2 medium beetroots,
    scrubbed and
    topped and tailed
1 tablespoon ghee
½ tablespoon fresh
    rosemary leaves
150g feta, crumbled
2 eggs, beaten
Sea salt and
    black pepper

1   Spiralize each beetroot using the small noodle blade.

2   Melt the ghee in a large frying pan over a medium-high heat. Stir in the rosemary and add the beetroot noodles. Season with a small pinch of salt and a big grind of pepper, tossing everything together to combine, and stir-fry for 3 minutes.

3   Flatten the noodles in the pan, neatening at the edges. Sprinkle over the feta and pour over the beaten egg, distributing it evenly.

4   Lower the heat and cook gently for 5–6 minutes until set. Use two spatulas to carefully turn the cake over to cook on the other side for a few minutes, or finish it under a hot grill. Delicious served hot or cold.

One of our go-to meals, this recipe takes no more than 15 minutes to put together (plus 10 minutes' marinating time). Based on the classic Greek salad, our version is loaded with protein-rich butterbeans, which soften and absorb the rich flavours of the dressing. We like to keep tinned beans in our cupboard for whipping up super-quick, nutrient-dense meals like this one. Indeed, you could swap the butterbeans for tinned chickpeas or cannellini, aduki or black beans. Delicious with or without feta, choose good-quality feta made from sheep's milk, or a mixture of sheep and goat's milk, and you will really taste the difference.

MARINATED BUTTERBEAN GREEK SALAD

SERVES 4 AS A MAIN OR 6 AS A SIDE

2 x 400g tins of butterbeans, drained and rinsed

1 large red onion, finely sliced

2 large red peppers, deseeded and roughly chopped

1 large cucumber, roughly chopped

250g cherry tomatoes, halved, or medium tomatoes, quartered

3 large handfuls of fresh parsley, leaves and stalks roughly chopped

1 large handful of mixed green olives and black Kalamata olives in oil, drained and pitted

300g feta

1 tablespoon fresh oregano leaves or 1 teaspoon dried

FOR THE DRESSING

120ml extra-virgin olive oil

4 tablespoons lemon juice or apple cider vinegar

2 garlic cloves, diced or grated

1 teaspoon mustard

Sea salt and black pepper (to taste)

1 Whisk all the dressing ingredients together in a bowl, or shake together in a jam jar with the lid on, and taste for seasoning.

2 Place the butterbeans and onion slices in a large serving bowl, add the dressing, toss gently to mix and leave to marinate for at least 10 minutes.

3 Add the remaining salad ingredients to the marinated butterbeans and onion, and mix everything together. Roughly chop the feta into cubes and scatter over the top, then sprinkle the oregano over the feta and serve.

Cauli rice is a revelation – simple to make and so much quicker to cook than standard rice. A great way to pack your meals full of vegetable goodness, it will have everyone fooled thanks to its incredibly fluffy texture. Here are four of our favourite ways to enjoy it, including our basic recipe, and each is completely different. We like serving the Coconut Lime Cauliflower Rice with dahl (page 78) or leftover chicken, while the Spiced Cauliflower Rice is great with some simple baked or smoked fish. Egg-fried Cauliflower Rice makes the perfect post-party late-night snack with some Homemade Sriracha (page 279).

CAULIFLOWER RICE 3 WAYS

SERVES 2

1 large cauliflower
1 teaspoon ghee
    or coconut oil
2 tablespoons water
Sea salt and
    black pepper

BASIC CAULIFLOWER RICE

1   Remove the cauliflower leaves and the tough end of the stalk. Use a food processor (the S-curved blade or grater attachment) or the coarse side of a grater to grate the cauliflower into rice-sized pieces.

2   Melt the ghee or coconut oil in a wide frying pan, add the grated cauliflower with the water and stir to mix.

3   Cook over a medium heat, with the lid on, to let the grated cauliflower steam for 4–5 minutes until tender but still with a little bite. Check after 3–4 minutes to make sure that there is still enough water in the bottom of the pan to stop the cauliflower catching.

4   Season with salt and pepper to taste and serve, or add the other ingredients to make one of the dishes on pages 242 and 243.

→ CONTINUED OVERLEAF

CAULIFLOWER RICE 3 WAYS (CONTINUED)

SERVES 2

1 teaspoon
    ground cumin
1 teaspoon sweet
    smoked paprika
A pinch of chilli
    flakes
1 tablespoon ghee
    or coconut oil
½ medium red
    onion, finely
    sliced
2 garlic cloves,
    finely diced
1 quantity of
    uncooked Basic
    Cauliflower Rice
    (page 240 – step
    1 only)
2 tablespoons water
1 large handful of
    cooked chickpeas
1 large handful of
    fresh coriander
    or parsley,
    leaves and stalks
    finely chopped
2 large handfuls
    of watercress,
    snipped
100g halloumi,
    cut into cubes
Sea salt and
    black pepper

FOR THE TAHINI DRESSING

1 garlic clove,
    crushed or
    finely diced
1 tablespoon tahini
1 tablespoon
    hot water
3 tablespoons
    extra-virgin
    olive oil
1 tablespoon
    lemon juice

OPTIONAL EXTRAS

1 tablespoon raisins,
    dried goji berries
    or pitted dried
    dates or dried
    apricots, chopped
1 tablespoon
    pomegranate
    seeds
1 tablespoon
    pistachios,
    roughly chopped

SPICED CAULIFLOWER RICE WITH HALLOUMI AND A TAHINI DRESSING

1   Toast the spices in a dry frying pan over a medium heat for a minute until fragrant.

2   Add half the ghee or coconut oil and the onion and fry for 2 minutes, then add the garlic and fry for a further minute.

3   Tip in the uncooked cauliflower rice and add the water. Give everything a stir, pop a lid on the pan and steam for 4 minutes until tender.

4   Stir through the chickpeas, herbs (reserving some for serving) and dried fruit (if using) and season with salt and pepper to taste.

5   Meanwhile, whisk all the dressing ingredients together in a bowl, seasoning to taste with salt and pepper. Set aside.

6   Divide the cauliflower rice mix between two plates, adding the watercress on the side, then wipe out the frying pan and place on a high heat to fry the halloumi.

7   Heat the remaining ghee/coconut oil to a high temperature and fry the halloumi cubes in batches for about a minute on each side until each piece takes on a golden-brown colour. (Keep your eye on them – too long in the pan and they'll toughen up.)

8   Serve the hot halloumi on top of the plated-up cauli rice, with pomegranate seeds or pistachios (if using) sprinkled on top, then drizzle over the dressing and scatter over the reserved herbs.

TIPS

+   You can always swap halloumi for crumbled feta or a fried egg, served on top. To keep it even simpler, just dress with extra-virgin olive oil and lemon juice.

SERVES 4 AS A SIDE

1 heaped
	tablespoon
	desiccated
	coconut
1 quantity of
	uncooked Basic
	Cauliflower Rice
	(page 240 – step
	1 only)
3 tablespoons full-
	fat coconut milk
Grated zest and
	juice of ½ lime
1 handful of fresh
	coriander, leaves
	and stalks finely
	chopped
A pinch of finely
	diced fresh red
	chilli (optional)
Sea salt and
	black pepper

COCONUT LIME CAULIFLOWER RICE

1 Toast the desiccated coconut in a dry frying pan over a medium
	heat for 2 minutes until fragrant and golden brown. Transfer
	to a plate and set aside.

2 Place the uncooked cauliflower rice in the same pan, add the
	coconut milk and stir together.

3 Cook over a medium heat, with a lid on the pan, to let the
	cauliflower steam for 4–6 minutes until tender. Check after
	3–4 minutes to make sure that there is still enough liquid in
	the bottom of the pan to stop the cauliflower catching.

4 When the cauliflower rice is cooked, squeeze in the lime
	juice, season with salt and pepper and stir to combine.

5 Serve immediately, sprinkled with the toasted desiccated
	coconut, coriander, fresh chilli (if using) and lime zest.

TIP

+ Save the rest of the coconut milk for
	smoothies, porridge, soups and stews.

SERVES 2

1 tablespoon
	coconut oil
2 spring onions,
	finely chopped
1 garlic clove,
	finely diced
1 quantity of
	uncooked Basic
	Cauliflower Rice
	(page 240 – step
	1 only)
2 tablespoons water
4 eggs
2 teaspoons tamari
1 teaspoon toasted
	sesame oil
	(optional)
Black or
	white pepper

EGG-FRIED CAULIFLOWER RICE

1 Melt half the coconut oil in a wide frying pan on a medium
	heat and gently fry half the spring onions and all the garlic
	for 1 minute.

2 Add the uncooked cauliflower rice and water and stir
	together. Put a lid on the pan and cook for 3–5 minutes until
	just tender – it will cook further when the eggs are added.

3 Push the cauliflower rice to one side of the pan to create
	a big space for scrambling the eggs.

4 Add the remaining coconut oil to the open space in the pan
	and crack the eggs in quickly. Stir the yolks into the whites
	and leave the mixture to set ever so slightly in the pan –
	about 30 seconds – before breaking it up with a wooden
	spoon into lovely egg chunks, stirring it through the
	cauliflower rice.

5 Stir through the tamari, pepper and toasted sesame oil
	(if using) and top with the remaining spring onions.

We're mad on pesto because it combines our love of fresh herbs, garlic, natural fats in the form of nuts and cold-pressed EVOO in a super-quick and simple-to-make way – just blend and go! Delicious as dips, drizzled onto grilled fish or roast meat, tossed with cooked beans and lentils, or generously dolloped into hot soups and stews, these are the three pestos that we make the most, worth committing to memory for quick meals. Courgettes are one of our favourite vegetables: versatile, affordable, easily available, and of course you don't need to cook them, so pair pesto with courgetti instead of standard pasta to cut down on refined foods and up your vegetable intake at the same time. These pestos are also delicious with cucumber noodles (page 173) – or branch out in the winter and try noodles made with beetroot (page 237), butternut squash (page 150) or celeriac spaghetti (page 198).

COURGETTI PESTO 3 WAYS

SERVES 4

6 large courgettes
Extra-virgin olive
    oil, for drizzling

COURGETTI

1   Use a spiralizer to turn the courgettes into long strips that resemble spaghetti, snipping any long strands in half to make them easier to eat. Alternatively, use a julienne peeler or standard vegetable peeler to peel the courgettes into long, wide strips before cutting in half lengthways.

2   Combine the courgetti with your chosen pesto (below and pages 246 and 247) in a large bowl and toss together.

3   Pile everything into a serving dish, drizzle with EVOO and serve immediately.

SERVES 4 WITH COURGETTI

18 cashew nuts,
    soaked in double
    the volume of
    water for 3 hours
    (page 341)
100g fresh basil
    (leaves and
    stalks)
2 garlic cloves
200ml extra-virgin
    olive oil
3 tablespoons
    lemon juice
Sea salt and
    black pepper

LEMON BASIL CASHEW PESTO

1   Rinse and drain the soaked cashews.

2   Place in the small bowl of a food processor with the remaining ingredients and blitz together, seasoning with salt and pepper to taste. Blitz to the desired consistency – sometimes we like it chunky, other times smooth and creamy.

3   Alternatively, finely chop the first three ingredients with a sharp knife and then mix together with the remaining ingredients.

→   CONTINUED OVERLEAF

COURGETTI PESTO 3 WAYS (CONTINUED)

SERVES 4 WITH COURGETTI

1 medium red
   pepper, halved
   and deseeded
400g cherry
   tomatoes
½ bulb of garlic
45g cashew nuts,
   soaked in double
   the volume of
   water for 3 hours
   (page 341), then
   drained and
   rinsed
30g Parmesan
   or pecorino,
   roughly chopped

1 tablespoon
   balsamic
   vinegar, or ½
   tablespoon apple
   cider vinegar
½ fresh red chilli,
   deseeded
   (to taste)
1 large handful
   of fresh basil
   (leaves and
   stalks)
Sea salt and
   black pepper

ROASTED TOMATO AND PEPPER PESTO

1 Preheat the oven to fan 170°C/Gas mark 5 and line a baking tray with baking parchment.

2 Place the red pepper in the prepared baking tray with the cherry tomatoes and garlic bulb. Roast in the oven for 1½–2 hours, removing the garlic after 25 minutes, to reduce the moisture in the red pepper and tomatoes and concentrate their sweet flavour.

3 Squeeze the roasted garlic out of their skins into a food processor, then add the roasted tomatoes and red pepper as well as the rinsed cashews, the cheese, balsamic vinegar or ACV, chilli and almost all of the basil (save some for sprinkling). Pulse or crush together using a pestle and mortar, adding salt and pepper to taste for a chunky pesto.

SERVES 4 WITH COURGETTI

200g spinach
   (preferably baby
   spinach)
60g fresh basil
   (leaves and
   stalks)
2 garlic cloves
35g Parmesan
   or pecorino,
   roughly chopped
2 tablespoons
   lemon juice, or
   1 tablespoon
   apple cider
   vinegar
80ml extra-virgin
   olive oil
Sea salt and
   black pepper

SPINACH AND BASIL PESTO

1 Place all the ingredients in a food processor and blend together until smooth and creamy, adding salt and pepper to taste.

TIPS

+ When storing this pesto, transfer to a sterilised jar (page 17) and add a layer of extra-virgin olive oil to preserve it for longer and keep the colour a vibrant green, then seal with the lid and store in the fridge.

+ Choose baby spinach, if you can, as it's less bitter.

Our one-pot broccoli risotto makes use of protein-rich quinoa in place of Arborio rice. We bulk it out with plenty of broccoli, which pairs deliciously with Parmesan for a comforting, weekday supper. Slow-cooked bone broth replaces commercially prepared stock as a soothing, nourishing base. If you have them to hand, peas or broad beans make a great addition.

EASY CHEESY BROCCOLI RISOTTO

SERVES 4

250g quinoa
1 tablespoon ghee
    or coconut oil
2 medium onions,
    finely diced
3 garlic cloves,
    diced
1 tablespoon fresh
    oregano or
    thyme leaves or
    1 teaspoon dried
2 large handfuls
    of fresh basil,
    leaves and stalks
    separated and
    roughly chopped
5 tablespoons
    tomato purée
1 litre Bone
    Broth (page 63)
    or water
2 large heads
    of broccoli
    (about 700g)

100g Parmesan,
    grated
2 tablespoons
    lemon juice,
    or 1 tablespoon
    apple cider
    vinegar
Sea salt and
    black pepper

1 Cover the quinoa in double the volume of water and leave to soak overnight, or a minimum of 8 hours, then drain and rinse. If you don't have time to soak the quinoa, rinse thoroughly and cook for longer, though we really recommend soaking (page 341).

2 Melt the ghee or coconut oil in a saucepan over a medium heat and fry the onions for 5 minutes until softened. Add the garlic and oregano or thyme and the basil stalks and cook for 1 minute. Add the rinsed quinoa and the tomato purée and stir well.

3 Add the bone broth or water and bring to the boil. Reduce the heat, pop a lid on the pan and simmer for 12 minutes until the quinoa is almost tender.

4 Meanwhile, prepare the broccoli by cutting into equal-sized florets and roughly chopping the stalks (after first slicing off the tough outer layer).

5 Stir the broccoli into the pan and cook for another 3–4 minutes until tender (you might want to add another 100ml of liquid at this point if the risotto is getting dry), then remove from the heat.

6 Season to taste with salt and pepper, add the Parmesan and lemon juice or ACV and stir through the chopped basil leaves.

This salad is a great way to pack lots of vibrant greens into one dish. A sesame, ginger and lime dressing and some nutty buckwheat noodles tie it all together. It is the perfect dish to make on a Sunday night for supper, giving you leftovers to keep in the fridge and use for a packed lunch the following day. Pile everything into a glass jar – the dressing at the bottom and the avocado slices and leaves on top so they're not crushed, then add the lid and take to go!

GREEN GODDESS NOODLE SALAD

SERVES 4

300g buckwheat (soba) noodles
1 tablespoon extra-virgin olive oil
300g broccoli florets or purple-sprouting broccoli, asparagus or green beans
1 medium green cabbage or pak choi, leaves finely shredded
1 medium fennel bulb, finely sliced
1 cucumber, halved lengthways, seeds scooped out with a spoon and flesh chopped
4 spring onions, finely sliced
1 large ripe avocado, sliced

2 handfuls of fresh greens (such as watercress, baby spinach, sliced lettuce or leftover cooked kale)
1 small handful of nuts (such as cashew nuts, peanuts or almonds) or seeds (such as sesame, sunflower or poppy seeds), preferably 'crispy activated' (page 341)
4 large handfuls of fresh herbs (such as coriander, mint or basil, or a mixture), roughly chopped

1 Cook the buckwheat noodles in a large pan of boiling water according to the packet instructions (about 7 minutes). Use two forks to tease the noodles apart during the first minute of cooking.

2 When they are tender, drain and rinse under cold water for 15 seconds. Drain again and then toss in the EVOO in a large serving bowl to stop the noodles sticking together. Set aside.

3 Using the same pan, after a quick rinse, steam the broccoli (or other vegetable), covered with a lid, in 4 tablespoons of boiling water for 4 minutes until tender.

4 Whisk all the dressing ingredients together in a bowl or shake in a jam jar with the lid on. Season to taste with salt and pepper, then drain.

5 Add the raw vegetables, spring onions and avocado to the noodles with the greens and steamed broccoli. Pour over the dressing and mix everything together. Top with the nuts or seeds, toasted in a dry pan for a minute if you like, and the fresh herbs.

FOR THE DRESSING

Grated zest and juice of 2 limes or 1 lemon

2 tablespoons toasted sesame oil

5 tablespoons extra-virgin olive oil

1 garlic clove, grated

4cm piece of fresh root ginger (unpeeled if organic), finely grated

2 teaspoons tamari

A pinch of cayenne pepper or chilli flakes (optional)

Sea salt and black pepper

Leftovers and store cupboard staples have become the inspiration for some of our favourite dishes, and quinoa falls into both those categories. We use this protein-rich powerhouse of a seed as a gluten-free alternative to refined grains such as couscous and pasta, as well as white rice (see 'Going Against the Grain', page 11). Cook up a big batch of this versatile pseudocereal as part of your Sunday Cook-Off (page 334) to create a base for meals throughout the week – just don't forget to soak it overnight, or earlier in the day, to get the most from it. Use 'leftover' quinoa in salads and soups, and as an alternative to rice in dishes such as vegetarian biryanis and risottos – to stay with 'simple food combining'.

QUINOA 3 WAYS

MAKES ABOUT 700G

250g quinoa, soaked
   in double the
   volume of water
   overnight or
   for a minimum
   of 8 hours
   (page 341)
250ml Bone
   Broth (page 63,
   vegetable stock
   or water
Sea salt

BASIC COOKED QUINOA

1   Using a fine-mesh strainer, drain and rinse the soaked quinoa until the water runs clear and with no foam.

2   Pour the bone broth, stock or water into a saucepan on a medium-high heat, cover and bring to a medium simmer.

3   Add the quinoa and a pinch of salt and stir. Continue to cook on a medium simmer for 12 minutes until tender.

4   Take off the heat and leave to stand for 5 minutes. Fluff up with a fork before serving.

TIPS

+   Uncooked quinoa roughly trebles in weight when it is cooked, producing about 700g cooked quinoa in this case. Keep in the fridge for up to 5 days to use in all three recipes on pages 254 and 255, or freeze in portions. Red or black quinoa will need an extra 5 minutes of cooking time, so add an extra 25ml cooking liquid.

→   CONTINUED OVERLEAF

QUINOA 3 WAYS (CONTINUED)

SERVES 2

2 tablespoons dried
   seaweed (such
   as wakame
   or dulse)
400g fresh shiitake
   mushrooms,
   sliced
1 tablespoon
   coconut oil
   or ghee
2 garlic cloves,
   diced
1 bunch of spring
   onions, finely
   sliced, or 1 small
   onion, diced
200g cooked quinoa
   (page 253)
300g spinach,
   roughly chopped
2 tablespoons
   tamari
2 tablespoons
   lemon juice,
   or 1 tablespoon
   apple cider
   vinegar

2 large handfuls of
   fresh coriander
   (or mixed
   coriander and
   parsley), leaves
   and stalks
   chopped
2 tablespoons
   extra-virgin olive
   oil or flaxseed oil
Sea salt and black
   or white pepper

SHIITAKE AND SEAWEED QUINOA

1   First soak the dried seaweed in water according to the packet instructions (about 10 minutes), then drain and roughly snip with scissors.

2   Fry the mushrooms in the coconut oil or ghee in your widest frying pan (the bigger the better for this dish) over a medium heat for 4 minutes. The mushrooms will release a lot of water as they cook, so keep frying until all the moisture cooks off.

3   Add the garlic and half the spring onions and cook for 1 minute. Add the cooked quinoa with a splash of water and stir into the mushrooms, cooking for 2 minutes until completely heated through.

4   Tip in the spinach, cover with a lid and steam for 3–4 minutes until the spinach has wilted, adding a little more water if the quinoa starts sticking to the bottom of the pan.

5   Remove from the heat, then stir through the tamari and lemon juice or ACV and season with salt and pepper to taste. Divide between warmed plates, then wipe out the pan and return to the hob.

6   Add the chopped seaweed to the dry pan and toast over a medium heat for 1 minute until crispy, removing from the heat as soon as the seaweed starts to turn green.

7   Top the quinoa with the coriander and a drizzle of EVOO or flaxseed oil and crumble over the crispy seaweed.

VARIATIONS

+   If you don't have shiitake mushrooms, substitute with any mushrooms that you have to hand.

+   Swap the spinach for chard or kale, steaming for a few minutes longer in step 4.

SERVES 2

1 tablespoon
    coconut oil
1 medium onion,
    diced
2cm piece of fresh
    root ginger
    (unpeeled if
    organic), finely
    diced
2 garlic cloves, diced
2 tablespoons
    tomato purée
2 medium carrots or
    courgettes, diced
90ml water or Bone
    Broth (page 63)
1 medium cauliflower
    or head of
    broccoli, cut into
    equal-sized
    florets and stems
    chopped (outer
    layer removed)
1 large handful of
    green beans
    (about 200g),
    trimmed and
chopped into
    thirds
200g cooked quinoa
    (page 253)
2 tablespoons lemon
    or lime juice
2 large handfuls of
    fresh coriander
    (or mixed
    coriander and
    mint leaves),
    leaves and stalks
    roughly chopped
Sea salt and
    black pepper

FOR THE SPICES

2 teaspoons
    garam masala
    or medium curry
    powder
1 teaspoon ground
    turmeric
A pinch of chilli
    powder or
    cayenne pepper
1 bay leaf

QUINOA BIRYANI

1 Melt the coconut oil in a medium pan, add the onion and cook over a medium heat for about 4 minutes until the onion begins to soften.

2 Add the ginger, garlic, tomato purée and spices. Cook for 2 minutes, stirring from time to time, until the ginger starts sticking to the bottom of the pan.

3 Add the carrots (if using) and pour in the water or broth. Pop a lid on the pan to steam for 4 minutes, stirring halfway through.

4 Add the courgettes (if using) with the cauliflower or broccoli and green beans and steam for a further 3 minutes until all the vegetables are tender.

5 Stir through the cooked quinoa with a couple of tablespoons of water (to stop it sticking) and place the lid back on the pan. Cook until the quinoa is warmed through, then remove from the heat.

6 Stir in the lemon or lime juice. Season with salt and pepper to taste and top with the coriander to serve.

SERVES 2

2 large Romano
    red peppers
    (or red peppers)
200g cooked quinoa
    (page 253)
1 handful of pitted
    green olives
    in oil, drained
    and diced
1 small red onion,
    finely diced
1 teaspoon fresh
    thyme leaves
    or 1 large pinch
    of dried
2 large handfuls
    of fresh parsley
    (or mixed
    mint, dill and
    coriander),
    leaves and stalks
    finely chopped
½–1 teaspoon finely
    diced fresh red
    chilli (to taste)
Juice of ½ lemon,
    or 1 tablespoon
    apple cider
    vinegar
1 small handful of
    crumbled feta
Sea salt and
    black pepper

QUINOA-STUFFED ROMANO PEPPERS

1 Preheat the oven to fan 200°C/Gas mark 7.

2 Slice the red peppers in half lengthways. Remove and discard the seeds and then roast, cut side up, on a baking tray in the oven for 12 minutes.

3 Combine all the other ingredients together (except the feta), adding salt and pepper to taste (bearing in mind that the feta is already salty). Preheat the grill to high.

4 Stuff the pepper halves with the quinoa mix, top with crumbled feta and cook under the grill for 3–5 minutes until golden and bubbling. (Serve any leftover quinoa mix on the side.)

TIP

+ A stuffed pepper half makes a pretty starter. Just add a sprig of watercress or some fresh parsley to finish.

We are serious advocates of the humble mung bean! Nutritious, cheap and easy to cook, this is our salad version of an Indian-spiced dahl. A wholesome meal in itself, it's perfect for packed lunches or with a selection of other salads as part of a mezze spread. You could also bulk it out more with roasted vegetables from your Sunday Cook-Off (page 334). Mung beans absorb different flavours really well, so if you play around with the spices you can skip the caramelised onions, and just replace with chopped spring onions or chives at the end if you like, but they do make this extra-special. The diced vegetables are all raw, so finely dicing is a must – as is chewing properly!

SIMPLE AND SPICED MUNG BEAN SALAD

SERVES 4

250g dried mung beans, soaked in double the volume of water overnight or for at least 8 hours (page 341)

4 large handfuls (about 500g) of raw, finely diced vegetables (such as French beans, fennel, carrots, red pepper, courgettes, cabbage or kale)

3 medium onions, halved and thinly sliced

1 tablespoon coconut oil or ghee

3 garlic cloves, grated or diced

3cm piece of fresh root ginger (unpeeled if organic), grated or finely diced

2 large handfuls of fresh coriander (or mixed coriander and mint leaves), leaves and stalks roughly chopped

Sea salt and black pepper

FOR THE SPICES

1 tablespoon ground turmeric

1 tablespoon garam masala or medium curry powder

A pinch of chilli powder or diced fresh red chilli

1 Drain and rinse the soaked mung beans, place in a medium saucepan and cover with cold water. Bring to the boil and then reduce the heat and gently simmer for 20–25 minutes until the beans are soft but still retain a little bite.

2 Meanwhile, whisk all the dressing ingredients together in a large mixing bowl until well combined, then add all the raw diced vegetables to the bowl.

3 Drain the mung beans once they are tender and add to the bowl, then mix everything together so that the hot beans soak up the dressing.

4 Using the same pan, fry the onion slices in the coconut oil or ghee over a medium heat for 10 minutes until softened and caramelised. (Stir only when you need to so that they caramelise but don't burn.)

5 Add the spices with the garlic, ginger and a pinch of sea salt, and cook for 2 more minutes, then tip half the spiced onion mixture into the bowl. Toss everything together with the fresh coriander and season with salt and pepper, then scatter over the remaining spiced onions to serve.

FOR THE DRESSING

120ml extra-virgin olive oil

4 tablespoons lemon or lime juice, or 3 tablespoons apple cider vinegar

1 tablespoon tamari (or sea salt to taste)

VARIATIONS

+ Swap the raw veggies with leftover cooked vegetables and add with the herbs in the final step.

+ Make your own spice mix: combining 2 teaspoons ground cumin, ½ teaspoon ground cinnamon, 1 teaspoon ground coriander and ½ teaspoon of fennel seeds and a pinch of chilli.

Dried lentils come in a wide variety of forms and they store well, so we like to keep a selection in our store cupboard, ready for action. Smaller than most beans, they cook more quickly, so for ease we tend to rely on a combination of dried lentils and tinned beans – just don't forget to soak lentils (except red ones) before cooking! What's more, they're inexpensive and great for bulking out a whole host of dishes, from stews to salads. This lentil and mushroom mix can be easily made into burgers or balls – great for stockpiling your freezer. While they're vegetarian-friendly, even the most avid meat eater will find the dense, chewy texture and nutty taste hard to resist. Serve the burgers in our Flaxseed Buns (page 136) with any of our dips (pages 262–281).

MUSHROOM LENTIL BURGERS/BALLS

MAKES 12 BURGERS OR 20 BALLS

250g dried brown or green lentils, soaked in double the volume of water overnight or for a minimum of 8 hours (page 341)
400ml water
1 large onion, diced
1 tablespoon ghee or coconut oil
250g mushrooms, roughly sliced
4 garlic cloves, diced
1 tablespoon mixed dried herbs (such as oregano, basil, thyme and rosemary)
A pinch of chilli powder or cayenne pepper (to taste)
2 tablespoons tomato purée
2 large handful of fresh parsley leaves, roughly chopped
1 egg
80g ground almonds
Sea salt and black pepper

1   Rinse and drain the soaked lentils and place in a saucepan with the water. Bring to the boil, then reduce the heat and simmer for 20 minutes until the lentils are just cooked. Drain any excess liquid, then pour two-thirds of the cooked lentils into a food processor, setting the rest to one side.

2   In the same pan, fry the onion in the ghee or coconut oil over a medium heat for 5 minutes. Add the mushrooms, garlic, fresh and dried herbs, chilli powder or cayenne pepper and tomato purée and fry for about 7–8 more minutes until the liquid released by the mushrooms has evaporated.

3   Add this mix to the food processor with some salt and pepper. Blend until the mixture is pretty well pulverised but still has some texture, then stir in the reserved lentils and the parsley.

4   In a big bowl, beat the egg and add the lentil mixture and almonds. Combine and taste for seasoning. Use your hands to scoop up a small handful of the mixture at a time, shaping it into 20 golf-ball sized balls, or scoop up larger amounts and shape into 12 burgers. Preheat the oven to fan 180°C/ Gas mark 6 and line a baking tray with baking parchment.

5   Place each 'meatball' or burger onto the baking tray, leaving space around each one. Bake the balls for 20 minutes, the burgers for 35 minutes or until golden brown. Or fry in batches in a frying pan in ghee or coconut oil over a medium-high heat for 2 minutes on each side for burgers, or 4–5 minutes all over for balls, to let them get a nice crust.

TIP

+ Any leftover cooked lentils can be turned into a dip or blended into a creamy dressing with garlic, extra-virgin olive oil, lemon juice and a pinch of sea salt and black pepper.

This recipe calls for a homemade sweet and sticky teriyaki sauce. We don't think we've met anyone who doesn't find it irresistible! Whether teamed with chicken, fish, beef or an assortment of vegetables, the sauce lends a deep flavour with just the right level of tang. There are lots of great grain- and gluten-free noodles available. We've used buckwheat here, but look out for chickpea, mung bean or seaweed spaghetti (seaweed that naturally grows like noodles). Or spiralize celeriac, butternut squash (pages 198 and 150) or beetroot (page 237) to make noodles, then steam in a saucepan with 4 tablespoons of water with the lid on for 4 minutes until tender.

TERIYAKI NOODLE STIR-FRY

SERVES 4

300g buckwheat (soba) noodles
1 tablespoon extra-virgin olive oil
300g raw diced vegetables (such as carrots, courgettes, red peppers, fennel or radishes)
1 tablespoon coconut oil
1 small cabbage or 2 big heads of pak choi, shredded
4 spring onions, finely sliced
1 large ripe avocado, sliced
1 handful of flaxseeds
1 large handful of fresh coriander (leaves and stalks) or fresh mint leaves, roughly chopped

FOR THE TERIYAKI SAUCE
4 tablespoons tamari
2 tablespoons apple cider vinegar or lemon juice
2 tablespoons maple syrup
1 garlic clove, finely grated or diced
1 teaspoon fresh root ginger (unpeeled if organic), diced
A pinch of white or black pepper or diced fresh red chilli or chilli flakes (optional)
1 tablespoon tahini or other nut or seed butter

1 Cook the buckwheat noodles in a large pan of boiling water according to the packet instructions (about 7 minutes). Use two forks to tease the noodles apart during the first minute of cooking.

2 When tender, drain and rinse in cold running water for about 15 seconds to stop them cooking further. Set aside to drain, then toss with the EVOO in a large serving bowl to stop the noodles sticking. Set aside.

3 Rinse the noodle pan and add all the teriyaki sauce ingredients. Bring to a medium simmer and cook for 10 minutes until the sauce reduces and thickens.

4 Meanwhile, stir-fry all the diced vegetables in the coconut oil in a large frying pan over a medium heat. If using carrots, fry these first, giving them a 2-minute head start, then add the rest of the diced veg and stir-fry for 4 minutes until tender.

5 Once the diced vegetables are just tender, add the cabbage or pak choi to the pan with the teriyaki sauce and heat through for 1 minute.

6 Tip the contents of the pan into the serving bowl and mix well with the noodles. Garnish with the spring onions, sliced avocado, sesame seeds and chopped fresh herbs and let everyone help themselves.

DIPS, DRESSINGS, SAUCES AND SPREADS

We really had to rein ourselves in with this chapter as we were bursting with ideas! That's the beauty of sauces, spreads, dips and dressings – the possibilities are endless, so feel free to allow your creativity to run wild using our recipes as a springboard for your imagination. These condiments are a great opportunity to use up whatever is in the store cupboard or fridge – which is where most of our inspiration comes from. The right condiment will make almost anything taste good – keeping even those wary of vegetables happy too.

We've got the 'better for you' versions of some classic condiments like BBQ Ketchup (page 278), Homemade Sriracha (page 279), ranch dressing (page 276) and mayonnaise (page 277) – sauces that you can whip up and then store, ready to bring to life the plainest of meals or to transform leftovers. They can be made in minutes and prepared ahead as most will keep for a week or so. Simply store them in the fridge in a sterilised glass jar (page 17) with a lid, and make sure you use a clean spoon every time you dip into them. Drizzling a layer of extra-virgin olive oil (EVOO) on top helps too, acting as a 'seal' for raw sauces that contain fresh ingredients like herbs and garlic. You'll be much more likely to throw together a home-cooked meal at the end of the day if you know you've got a tasty homemade condiment ready to go in the fridge.

We've also included some delicious dips – thick, creamy and full of flavour – for serving with crudités and meatballs or lentil burgers (pages 214 and 258), or for spreading on bread (pages 136) or crackers (page 127) for a wholesome snack. Try our butterbean hummus (page 273), vibrant green from the fresh spinach, or our take on baba ghanoush (page 272), using miso for a Japanese twist. Have a go at creating your own dips. You just need a thick, creamy base to flavour, from cream cheese, egg and yoghurt to avocado, nuts, seeds and pulses. Some of our favourites include mung beans (page 256) or cannellini beans – popped into the blender straight from the tin – or red lentils (page 259) saved from another dish. Whizzed up in a food processor or high-powered blender, many vegetables also make a good base. Try those with a low water content – raw fresh peas or broccoli, or cooked squash, celeriac, beetroot or carrots. Just add some natural fat – butter, extra-virgin olive oil or coconut oil – for a creamy texture.

If you've got a bit of dip left, a few spoonfuls or so, don't throw it away! Add it to a homemade pot noodle or stir in some more EVOO and lemon juice or a dash of apple cider vinegar (ACV) and swirl it through soups and stews to make them creamy and give them a lift. That's why we love dips and dressings – they are transformative and endlessly versatile.

TIPS AND TRICKS

CHOP AND CHANGE You can really get away with changing things up with a 'bit of this and a bit of that' in dips and dressings. If you don't have lemons, use limes or other citrus fruits such as oranges or clementines, or swap for ACV. Mix up the herbs and the spice combos too. Try blending in leftover caramelised onions or roasted red peppers or adding anchovies, olives, capers or sliced jalapenos for a hit of flavour. Instead of mixing in chopped garlic, try blending in roasted garlic, or drop a whole, lightly crushed garlic clove into a dressing to infuse for a subtler effect.

FREEZER Don't try to freeze fresh herbs as they are – they just go dark and crumbly. Instead blend with EVOO, ready to add to future dressing and dips, or make into a dressing and freeze for future use. Ginger makes a frequent appearance in our recipes and we've always got some in the fridge, but you can also keep knobs of ginger in the freezer and grate straight from frozen.

SPICE CUPBOARD Dried spices last well if kept somewhere cool and dark, so they are store cupboard essentials for whipping up meals when you aren't able to get to the shops. Look for a good brand to get the maximum health benefits and flavour. (See page 339 for our store cupboard favourites.)

GO FOR QUALITY Always choose good-quality oils for their superior flavour and health-giving properties. (See our fats chart on page 339 for our store cupboard favourites.)

A FOOD PROCESSOR OR HIGH-POWERED BLENDER (one that is easy to wash) is your friend here. If not, you can still enjoy many of these recipes. Look out for alternative methods involving some fine chopping or mashing with a fork.

ON THE GO When you're out and about, you want to minimise any chance of sauces leaking out and making a mess. Rather than the looser dressings and sauces, coat lentils or quinoa and veggies in a thick tasty dip – a good one to remember if you're flying, to avoid having your lovingly made food confiscated at security!

AT YOUR DESK Take a couple of jars of different dressings or dips to work (keep in the fridge) on a Monday to jazz up your lunch throughout the week. This is a good stopgap if you find that you have to rely on shop-bought salads or other meals. A homemade dressing adds high-quality fats to your food that will not only make it tastier and more nutritious but keep you fuller for longer.

ANYTHING GOES Along with guacamole (page 50), hummus is one of the ultimate dips and pesto (pages 245–246) is one of the best sauces. See the ideas section opposite for our versions of some of these classic condiments and have a go at experimenting yourself!

Combining two fantastically good-for-you ingredients, avocado and ginger, this Japanese-inspired sauce is both creamy and zingy. It brings any dish or simple vegetable side to life, whether tossed into Asian-style raw vegetable salads or spooned over grilled or barbecued fish. For a quick meal, spoon it over Egg-fried Cauliflower Rice (page 243).

AVOCADO AND GINGER SAUCE

MAKES 300ML

5cm piece of
    fresh root ginger
    (unpeeled if
    organic), grated
1 ripe avocado
2 tablespoons
    lemon or
    lime juice
1 teaspoon
    grated lemon
    or lime zest
1½ teaspoons
    raw honey
2 teaspoons tamari
200ml water
Sea salt and black
    pepper (to taste)

1   Place all the ingredients in a food processor, adding half the water, and blend until smooth.

2   Add the rest of the water a little bit at a time until you have a thin sauce consistency and taste for seasoning.

The distinctive texture and gentle spiciness of our Quick Coconut Dahl (page 78) inspired us to think of dahl as a dip! Using red lentils means that you don't have to do any pre-soaking for this dip and the lentils are cooked in just 20 minutes, making it brilliant for when you forget to plan ahead or have an unexpected guest. Enjoy this filling dip with seasonal crudités – carrots in winter or cucumber in summer – or use to add a burst of flavour and creaminess to a salad, stew or soup. The recipe makes enough dip to last a week or for a party. If you need less, you can either freeze half or just halve the quantities in the recipe.

SPICY TURMERIC AND RED LENTIL DIP

MAKES 800ML

250g dried red
    lentils, rinsed
    and drained
600ml water
3 garlic cloves
Juice of
    1–1½ lemons
2 teaspoons
    garam masala
    or medium
    curry powder
2 teaspoons ground
    turmeric
½ teaspoon chilli
    powder or
    cayenne pepper
    (or to taste)
4 tablespoons
    extra-virgin olive
    oil, plus extra
    to cover
Sea salt and black
    pepper (to taste)

1 In a large pan, cover the lentils with the water and simmer over a medium heat for 20 minutes until tender, then drain off any excess water.

2 Add to the food processor with all the other ingredients and blend until you have a thick, creamy dip.

3 Place in a sterilised jar (page 17), then cover with a layer of EVOO and the lid. Stored like this, it will keep for a week in the fridge.

In the summer, take advantage of vibrant-green, fresh, young broad beans. When they aren't available, the frozen kind are great too – keep a stash in your freezer. For a cheaper version, replace half with frozen peas. Enjoy this creamy dip as a spread, as a sauce with spiralized vegetable noodles, or have it as a mash with some veggie curry for a weekday dinner. Play around with other herbs too: a combination of basil and dill is amazing, and whenever we have a little leftover cheese, such as pecorino or goat's cheese, we add that as well. We even use it as a white sauce (minus the mint) for our Courgette and Cannellini Bean Lasagne (page 226).

MINTY BROAD BEAN DIP

MAKES 500ML

400g fresh or frozen
    broad beans
    (or mixed broad
    beans and peas)
1 garlic clove or
    1 handful of wild
    garlic (when in
    season)
12 fresh mint leaves
4 tablespoons
    lemon juice
120ml extra-virgin
    olive oil, plus
    extra to serve
6 tablespoons water
    (to steam fresh
    beans, if using,
    and enough for
    blending to the
    preferred
    consistency)

1 small handful of
    grated pecorino
    /Parmesan or
    crumbly goat's
    cheese (optional)
Sea salt and
    black pepper

1   Very young broad beans won't need cooking; steam fresh older beans with 4 tablespoons of water over a medium heat, in a pan covered with a lid, for 3 minutes until just tender, then rinse under cold water. If using fresh peas, follow the same method, steaming them for just a minute. If using frozen beans or peas, sit them in a bowl of warm water to defrost (about 10 minutes) – no need to cook.

2   Blend all the ingredients together in a food processor, adding a pinch of salt and pepper and saving a few mint leaves (chopped) to garnish. Add a little more water if it is too thick, and taste for seasoning.

3   Serve with a swirl of EVOO, a grind of pepper and salt and the reserved chopped mint.

This dip came about from having a few handfuls of roasted squash left over in the fridge. During a Sunday Cook-Off (page 334) we like to roast any leftover veggies that are hiding in the fridge – often a whole squash, a few carrots or a beetroot or two. Once roasted, we add them to cooked quinoa (page 253), or use them to make soup (page 82). And any left after that are given a new lease of life as a smooth and creamy dip – a few seconds in the food processor and it's done. Try this in a Flaxseed Bun (page 136), with slices of avocado, or spread onto some Quinoa Courgette Toast (page 32) topped with fresh and crunchy salad leaves, a crumble of feta or some toasted pumpkin seeds.

SWEET AND EARTHY ROASTED SQUASH DIP

MAKES 500ML

350g roasted
   butternut squash
   (see tip on
   page 34)
3 tablespoons tahini
4 tablespoons
   lemon juice
2 garlic cloves
   (or roast them
   unpeeled with
   the squash and
   squeeze out the
   flesh), crushed
5 tablespoons water
   (or enough for
   blending to the
   preferred
   consistency)
Sea salt and black
   pepper (to taste)

TO SERVE

½ teaspoon smoked
   paprika and/or
   ground cumin
   (optional)
Extra-virgin olive oil

1   Place the roasted squash in a food processor or mash in a bowl for a chunkier version. Add all the remaining ingredients and blend until thick in the machine or by hand. Add more water if you want a smoother, lighter dip.

2   Sprinkle with one or both the spices and drizzle with EVOO to make a beautiful, earthy orange dip.

This dip is an earthy, sweet and salty combination inspired by the Middle Eastern baba ghanoush and by Japanese miso-glazed baked aubergine dishes. You can use any traditionally fermented miso paste in this dish for varying flavours, but since the miso remains uncooked we like to take advantage of the unpasteurised form for its probiotic benefits. Serve this dip chunky with Quinoa Courgette Toast (page 32) or Multiseed Crackers (page 127), or blended smooth to accompany crunchy crudités. Especially good served alongside fried fish, roasted chicken or with a simple quinoa salad (page 254).

MISO AND AUBERGINE DIP

MAKES 400ML

3 large aubergines
1 garlic clove
   (unpeeled if
   roasting)
4 tablespoons
   lemon juice
   or apple cider
   vinegar
2 tablespoons
   quality sweet
   white miso paste
   (or to taste)
3 tablespoons tahini
2 teaspoons raw
   honey or maple
   syrup (optional)
Sea salt and
   black pepper

TO SERVE
2 tablespoons black
   sesame seeds
Extra-virgin olive oil

1   Preheat the oven to fan 180°C/Gas mark 6.

2   Place the whole aubergines on a baking tray and roast in the oven for about 30 minutes until a knife slides in easily. Halfway through, add the garlic clove, if you like, so it roasts a little.

3   Slice the aubergines in half, then scoop out the hot flesh and roughly chop. Peel the garlic and finely chop, or crush the raw garlic if you didn't roast it.

4   Combine everything in a bowl for a chunky dip or blend with a little water until smooth if desired – we like it chunky – and season with salt and pepper to taste (bearing in mind that the miso is already salty).

5   Serve topped with a sprinkling of black sesame seeds and a drizzle of EVOO.

Instead of the traditional chickpeas we've used butterbeans in this hummus to mix things up, along with spinach to supercharge it. You can use any leftover cooked beans or herbs in this recipe and, if you have a high-powered blender, any greens such as kale or chard. The lemon, garlic and tahini are of course a must for hummus and boost the nutrients of this smooth dip as well as the flavour. Great as a snack or part of a packed lunch, served with crudités or crackers (page 127).

SPINACH AND BUTTERBEAN HUMMUS

MAKES 500ML

1 x 400g tin of
   butterbeans,
   drained and
   rinsed
150g spinach
3 tablespoons tahini
4 tablespoons
   lemon juice
2 garlic cloves
5 tablespoons
   water (or enough
   for blending to
   the preferred
   consistency)
Sea salt and
   black pepper

TO SERVE
1 teaspoon sumac
   or za'atar
   (optional)
Extra-virgin olive oil

1   Blend all the ingredients together in a food processor and season with salt and pepper to taste. Add enough water to give a thick, creamy hummus.

2   To serve, add the hummus to a bowl, sprinkle with your spice of choice and drizzle with a swirl of EVOO.

3   To store, spoon into a sterilised jar (page 17) and cover with a layer of EVOO and the lid. It will keep like this for a week in the fridge.

A delicious paste made from ground sesame seeds, tahini is rich in minerals, including magnesium, potassium and iron. We love how versatile it is, working just as well in sweet dishes as it does in savoury. Try Lemon and Parsley Tahini Dressing with a quinoa salad, cauliflower tabbouleh or roasted veg. While Lime and Coriander Tahini Dressing is brilliant drizzled over roast chicken or cooked lentils. For a taste of the sweeter side of tahini, try our Tahini Applejacks (page 124) or Tahini Date Fridge Fudge (page 287).

HERBY TAHINI DRESSING 2 WAYS

MAKES 300ML

1 large handful
   of fresh parsley
   (leaves and
   stalks)
3 tablespoons tahini
1 garlic clove
180ml extra-virgin
   olive oil

4 tablespoons
   lemon juice
   (juice of 1 lemon)
A pinch of diced
   fresh red chilli
   (to taste)
Sea salt and black
   pepper (to taste)

LEMON AND PARSLEY TAHINI DRESSING

1   Place all the ingredients in a food processor or high-powered blender and whizz together until creamy.

MAKES 300ML

1 large handful of
   fresh coriander
   (leaves and
   stalks)
3 tablespoons tahini
1 garlic clove
180ml extra-virgin
   olive oil

4 tablespoons
   lime juice
   (juice of 2 limes)
A pinch of diced
   fresh red chilli
   (to taste)
Sea salt and black
   pepper (to taste)

LIME AND CORIANDER TAHINI DRESSING

1   Place all the ingredients in a food processor or high-powered blender and whizz together until creamy.

This creamy-white, dairy-free dressing is amazing drizzled over our Mushroom Lentil Burgers (page 258) or just served with some cucumber and carrot crudités.

CREAMY CASHEW RANCH DRESSING

MAKES 500ML

200g cashew nuts, soaked in double the volume of water for 3 hours (page 341)
2 garlic cloves
2 tablespoons apple cider vinegar, or 3 tablespoons lemon juice
1 tablespoon maple syrup or raw honey
1 small handful of fresh chives, spring onions or chopped onion
300ml water (or enough for blending to the preferred consistency)
Sea salt and black pepper (to taste)
Extra-virgin olive oil, to cover

TO SERVE
1 small handful of fresh parsley, leaves and stalks finely chopped
½ teaspoon dried dill or 1 tablespoon finely chopped fresh dill

1   Drain and rinse the cashews under cold running water.

2   Blend everything except the EVOO together in a food processor, adding the water slowly until the dressing is thick and creamy in consistency.

3   Sprinkle the herbs over your dressing to serve. Keep stored in the fridge in a sterilised jar (page 17) and covered with a layer of EVOO with the lid on; give it a stir before using.

Making your own mayonnaise means that you have all the nutrition from fresh egg yolks and unrefined oils – everything about mayo is nourishing if the ingredients are top quality. It's an excellent fat to add to a salad to help you absorb all those vitamins while making it tasty and satisfying, and we all know how good mayo is in a sandwich. We've come up with a recipe that uses whole eggs for extra protein and it's also cooked, which means it lasts longer in the fridge and is better for picnics and packed lunches if you're transporting your food around unrefrigerated (though a cool bag is best!). It's thick and creamy too, just like a shop-bought mayo but without the starchy additives. Mix it up with a little of our BBQ Ketchup (page 278) for a take on a smoky Marie Rose sauce for your parsnip chips (page 100).

QUICK-COOKED MAYO

MAKES 150ML

2 eggs, beaten
2 tablespoons
   lemon juice
2 tablespoons water
2 teaspoons
   mustard or
   1 teaspoon dried
About ½ teaspoon
   sea salt
A pinch of
   black pepper
65ml extra-virgin
   olive oil

1 Place all the ingredients except the EVOO in a small saucepan and whisk together until blended.

2 Set over a very low heat and cook, stirring constantly, until the mixture begins to bubble. Remove from the heat immediately and allow to cool for 5 minutes. Don't worry if you almost get scrambled eggs!

3 Pour the mixture into a tall jug or deep bowl, immerse a hand-held stick blender or electric whisk in the jug or bowl and start blending.

4 Add a few drops of the EVOO and continue blending until thickened. Continue to add the oil slowly, in a thin stream, and blend until the mayonnaise is thick and smooth.

5 Keep in the fridge in a sterilised jar (page 17), covered with a lid, for up to a week.

VARIATIONS

+ This makes a really thick mayo that you'll be proud of. Add more mustard to taste, or any other flavours that you fancy. Add more EVOO to thin, if you like, or stir in some yoghurt for a tang.

This recipe uses a whole pot or tube of tomato purée to create a quick dump-and-stir sauce that makes everything taste like it's straight from an American diner! In fact it's all straight out of the store cupboard, with no need to cook or chop onions or buy the commercial stuff that's loaded with sugar. It will keep in a sealed jar in the fridge for up to a month – just be sure to use a clean spoon when you dip into it. If you don't think you'll get through it quickly enough, freeze it in mini jam jars so it's ready to use when you need it.

BBQ KETCHUP

MAKES 450ML

200g tomato purée
120ml extra-virgin
  olive oil
6 tablespoons
  balsamic vinegar
2 teaspoons
  smoked paprika
  (or to taste)
2 teaspoons
  mustard
Sea salt and
  black pepper

1   Whisk together all the ingredients in a bowl, then season with salt and pepper to taste.

2   Transfer to a sterilised jar (page 17), cover with the lid and chill in the fridge until needed.

TIP

+   Try this ketchup fermented for some probiotic goodness: Stir through 1½ teaspoon of sauerkraut juice or whey (strained from live dairy yoghurt) before pouring into the sterilised jar. Cover the top of the jar tightly with a muslin cloth (not a lid) and leave in a warm place for 4–5 days. Remove the muslin and seal with a lid. Transfer the ketchup to the fridge. Fermented BBQ Ketchup will keep for up to 2 months.

A Hemsley homemade version of the fiery original. If you've never tried Sriracha, you must give it a go! It's an amazing hot and vinegary sauce from Si Racha in Thailand (hence the name). We use it as a dipping sauce, add a little to stir-fries, stews and broths for a burst of flavour, or drizzle over Egg-fried Cauliflower Rice (page 243) for warming comfort food. This sauce can be kept in the fridge for a few weeks due to the preservative qualities of the vinegar. We also make double or triple the recipe and freeze in batches because it's a great one to have to hand, adding a kick to anything and everything.

HOMEMADE SRIRACHA

MAKES 500ML

300g fresh red
   chillies
6 garlic cloves,
   diced
2 tablespoons
   tomato purée
2 tablespoons
   maple syrup
4 tablespoons apple
   cider vinegar
180ml water
Sea salt (to taste)

1   Chop the ends off the chillies and add to a food processor with the garlic. Blend together, then add the remaining ingredients and blend together until smooth.

2   Add the sauce to a pan and simmer for 10 minutes, then let it cool and taste for seasoning – you should taste hits of spice, garlic, tanginess and sweetness.

3   Pour into a sterilised jar (page 17), cover with the lid and keep refrigerated until needed.

This recipe has become a winter staple that sees us through to the following year. Chutneys develop a deeper, richer flavour as they mature, so we like to cook a big batch in the autumn when apples are plentiful. There is nothing like a kitchen table piled high with jars of homemade chutney to let you know that Christmas is around the corner! Not just for enjoying with cheese and cold cuts, a spoonful of sweet and spicy chutney is a delicious condiment to curries or stirred into stews for another layer of flavour. It makes the perfect hamper filler, so halve the recipe if you like, but we suggest you make the full amount and divvy up the jars as presents to others and to yourself.

SPICED WINTER APPLE CHUTNEY

MAKES 8 X 250ML JARS

500g cooking apples
    and 1.5kg eating
    apples (or 2kg
    eating apples)
800g onions
300g dried
    dates, pitted
1 tablespoon ghee
    or coconut oil
300g raisins
300ml maple syrup
3 large pinches
    of sea salt
3 teaspoons
    ground turmeric
2 teaspoons
    ground cumin
3 teaspoons
    ground coriander
4 teaspoons
    ground ginger
½ teaspoon
    ground cloves
½–1 teaspoon
    cayenne pepper
    (or to taste)

Grated zest
    and juice of
    1 medium orange
2 tablespoons
    tomato purée
250ml port
800ml apple
    cider vinegar

1   Core the apples and chop into chunks of varying sizes to give texture to the chutney.

2   Finely chop the onions – we use the S-blade attachment on our food processor for ease.

3   Chop the dates – again we chop them in the food processor (no need to wash it out first).

4   Melt the ghee or coconut oil in a very large saucepan, add all the ingredients and stir to coat them in the ghee/coconut oil. Bring to the boil, then reduce the heat and cook on a slow simmer for about 45 minutes, stirring occasionally to prevent the mixture catching on the bottom of the pan, until the apples are tender. Remove from the heat and give everything a good mix.

5   Meanwhile, sterilise the jars (page 17) and while they are still hot, pour in the hot chutney then allow to cool, before adding wax paper discs and sealing with the vinegar-proof lids. Store in a cool, dark place and, once opened, keep them in the fridge.

BAKING, DESSERTS AND SWEETS

There's no denying that baking cakes and making desserts and sweets is good for the soul. Traditionally associated with celebrations, for sharing with family and friends, they're fun to create and provide a joyful end to a meal or a comforting pick-me-up. Our sweet recipes are as good for you as they are tasty, so there's no need for guilt when you tuck into them.

This chapter is filled with sweet things that we've made better for you. There's something for every occasion, from muffins, cookies and biscotti (pages 308, 302 and 306), for a tasty snack, to delicious date fudge and chocolate bars (pages 287 and 290) for a special treat. Not to mention the 'secret' recipe that everyone's been waiting for – our Cannellini Vanilla Sponge Cake with Chocolate Avo Frosting (page 312)! A favourite of many of our clients, whether they have something special to celebrate or not.

In these recipes, we've avoided the usual refined sugars found in commercial confectionery and replaced them with honey, maple syrup and fruit (see our sweeteners chart, page 13) – in small amounts to complement and enhance the natural flavours of food without overpowering it. These wholefood sweeteners come with vitamins and minerals, as well as a more complex, well-rounded flavour. All forms of sugar can be addictive, however, and our bodies are hard-wired to want sweet things which provide instant, easily accessible energy. We say stick to the more natural sweeteners and use as little as you can get away with. Reduce quantities bit by bit to tame your taste buds and wean yourself off sugar and you'll be surprised at how quickly you adapt. You'll see that some of our recipes suggest varying amounts of sweeteners for this very reason.

By now you're probably well acquainted with our attitude towards fat – we love it! The sweets and desserts in this chapter all include fat (as well as protein), so that flavour and texture are never compromised. Beneficial fats like coconut oil or butter make a sweet recipe really satisfying too – nutrient dense rather than full of empty calories – so that you don't need a huge portion to hit that sweet spot.

In these recipes we try to give different 'free from' options when we can. While our carrot cake (page 300) uses ground almonds to replace standard flour, for instance, you can easily substitute with flour made from ground sunflower seeds if you have a nut allergy. Likewise in the Frozen Banana Man Bites (page 299), you can swap the peanut butter for a mixture of tahini and honey. Apart from soaking the odd ingredient overnight, most of the recipes are simply 'dump and stir', so that you can speedily knock up treats and snacks to see you through the week. We've designed these to fit into a busy lifestyle – some recipes keep well in the freezer – and worked hard to make them foolproof and easy to prepare. Enjoy!

TIPS AND TRICKS

COMBAT THE CRAVINGS When sugar cravings hit, make sure that you are well hydrated before reaching for a snack. Try Rehydrate Mate (page 320) for a refreshing hit to the taste buds. A cup of Salabat (page 329), a Filipino thirst-quencher, or a cinnamon-based herbal tea really helps, or go sour with a squeeze of lemon or lime juice in water.

READ LABELS Always read the labels on food and drinks before you buy them, because sugar is used in all types of foods (even savoury) to make them taste better. Sugar can come under many different guises, so look out for terms such as fructose, corn syrup, cane juice, erythritol, malted barley and rice syrup.

SUGAR- AND GLUTEN-FREE Our recipes are not bulked out and flavoured with sugars, nor do they rely on the powers of gluten to bind or form crumb and crust, so don't expect the same results. Because of the lack of gluten, always allow baked goods to cool completely before removing from the tin unless we suggest serving it /them warm.

RAISING AGENTS Apple cider vinegar and lemon juice are used as raising agents when combined with bicarbonate of soda and are interchangeable in the baking recipes.

DARK CHOCOLATE IS A FEEL-GOOD FOOD with plenty of antioxidants, magnesium and good fats from the cocoa butter. We use chocolate with a minimum of 85 per cent cocoa solids in our recipes: the higher the percentage, the better as it means less room for additives.

FRESH FRUITS ARE NATURE'S SWEETS As well as enjoying them as they are, we use fruit to sweeten and enhance the flavour of other foods. Bananas make a fantastic base for dairy-free ice creams, for instance. It's easy to eat too much fruit, however, especially if you choose it over vegetables or have a sweet tooth that needs taming. If you have poor digestion, it's best to eat fruit on an empty stomach and not for dessert or in meals.

DRIED FRUIT We make sure all the dried fruit we buy is entirely natural and free from sulphur dioxide – a preservative used to keep dried fruits like apricots brightly coloured. Rich and sticky, dried fruit is great for sweetening dishes, but beware of overindulging: imagine each piece of dried fruit is a fresh fruit and drink the equivalent amount of missing water.

HONEY We use the raw variety because it hasn't been heat-treated or 'purified', which means that it's still highly nutritious, full of vitamins, minerals and amino acids. Heating honey destroys the enzymes and ruins its health-giving properties, so we like to save it for raw desserts and salad dressings.

MAPLE SYRUP Mineral-rich maple syrup is sweeter than sugar, so a little goes a long way. Unlike honey, its nutrients aren't affected by heating, so we use it in all cooking and baking. Make sure that the syrup you buy is pure and not a blend.

STEVIA AND XYLITOL These natural sweeteners (page 12) can be helpful for people who cannot tolerate large amounts of any kind of sugar, or for those wanting to cut down on the amount of sweetener they use. As stevia and xylitol are many times sweeter than sugar, adding just a few drops of either to one of our dishes means you can cut down the amount of maple syrup or raw honey you use while still retaining the more complex flavour.

Sweet and nutty, this is a cross between halva and fudge with a melt-in-the-mouth texture – much easier to make (just blend and set in the fridge) and of course better for you! We love the unique creamy and nutty flavour that the tahini gives and the fudgy texture from the dried dates, used in place of sugar. You could sub in almond butter for the tahini and use dried apricots (dark unsulphured ones) or prunes instead of the dates. Choose a wholefood tahini – see our website – which contains no emulsifiers (the tahini should naturally separate in the jar) otherwise your fudge might not set properly. We usually make this by eye with a mug, rather than get the scales out. Blend, taste and then adjust – not forgetting to try to reduce the sweet flavour by a date or two every time you make it.

TAHINI DATE FRIDGE FUDGE

MAKES ABOUT 18 FUDGE SQUARES

85g (about ½ mugful) of pitted dates (chewy dried dates rather than the larger soft ones), or to taste

110g (about ½ mugful) light tahini (make sure it doesn't contain emulsifiers – see intro above)

2 tablespoons coconut oil, at room temperature, or extra-virgin olive oil

Sea salt flakes

1 tablespoon white sesame seeds or desiccated coconut, to decorate (optional)

1 Line a small baking tin – about 11cm x 17cm – or similar-sized container (we use a glass lunchbox) with baking parchment.

2 Slice one of the dates finely and set aside to decorate the top of the fudge. Place the rest of the dates in a food processor with the tahini, coconut oil or EVOO and ⅛ teaspoon of salt flakes and blend to a smooth, thick paste. Taste and add more salt if desired.

3 Transfer the mixture to the prepared tin and use a spatula to press the mixture down evenly.

4 Decorate the top with the date slices and a sprinkle of sesame seeds or desiccated coconut (if using), pour over any leftover oil from the food processor and press down gently.

5 Freeze or chill in the fridge until firm – about 15 minutes in the freezer and 30 minutes in the fridge. Slice into squares, then store in the fridge or freezer. Eat chilled/frozen straight from the fridge/freezer.

TIPS

+ You can upgrade to the more nutritious dark tahini which has a bitter flavour, if you like.

+ This keeps really well in the fridge or freezer, so make double!

Deliciously chewy coconut macaroons decorated with a drizzle of dark chocolate – perfect for tea parties, petits fours after dinner, or a light dessert. If you want to make the macaroons in advance, then re-crisp in the oven just before serving and drizzle over the melted chocolate to serve. We like to make these around the same time as Frozen Banana Man Bites (page 299) (using the leftover melted chocolate to drizzle over the macaroons) and when we're making carbonara (page 204) so that we can add the extra egg yolks into the sauce!

CHOCOLATE DRIZZLE COCONUT MACAROONS

MAKES 18 MACAROONS

4 tablespoons
    maple syrup
1½ teaspoons
    vanilla extract
150g desiccated
    coconut
3 egg whites
A tiny pinch
    of sea salt
50g dark (85%
    cocoa solids)
    chocolate,
    broken into
    squares

1   Preheat the oven to fan 170°C/Gas mark 5 and line a large baking sheet with baking parchment.

2   In a large bowl, mix together the maple syrup, vanilla extract and desiccated coconut, then set aside.

3   In a squeaky-clean mixing bowl, whisk the egg whites with the salt until stiff peaks form. Gently fold the egg whites into the coconut mixture with a metal spoon to form a loose mixture.

4   Use a tablespoon to scoop the mixture onto the prepared baking sheet, making 18 mounds, spaced at least 2cm apart. Every now and then stir the mixture gently between scoops, to prevent it from separating. Use your fingers or two teaspoons to carefully neaten the little mounds on the baking sheet.

5   Bake in the oven for 12–15 minutes until the macaroons are lightly browned. Remove from the oven and allow to cool on the baking sheet.

6   Meanwhile, melt the chocolate in a bowl set over a pan of gently simmering water (the water shouldn't touch the base of the bowl). Drizzle the melted chocolate over the top of each cooked macaroon using a spoon and allow to set. Store in an airtight tin somewhere cool or in the fridge.

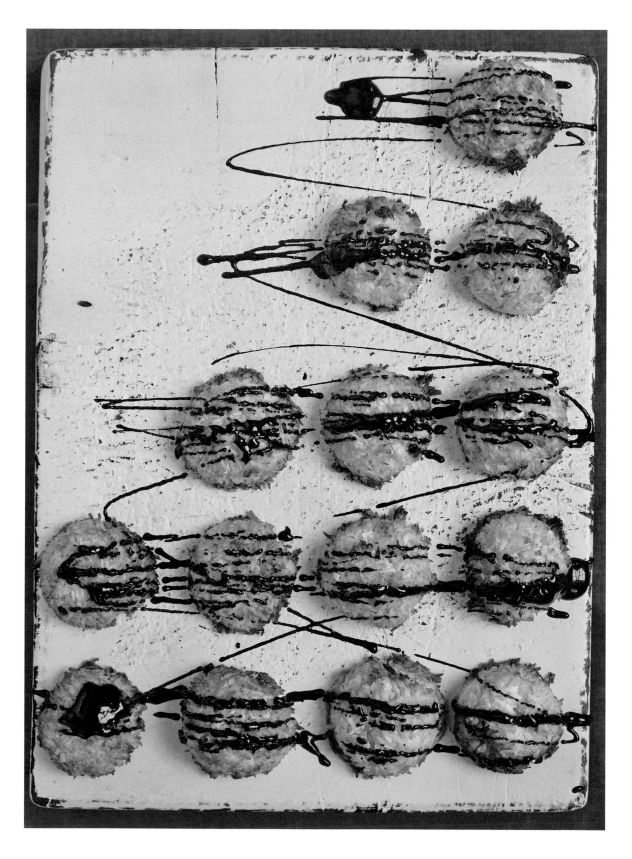

This recipe is just so good and yet so easy to make. Whole, fresh and juicy clementine pieces enrobed in melt-in-the-mouth chocolate infused with coconut, vanilla and orange extract. As always, a pinch of salt goes a long way in this sweet recipe – it makes the citrus even zingier, cuts through the bitterness of the chocolate and adds complexity to the maple syrup's sweetness. The homemade chocolate is very easy to make – no temperamental cocoa solids to contend with. Just whisk cocoa powder, and a little maple syrup for sweetening it, into gently melted coconut oil. Pour over the clementines and leave to set in the fridge. Present the whole bar as a beautiful gift or serve on a slab of chilled marble with a sharp knife at the end of a dinner.

CHOCOLATE ORANGE BAR WITH CLEMENTINES

SERVES 6

1 organic
    clementine (or
    see tip opposite)
100g coconut oil
50g cocoa powder
3 tablespoons
    maple syrup
1 teaspoon vanilla
    extract
½ teaspoon orange
    extract (not
    essence)
A tiny pinch
    of sea salt

1. Line a small baking tin – about 11cm x 17cm – or similar-sized container with baking parchment.

2. Zest the clementine with a grater or zester and place the zest to one side. Peel the clementine, break into segments and arrange in the bottom of the prepared tin.

3. Gently melt the coconut oil in a saucepan over a low heat. Remove from the heat and whisk in the cocoa powder until smooth, then stir in the remaining ingredients until well combined.

4. Pour the fudge mixture over the clementine segments in the tin, then sprinkle over the clementine zest, pressing it gently onto the surface of the chocolate mixture.

5. Chill in the fridge for 1 hour, or until set. Slice with a sharp knife and serve immediately as the chocolate becomes very soft at room temperature, or store in the fridge and eat within a day or two.

TIP

+ To remove the wax from a non-
organic clementine, place the fruit
in a colander and pour over recently
boiled water. Scrub with a brush,
then rinse under cool water and dry.

VARIATION

+ You can replace the cocoa powder
with carob for a caffeine-free treat.
Use 40g carob powder, sifting it into
the melted coconut oil in step 3, and
reduce the maple syrup to 1 tablespoon.
The coconut oil sometimes separates
on top of the finished bar.

Growing up, we both loved chocolate hazelnut spread as a treat for breakfast. We still do and here is our own wholefood version! Try this creamy spread, made with black beans and roasted hazelnut butter, in a thick layer on your toast (page 32) and enjoy for breakfast, teatime or as a snack. Deliciously rich and decadent, it's divine on its own – we like to enjoy a tiny pot or small scoopful for dessert, delicious with some fresh berries and a drizzle of cream. Remember to team it with our Chestnut Pancakes (page 30) for a chocolate crêpe, or just spread it onto thickly sliced apple rings.

BBTELLA SPREAD

MAKES 550G

100g hazelnut butter
1 x 400g tin of black beans, drained and rinsed
4 tablespoons cocoa powder
2 tablespoons butter or coconut oil
4 tablespoons raw honey
2 teaspoons vanilla extract
A small pinch of sea salt

1   Add all the ingredients to a food processor or high-powered blender and pulse to the desired consistency.

2   Transfer the spread to a sterilised jar (page 17) and store in the fridge for up to 3 weeks.

VARIATIONS

+   Add extra honey or a few drops of liquid stevia (page 12) if you'd like the spread to be a little sweeter.

+   Try replacing the hazelnut butter with almond butter and ¼ teaspoon of almond extract. Or leave out the hazelnut butter altogether for a nut-free version – it works just as well!

+   Instead of using hazelnut butter, roast your own hazelnuts. Add a couple more tablespoons of butter or coconut oil, if needed, to get the right consistency.

+   For a caffeine-free spread, replace the cocoa with carob powder and halve the quantity of honey.

This dessert was inspired by leftover chocolate buckwheat porridge, which thickens as it cools. To give it an extra fudgy bite, we replaced the cocoa powder with bars of dark chocolate – the cocoa butter gives it an even thicker bite – and a new dessert was born! Just spoon the freshly cooked chocolate porridge into a lined cake tin and set in the fridge for a deliciously dark and subtly flavoured pudding that's offset by its cool, smooth texture. We like to pour over some melted chocolate to give it a crisp top – an idea from our friend Sjaniel, the dessert queen – and, for an even more decadent touch, serve with fresh cherries and coconut yoghurt or full-fat cream. Gluten-, dairy- and egg-free (and made without nuts), this recipe is great for vegans and anyone with these common food sensitivities.

CHOC MUD FRIDGE TART

SERVES 12

200g buckwheat
    flour (or whole
    buckwheat
    groats – see tips
    opposite)
6–7 tablespoons
    maple syrup
    (to taste)
¾ teaspoon ground
    cardamom,
    allspice or
    freshly grated
    nutmeg
1 tablespoon
    ground
    cinnamon
2 pinches of
    cayenne pepper
    (optional)

¼ teaspoon sea salt
1 litre water
5 tablespoons
    (about 75g)
    coconut oil
2 tablespoons
    vanilla extract
200g dark (85%
    cocoa solids)
    chocolate
2 handfuls of
    cherries or fresh
    berries (optional)

1   Line a deep 20cm-diameter cake tin with a baking parchment cake liner.

2   Whisk the buckwheat flour, maple syrup, spices and salt in a large saucepan with half the water until smooth, then whisk in the rest of the water.

3   Cook on a medium heat for 5 minutes, stirring continuously so the mixture doesn't go lumpy, to make a very thick porridge. (You can always smooth out any lumps in a blender or using a hand-held stick blender.) Remove from the heat when the porridge is so stiff that you can stand your spoon up in it.

4   Stir in the coconut oil with the vanilla extract and 150g of the chocolate, broken into pieces, and mix in until melted, incorporated and smooth.

5   Spoon the mixture into the prepared tin, smoothing it to the edges. Use a damp spatula to smooth over the top.

6   Grate the remaining chocolate over the tart and chill before serving. Alternatively, chill the tart in the fridge while you melt the remaining chocolate in a bowl over a pan of gently simmering water (without letting the base of the bowl touch the water). Pour the melted chocolate over the cold tart, smooth with a spatula and allow to set in the fridge. Serve chilled, topped with cherries or fresh berries (if using).

TIPS

+ If using buckwheat groats, soak in double the volume of water overnight or for a minimum of 8 hours (page 341), then rinse and drain before blending in a food processor or blender with 500ml. Place in a saucepan with all the other ingredients and whisk together with the remaining 500ml water, as in step 2.

+ It's important to keep stirring the porridge as it cooks – we use a wooden spatula to stop it sticking to the bottom of the pan.

We've reduced the sweetness in our version of this classic French pudding to enjoy the natural sweetness of the plums. Baking in a very hot oven means it's ready in just 15 minutes, puffed up and beautifully browned. As well as a delicious dessert, served hot or cold, this makes a gorgeous and easy breakfast to feed guests or a quick and easy teatime treat – everyone loves it.

PLUM CLAFOUTIS

SERVES 6

Butter or coconut
   oil, for greasing
6 large ripe plums,
   halved and
   stones removed

FOR THE BATTER
50g ground
   almonds
1 tablespoon
   coconut flour
2 tablespoons
   maple syrup
3 eggs
200g full-fat organic
   double cream or
   coconut cream
   (see tip below)

1   Preheat the oven to fan 220°C/Gas mark 9 and grease a 23cm-diameter flan dish with butter or coconut oil.

2   Whizz all the batter ingredients together until smooth in a blender or food processor or whisk by hand in a bowl.

3   Pour the batter into the prepared flan dish and arrange the plums, cut side up, on top. If you can't fit them all in, neatly chop them to fit.

4   Bake in the oven for 15 minutes until risen and golden brown. Serve warm.

TIP

+   For coconut cream, scoop all the cream from the top of a chilled tin and make up the weight required using the coconut water left in the bottom of the tin, saving the rest of the water for smoothies.

VARIATION

+   For an extra-nutty taste, use ground walnuts or unsalted pistachios instead of the almonds. Vary the fruit by using berries or apricots.

Little banana ice-cream 'sandwiches' filled with peanut butter and coated in dark chocolate. Fun to make, these have become a new favourite with children and adults alike. Dip the whole of each sandwich in chocolate or just half and decorate the tops, if you like. We think these taste their best when they've had 10 minutes out of the freezer to soften slightly. Also delicious with almond or hazelnut butter or BBtella Spread (page 293).

FROZEN BANANA MAN BITES

MAKES ABOUT 16 SANDWICHES

2 large ripe bananas
5 tablespoons
    peanut butter
    (100% roasted
    nuts with only
    salt added)
100g dark (85%
    cocoa solids)
    chocolate,
    broken into
    squares

1   Line a baking tray with baking parchment.

2   Peel and slice the bananas into 5mm-thick rounds. Spoon a little peanut butter onto half the banana slices and top each with another slice to make a sandwich, before placing them on the prepared baking tray.

3   Place the tray in the freezer – set to fast freeze if you have the option – and leave for at least 15 minutes so that they start to set.

4   Meanwhile, melt the chocolate in a bowl set over a pan of gently simmering water (making sure that the bottom of the bowl does not touch the water). Remove from the heat and allow to cool slightly until just warm.

5   Using two forks, dip each semi-frozen sandwich into the melted chocolate, allowing any excess to drip off and working quickly so that the chocolate doesn't harden. Place each coated sandwich back on the lined tray and return to the freezer to freeze fully.

6   Store in a sealed container in the freezer and serve frozen.

VARIATION

+   Replace the peanut butter with a mixture of tahini and a little honey, to make this nut-free. Also try it with our BBtella (page 293).

From teatime to birthdays, everyone loves a carrot cake. With only a few tablespoons of maple syrup in the sponge, we rely on the carrots, raisins and spices to provide sweetness. We've kept the recipe simple, but feel free to add other flavourings – allspice and orange zest, or a splash of brandy. This cake is a delicious recipe for anyone trying H+H for the first time. For anyone with less of a sweet tooth, reduce the maple syrup and raisins right down for a more nutty bake. It's good without the frosting too, but if you want the frosting, remember to strain the yoghurt the night before; otherwise a blend of cream cheese or goat's curd with yoghurt works just as well. This cake would be equally delicious with chocolate avocado frosting (page 312), making it completely dairy-free, or use coconut yoghurt.

CARROT CAKE WITH HONEY YOGHURT 'CREAM CHEESE'

MAKES 1 LARGE CAKE OR TRAYBAKE

FOR THE CAKE

2 tablespoons coconut oil or butter, melted, plus extra for greasing
250g ground almonds
¼ teaspoon sea salt
¾ teaspoon bicarbonate of soda
1½ tablespoons ground cinnamon
¾ teaspoon freshly grated nutmeg
3 eggs
3½ tablespoons maple syrup
300g carrots (about 2 large carrots), grated
75–100g raisins
75g walnuts, plus extra to decorate

FOR THE FROSTING

500g full-fat probiotic yoghurt, strained for 24 hours (see tip opposite), or 200g full-fat cream cheese, quark or goat's curd mixed with 80g full-fat probiotic yoghurt
2½ tablespoons raw honey
½ teaspoon vanilla extract
A tiny pinch of sea salt (optional)

1 Preheat the oven to fan 180°C/Gas mark 6 and line the base of two 23cm-diameter cake tins (for a whole cake) or a 20cm x 40cm baking tin (for a traybake) and grease the sides with coconut oil or butter.

2 In a large bowl, combine the ground almonds with the salt, bicarbonate of soda, cinnamon and nutmeg.

3 In a separate bowl, beat the eggs with the maple syrup and melted coconut oil or butter, then stir in the carrots, raisins and walnuts before mixing with the dry ingredients in the large bowl.

4 Pour the batter into the prepared cake tins or tin, spreading it out evenly, and bake in the oven for 35 minutes until springy to the touch and golden brown on top. Remove from the oven and place the tins on a wire rack to cool.

5 While the cakes are cooling, make the frosting. Add the strained yoghurt or cream cheese/quark/goat's curd mixture to a bowl and mix in the honey and vanilla extract. Taste, adding a tiny pinch of salt if needed, then leave in the fridge until the cakes have cooled down completely. Remove the cakes from the tins.

6 Spread the cooled cakes with the frosting. (Or freeze the cakes until needed, defrost, then add the frosting to serve.) Place one round cake on top of the other (cut into 15 slices) or slice the traybake into 30 small squares. Crush the additional walnuts and sprinkle over to decorate.

+ If you're making yoghurt 'cream cheese', line a sieve with two pieces of kitchen paper and place over a bowl. Pour in the yoghurt, cover with a plate and leave to strain in the fridge for 24 hours or longer. When the yoghurt has strained and thickened, mix with the rest of the frosting ingredients in step 5

VARIATIONS

+ You can substitute the raisins and ground almonds for dried fruit and ground nuts of your choice.

+ For anyone with a nut allergy, use 'sun flour' in place of the ground almonds and substitute pumpkin seeds for the walnuts. To make 'sun flour', blend 250g sunflower seeds in a high-powered blender (for a fine flour) or a food processor (for a coarser texture). Pulse-blend the seeds and use a spatula to regularly move the mixture around so that you have a uniform crumb and avoid sunflower seed butter! Store in the fridge until needed. **NB:** The chlorophyll in sunflower seeds can react with bicarbonate of soda in this recipe, giving a green tint, but this doesn't affect the nutrients or flavour.

+ You can also substitute 3 x flaxseed eggs (page 17) for an egg-free version. Bake for 40 minutes in a single 23cm-diameter cake tin or half-size rectangular tin, as it won't rise as much.

Our dear friend Nicky makes the most delicious grain- and gluten-free cookies. They are free from refined sugars too, and contain no eggs, which makes these little treats ideal for vegans. Rich and chocolatey from the coconut oil and dark chocolate, they are so moreish we *had* to put them in this book – with Nicky's permission of course. Best enjoyed on a lazy afternoon over a cup of tea with a loved one. Bliss!

NICKY'S CHOCOLATE CHIP COOKIES

MAKES ABOUT 12 COOKIES

85g dark (85% cocoa solids) chocolate, broken into squares
200g ground almonds
½ teaspoon bicarbonate of soda
½ teaspoon sea salt
4 tablespoons coconut oil or butter, melted and cooled slightly
2½ tablespoons maple syrup
2 teaspoons vanilla extract

1 Preheat the oven to fan 180°C/Gas mark 6 and line a large baking sheet with baking parchment.

2 Wrap the chocolate squares in a clean tea towel or between two pieces of baking parchment and, using a rolling pin, bash into small chips.

3 In a large bowl, mix together the ground almonds, bicarbonate of soda and salt. Add the remaining ingredients except the chocolate chips and mix into a soft dough.

4 Scoop up pieces of the dough in your hands and shape into round cookies, each about 5cm wide. Place on the prepared baking sheet, well spaced apart, and push chocolate chips into the top and bottom of each cookie.

5 Bake in the oven for 12 minutes until golden brown. Remove from the oven and leave to cool on the baking sheet, on top of a wire rack, so that the cookies set. (They will still be soft when they first come out of the oven.) Eat warm or cold.

An inventive new way to make a simple apple taste like apple pie! You'll need a spiralizer to create this quick dessert, which also makes a fab topping for porridge or stuffing for pancakes (page 30). Eat it by itself or with a dollop of something creamy like yoghurt (full-fat probiotic or coconut) or our yoghurt 'cream cheese' frosting (page 300). Use the small noodle blade to make spaghetti-like strands, or try the ribbon blade for a beautiful variation (see photo on page 31). If you're using a green apple, you might want to add the lightest drizzle of honey to offset any tartness. Red apples look really pretty and are usually sweeter – try making pear spaghetti too!

APPLE SPAGHETTI

SERVES 3

90g flaked almonds
3 apples
¾ teaspoon ground
    cinnamon
1½ teaspoons
    vanilla extract

1 Toss the flaked almonds in a dry pan over a medium-high heat for 2–3 minutes until lightly toasted.

2 For each apple, line up the core in the spiralizer, using the small noodle blade, and spiralize.

3 Place the apple spaghetti in a bowl with the cinnamon, vanilla extract and toasted almonds and toss gently to serve.

TIPS

+ It's best to serve this straight away before the apples go brown.

+ If you don't have a spiralizer, you can grate the apples instead. This won't make apple spaghetti but it will taste just as good!

Unlike cacao, carob contains no caffeine, making it a great alternative for kids or those who are caffeine-sensitive. These delicious snacks with chunks of nuts, seeds and dried fruit have a malty chocolate taste and because they are caffeine-free they can be enjoyed as a snack or dessert later in the day. We like to use activated crispy nuts and seeds in this recipe to aid digestion (see the tip below and page 341). For speed you can also smooth the mixture into a tray lined with baking parchment, chill and slice into squares. We usually make a double batch because these keep well in the fridge or freezer, ready to go when you are.

CAROBY FRUIT AND NUT BALLS

MAKES ABOUT 18 BALLS

10 tablespoons carob powder (about 65g)

¼ teaspoon sea salt

3 tablespoons butter, softened, or coconut oil

1 tablespoon vanilla extract

2–3 tablespoons raw honey (to taste)

100g almonds, 'crispy activated' (see tip below)

100g peanuts or pecans, 'crispy activated' (see tip below)

50g sunflower seeds, 'crispy activated' (see tip below)

50g raisins, sultanas or dried cranberries

1 Line a baking tray with baking parchment.

2 Place all the ingredients in the small bowl of a food processor and pulse until roughly chopped.

3 Scoop up single tablespoonfuls of the mixture and shape into balls, then place on the prepared baking tray and chill in the fridge until set. Serve chilled. Store in an airtight container in the fridge or freeze until needed.

VARIATION

+ Substitute the carob with 6 tablespoons of cocoa powder and reduce the butter to 1 tablespoon.

TIPS

+ Soak the nuts and seeds in double the volume of water overnight or for a minimum of 8 hours, rinse and drain well and then dehydrate until crispy in a dehydrator, or in the oven set to low, for a minimum of 12 hours.

+ You could make this recipe using half carob powder and half cocoa powder. As well as being lower in caffeine, carob powder is naturally sweeter than cocoa powder, so if using cocoa in place of carob, check the sweetness and add a little more honey, if you need to.

Sweet, lemon-scented biscotti with sour cranberry pieces, these are perfect for a tea break – delicious with a Chicory Bullet with Cinnamon (page 327)! Dried cranberries are almost always sweetened in some way because they are such a sour fruit. Choose those sweetened with apple juice, rather than refined sugar, to retain the tartness needed in this recipe. Double-baked to make them super-crunchy, these biscotti keep well stored in an airtight container in the fridge and will become chewy after a few days. If you want to make them in advance, then you might as well double the recipe, freeze and defrost to serve. You can always re-bake in the oven to crisp them up again.

LEMON AND CRANBERRY BISCOTTI

MAKES ABOUT 14 BISCOTTI

150g ground
    almonds
1½ tablespoons
    coconut flour
¼ teaspoon sea salt
¼ teaspoon
    bicarbonate
    of soda
2 tablespoons
    maple syrup
1 tablespoon grated
    lemon zest (from
    about 2 lemons)
30g dried
    cranberries
    (sweetened
    with apple juice),
    sliced in half

1 Preheat the oven to fan 180°C/Gas mark 6 and line a baking sheet with baking parchment.

2 Place all the ingredients except the cranberries in a food processor and pulse until well mixed, or combine the dry ingredients in a bowl and mix in the rest of the ingredients using a fork. Collect together between your hands and compact to form a dough, then work in the cranberry pieces.

3 Split the dough into two, place on the baking sheet and roll each piece into a log about 10cm long and 3cm in diameter. Press down gently to flatten each log to 5cm wide so that the biscotti will be the right shape when you cut the log. Transfer to the prepared baking sheet and bake for 15 minutes. Remove from the oven and allow to cool for 1 hour.

4 Carefully slice each log into 15mm-thick biscotti at an angle and spread out, cut side up, onto a wire rack. Reduce the oven temperature to fan 140°C, gas mark 3 and bake for a further 12–15 minutes until golden on the edges.

5 Remove from the oven (they will still be soft) and allow to cool on the wire rack and become crispy. Store in a sealed container in the fridge.

VARIATIONS

+ You can substitute the cranberries
  with different dried fruits, such as
  raisins, remembering to adjust the
  amount of maple syrup as most dried
  fruits will be much sweeter than
  dried cranberries.

+ If you prefer biscuits with a chewier
  texture, make the dough into cookies
  instead. Roll the dough into balls,
  flatten/shape into rounds and bake
  once for 10–12 minutes until golden
  at the edges.

Everyone loves an all-American blueberry muffin! You'll love these all the more when you know they're packed with protein, good fats, whole fruit and very little sugar – just 2 tablespoons of maple syrup for six muffins. Coconut flour may seem expensive but it's very good value for money. Not only does it treble in size when combined with liquids, but it's more nutritious than other white flours and a good alternative for ground almonds – just bear in mind that you cannot substitute the same quantity of one for the other. Be sure to weigh your coconut flour accurately as a little more or a little less makes a massive difference to the end result. This batter tends to stick to the usual muffin liners, even if you grease them, so look for liners made from baking parchment for a perfect muffin. Delicious served warm as elevenses with a cup of tea.

BLUEBERRY MUFFINS

MAKES 6 MUFFINS

3 eggs
2 tablespoons
    butter or coconut
    oil, melted
2 tablespoons
    maple syrup
½ teaspoon
    vanilla extract
1 tablespoon apple
    cider vinegar
    or lemon juice
A pinch of sea salt
40g coconut flour
¼ teaspoon
    bicarbonate
    of soda
150–200g
    blueberries,
    rinsed and dried
    thoroughly

1   Preheat the oven to fan 200°C/Gas mark 7 and line a six-hole muffin tin with baking parchment liners or squares of baking parchment.

2   Add all the ingredients except the blueberries to a food processor and blend until smooth. Alternatively, beat the eggs in a large bowl, then stir in the melted butter or coconut oil with the maple syrup, vanilla extract, ACV or lemon juice and salt. Sift the coconut flour and bicarbonate of soda into the batter and fold in well to ensure there are no lumps.

3   Once blended, divide the runny batter between the paper liners in the tin, then distribute the blueberries evenly between the liners, pushing most of the berries down into the batter and leaving a few studding the top of each muffin for decoration.

4   Bake in the centre of the oven for 20 minutes until lightly golden at the edges, then remove from the oven and transfer to a wire rack to cool completely before serving.

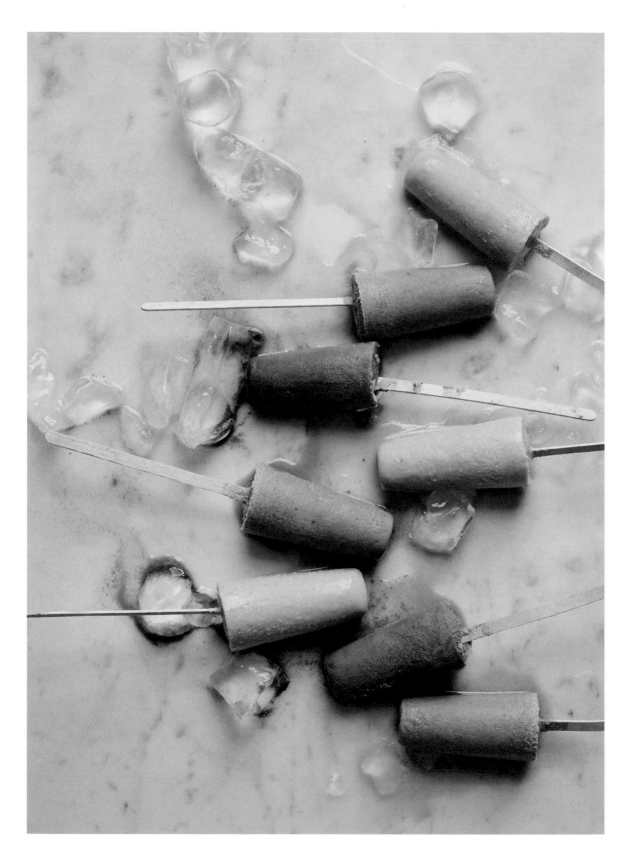

Aimed squarely at kids (though, let's face it, we'd all like one!), these creamy little lollies come in three classic flavours – vanilla, strawberry and chocolate. The lollies are on the sweet side, but the creamy coconut milk base means that they will still be delicious with less honey, so gradually reduce the amount you use until the mixture is just sweet enough; you can do the same with the cocoa powder too. To ensure the lollies are visually appealing, we've suggested adding turmeric to boost the colour of the vanilla version, and beetroot to make the strawberry one a brighter pink. Both of these additions are also good for you, but not necessary if the kids enjoy the ice-cream lollies just as they are.

MINI MYLKS

**MAKES 9 LOLLIES
(3 OF EACH FLAVOUR)**

1 x 400ml tin
  of full-fat
  coconut milk
A pinch of sea salt

FOR VANILLA
½ small banana,
  peeled
1 teaspoon
  vanilla extract
1½ teaspoons
  raw honey
A pinch of ground
  turmeric
  (optional)

**FOR
STRAWBERRY**
2 tablespoons sugar-
  free strawberry
  jam (lightly
  sweetened with
  apple juice)
¼ teaspoon
  vanilla extract
Raw honey (to taste)

A pinch of beetroot
  powder or
  scrape a sharp
  knife against the
  cut side of a raw
  beetroot to get a
  few drops of
  colour (optional)

FOR CHOCOLATE
1 teaspoon cocoa
  powder
½ teaspoon vanilla
  extract
¾ tablespoon
  raw honey

1 Whizz the coconut milk and salt in a blender until well mixed then pour 300ml of the milk into a measuring jug to reserve.

2 Add the ingredients for the vanilla flavouring to the remaining 100ml of coconut milk in the blender and blend until smooth. Distribute equally between three lolly moulds.

3 Pour 150ml of the reserved coconut milk into the blender (no need to wash it first!) and add the ingredients for the strawberry flavouring. Blend until smooth and then distribute equally between three more lolly moulds.

4 Pour the remaining coconut milk into the blender (no need to wash it!) and add the ingredients for the chocolate flavouring. Blend until smooth and then distribute equally between three more lolly moulds.

5 Freeze the lollies for 5 minutes or until they start to stiffen, then add the lolly sticks to each mould and freeze again until solid.

6 Store in the freezer and remove one whenever you like, briefly running warm water over the mould to help release the lolly.

TIP

+ In cold weather, you might need to gently warm the coconut milk through first in a pan to melt the fat, which may have separated and solidified in the tin.

Just like our Paradise Bars from *The Art of Eating Well*, this cake is a unanimous favourite with our clients – so much so that we are repeatedly asked to share the recipe. So here it is! This simple recipe is great, just add fresh raspberries, and candles if you wish, and bam! This cake is just sweet enough; it's also nut-free and as light as a wholefood sponge can possibly be. The chocolate frosting is wonderfully creamy thanks to the avocado. Swap the avocados for banana if avocados are out of season; or go half and half to save money. Just like the rest of our desserts, a little goes a long way, so slice on the small side and enjoy!

CANNELLINI VANILLA SPONGE CAKE WITH CHOCOLATE AVO FROSTING

SERVES 25–30

FOR THE CAKE
125g butter or coconut oil, melted, plus extra for greasing
3 x 400g tins of cannellini beans, drained and rinsed
9 medium eggs
1 tablespoon vanilla extract
220ml maple syrup
5 teaspoons apple cider vinegar or lemon juice
90g coconut flour
2½ teaspoons bicarbonate of soda
¼ teaspoon sea salt
150g punnet of fresh raspberries, to decorate

FOR THE CHOCOLATE AVO FROSTING
4 medium ripe avocados
5 tablespoons (about 75g) coconut oil, melted
8 tablespoons raw honey (to taste)
10 tablespoons cocoa powder
1 tablespoon vanilla extract
2 tablespoons lemon juice
½ teaspoon orange extract (not essence)
A pinch of sea salt

1. Preheat the oven to fan 180°C/Gas mark 6, then line the bases of two 25cm-diameter cake tins with baking parchment and grease the sides with butter or coconut oil.

2. Blend all the ingredients for the frosting together in a food processor until smooth, adding a dash of cold water if needed. Taste, adjusting the flavourings to taste, then transfer to a bowl and set aside in the fridge.

3. For the cake, add the cannellini beans to the cleaned food processor bowl with the eggs, vanilla extract and maple syrup and blend until smooth. Add the remaining cake ingredients, except the raspberries, and blend to combine.

4. Divide the cake batter between the prepared cake tins, spreading out evenly and smoothing the surface. Bake in the oven for 35 minutes until well risen and lightly golden on top. (Check the cakes after 25 minutes and swap the tins between shelves, if necessary, as they will cook at different rates.)

5. Remove from the oven, transfer to a wire rack and allow to cool completely in the tins before turning out.

6. While the cakes are cooling, gently wash the raspberries and dry them carefully using kitchen paper or leave to air dry. (They must be thoroughly dry before adding to the cake.)

7. Spread half the frosting on one of the cooled sponges, top with the other sponge and spread over the rest of the frosting. Store in the fridge and bring to room temperature to serve. Decorate with the fresh raspberries just before serving.

DRINKS

**FOR MORE DRINKS
IDEAS TRY:**

BONE BROTH
63

We have something for every occasion here, from refreshing wake-up breakfast lifts, such as the Ginger Zinger Smoothie (page 324) or Berry Brain Booster (page 325), to soothing brews like Salabat (page 329) for later in the day. As for hot chocolate, we've got a naturally caffeine-free version that uses carob and lavender to send you off for a good night's sleep (page 328), and if you're looking to cut down on or avoid coffee, we recommend the Chicory Bullet with Cinnamon (page 327) for a pick-me-up.

When it comes to alcohol, be selective and look for the 'better than' choices. Try organic and biodynamic wines, for example, to avoid unwanted tannins and sulphites. Steer clear of sugary sodas and juices in your cocktails too. They increase the likelihood of your getting a hangover and all that sugar will leave you with a sweeter tooth than you started with. For a healthier cocktail, nothing can beat our Beetroot Bloody Mary (page 332): full of goodness but still packing a punch!

Making sure you're well hydrated is key to curbing cravings, easing headaches and avoiding energy slumps, so for those who find drinking water a chore, make it more appealing by adding slices of citrus fruit, ribbons of cucumber or sprigs of fresh mint or rosemary to a glass jug of water to infuse. A decorative jug like this makes a beautiful table centrepiece. If you find that cutting out that takeaway coffee or your favourite fizzy drink leaves you with a hole in your life that herbal tea bags just don't fill, then a refreshing, vitamin-rich homemade juice is for you.

Juices are a wonderful way to pack in more veg, especially for those who don't always relish the thought of sitting down to a bowl of greens. Play around with the flavour until you're happy – adding a little extra fruit if you are still working on that sweet tooth. Over time, as your taste buds adapt, you can introduce more greens and reduce the fruit – just a little bit of apple will be all that's needed to make them taste delicious – and you can start upping the parsley, coriander, ginger and turmeric.

A well-balanced smoothie is a meal in itself and, done right, one for breakfast will keep you full until lunchtime. They're a great quick way to get greens, essential fats and proteins in at the start of the day – and all under the guise of something creamy and delicious! The combinations are endless, too: if you run out of coconut oil but have some coconut milk left over from a recipe, add that, or swap almonds for cashews or add a scoop of tahini.

Ideally, we would make fresh juices and smoothies daily and drink them immediately, but when we've gone to the effort of making one in the first place, we'd rather make double and store one half in the fridge for the next day. Just remember that they are not an overall substitute for food, so drink responsibly!

TIPS AND TRICKS

KEEP COLD OR FREEZE Smoothies and juices will keep for 48 hours in the fridge (72 hours max). You can always freeze them in portions (allowing 2.5cm space in the container for expansion). Make sure they come to room temperature first before drinking, as ice-cold drinks shock the system and disrupt digestion.

ON THE MOVE Store your juice or smoothie in a stainless-steel flask or glass jar (we love jam jars!) for short journeys. Combine with a cool bag and freezer block or even freeze before transporting for longer journeys. Vacuum flasks are also useful for keeping drinks cold. Just chill your fresh juice or smoothie in the flask before transporting.

CHECK DRINKS LABELS When you are out and about, read drinks labels very carefully. Look for organic, cold-pressed, unpasteurised juices, and choose freshly made smoothies with no added sugar, limited fruit and a good balance of fats, such as nuts, avocado or coconut milk.

KEEPING EVERYONE HAPPY If you're making them for the whole family or for people new to greens in juices or smoothies, pour out your portion first with the amount of greens you like, then add more fruit to the remaining drinks, mix and blend again.

BLENDING SMOOTHIES You'll need a high-powered blender for a quick and (completely) smooth result. We've included tips to suggest how to adapt each recipe if you're using a food processor instead. Don't leave the motor on the blender running when you're making smoothies. Blending too long will begin to heat up the smoothie and can damage the nutrients.

Use a tamper, if your blender has one, to keep the mixture moving while it blends, or switch the machine off at regular intervals (or use the pulse button) and use a spatula to push down the sides.

SOAK IT Remember to soak whole nuts and seeds where appropriate (page 341). We soak them in the blender overnight, then rinse, drain and add the other ingredients to blend the next morning.

JUICING Although you can store juices (see above left), we like to drink one portion of juice immediately to ensure we get the best from the ingredients right away. Cold pressing is best for nutrient preservation, but these machines are more expensive, slightly slower and more fiddly to clean. If this puts you off, a centrifugal juicer is your best bet.

ALTERNATE HARD AND SOFT Remember when juicing to put leaves and soft vegetables between harder fruit and vegetables to get the most from them, such as sandwiching mint between two pieces of celery.

PASS THE PULP If the pulp left over from juicing is still damp, you can re-juice it. Leftover pulp can be used to bulk out stews, soups and even baking!

SPACE YOUR DRINKS Just as with alcoholic drinks, don't down juices and smoothies too quickly too close to meals. It's important to 'chew' your drinks – not just to experience their flavour and texture but to help digestion, maximise what you get from them and to avoid flooding your stomach.

GINGER AID

This vibrant green summer drink is soothing on the digestive system and refreshing on the taste buds, making it the perfect accompaniment to a barbecue feast, or whenever you feel you have overindulged. Think of it as the hot-weather version of Salabat (page 329). This sparkling drink makes a lovely mocktail at dinner parties, or add a splash of your favourite spirit to take it up a level. Make sure to juice the mint leaves with the apples, sandwiching them between two pieces of apple, to ensure you get the most from them, especially if using a centrifugal juicer.

SERVES 5 (250ML EACH)

4 green apples
1 small handful
   of mint leaves
   (about 15g)
70g (8cm piece)
   fresh root ginger
   (unpeeled if
   organic)

1 litre sparkling
   water
1 handful of frozen
   berries, to serve

1   Wash the apples, mint and ginger, then chop the apples to fit your juicer. Juice the mint leaves between the harder apples and ginger.

2   Pour into a large jug with the sparkling water and mix together. Add the frozen berries, just before serving, as colourful ice cubes.

REHYDRATE MATE

After a workout it's easy to turn to sugar-laden 'sports drinks' for a quick recovery. With a good diet and plenty of water, most of us can stay properly hydrated and recover from sweating in the gym without having recourse to such drinks. For those times when you want more than just plain water, however, try our favourite recovery drink, made with revivifying coconut water, citrus fruits and Himalayan salt (which contains the same 84 trace minerals and elements found in our bodies) or a good sea salt. If you have had a particularly hard workout, you could also add a scoop of protein powder, or sip a mug of hot Bone Broth (page 63) as the ultimate recovery drink.

SERVES 2 (500ML EACH)

1 litre coconut
   water (with no
   added sugar
   or other
   ingredients,
   preferably raw
   /unpasteurised)

Juice of 1 lemon
   and 1 lime
¼ teaspoon
   Himalayan salt
   or sea salt

1   Combine the coconut water with the lemon and lime juices and add the salt.

2   Mix together or shake thoroughly before drinking.

TUMMY TONIC

Don't let the sound of this put you off! Team it with the zingy flavours of ginger (proven to be effective in combating symptoms of gastrointestinal distress and nausea) and sweetness from apples and carrots and you have a powerful anti-inflammatory – and that makes one mighty tummy tonic!

SERVES 1 (300ML)

10g (3cm piece)
    fresh root ginger
    (unpeeled if
    organic)
¼ small cabbage
    (about 150g)

1–2 green apples
2 medium carrots
    (about 200g)

1   Wash all the ingredients and chop to fit your juicer.

2   Juice everything together and pour into a glass to serve.

PURE PINK LIVER CLEANSE

This juice is a real pick-me-up, perfect if you are feeling under the weather or struggling after the night before. Fresh beetroot is a powerful cleanser and helps to support liver function. In modern life, the liver can often get overwhelmed and toxins can build up, so it's good to give it a helping hand whenever possible. The celery, carrot and cucumber add to the nutrients, helping you feel energised, while your immune system will get a boost from the antibacterial and antiviral properties of basil, parsley and the optional garlic. If you do add the garlic, be sure to save a sprig of parsley to chew on afterwards as it may not be only vampires who try to avoid you!

SERVES 1 (300ML)

1 large carrot
    (about 150g)
2 celery sticks
    (about 80g)
1 medium beetroot
    (about 120g)
½ large cucumber
    (about 150g)

1 small handful
    of fresh parsley
    (15g), leaves
    and stalks
1 small handful of
    fresh basil (15g),
    leaves and stalks
1 garlic clove
    (optional)

1   Wash all the ingredients and chop the vegetables to fit your juicer, placing the leaves/herbs between the harder veg.

2   Juice all the ingredients together, stir well and drink immediately.

DRINK YOUR GREENS

This is an everyday favourite as the ingredients are available all year round. Celery and parsley are known detoxifiers and we love their taste. Use mint instead of the parsley, for a sweeter taste, and if you're just starting out, add as much or as little apple as you need to make the juice more palatable. Once you've got used to the bracing flavour, up the vegetables and reduce the apple and play around with the herbs and greens you use.

SERVES 4 (300ML EACH)

1 lemon (unpeeled if organic)
12 celery sticks (2 bunches)
2 large cucumbers
100g (12cm piece) fresh root ginger (unpeeled if organic)
1–2 green apples (optional)
1 large handful of fresh parsley (leaves and stalks) or fresh mint leaves (30g)

1   Wash all the ingredients and chop the fruit, vegetables and ginger to fit your juicer, placing the leaves/herbs between the harder veg.

2   Juice all the ingredients together and stir well before drinking.

TIP

+   Don't throw away the celery leaves: juice them too or save and put into salads, or packed lunches. Since a juicer removes all the tough bits, you don't need to trim celery at all except to remove any bits that have gone brown.

HEMSLEY GREEN MACHINE

This smoothie is one of our favourites for getting revved up, ready to tackle the day. It's a filling powerhouse of nutrients, with anti-inflammatory turmeric, iron-rich spinach and creamy fats, in the form of avocado and coconut oil. Mint boosts the flavour as well as the digestive effects. If you're not drinking the smoothie straight away, add another 100ml water, as the chia seeds or flaxseeds will thicken the smoothie over time.

SERVES 2 (400ML EACH)

1 ripe avocado (or ½ avocado and ½ banana)
2 large handfuls of fresh or frozen spinach (no need to defrost) or kale (stems removed)
10 fresh mint leaves
1 teaspoon ground turmeric
1 tablespoon chia or flaxseeds
1 tablespoon coconut oil
2 tablespoons lemon juice
700ml water

1   Place all the ingredients in a high-powered blender and blend until smooth. Pour into glasses to serve.

TIP

+   If blending in a food processor, use ground chia or flaxseed, and spinach instead of kale.

A great starter smoothie for people who are new to the 'green' smoothie. We love avocados but bananas help offset the bitterness of the spinach, so for those still getting used to the taste of veg in drinks, it's ideal. We chop up very ripe, peeled bananas (you can often get a good deal on them) and freeze, which makes our breakfast smoothie that much easier and quicker – and gives it a cool texture that will feel more like a commercial smoothie. (Just don't forget to warm it in your mouth before swallowing.) This one's great for breakfast: it injects a big dose of healthy greens, rejuvenates with immune-boosting lemon and ginger, adds coconut oil for energy and maca for stamina, helping you to power through the day!

GINGER ZINGER SMOOTHIE

SERVES 2 (400ML EACH)

1 small ripe avocado
   or 1 small banana
200g fresh or frozen
   spinach (no need
   to defrost)
50g (6cm piece)
   fresh root ginger
   (unpeeled if
   organic)
4 celery sticks
1½ tablespoons
   coconut oil
2 teaspoons
   chia seeds
   or flaxseeds
2 tablespoons maca
   powder (optional)
Juice of
   1 small lemon
600ml water

1   Peel the avocado or banana, removing the avocado stone, then place in a high-powered blender with all the other ingredients and blend until smooth. Pour into glasses to serve.

TIPS

+   If blending in a food processor, use ground chia or flaxseed, grate in the ginger and replace the celery with handfuls of watercress or more spinach.

+   If you're not drinking the smoothie straight away, add another 100ml water, as the chia seeds or flaxseeds will thicken the smoothie over time.

This smoothie was created to keep the body topped up with vital vitamins and minerals and the brain firing and focused. Berries may be small but they pack a powerful nutritional punch. Feel free to mix up the varieties you use, as different coloured ones offer different phytochemicals and hence differing health benefits. Fresh berries can be expensive, but we try to buy them when they are in season and cheaper, and then freeze in portions. In this smoothie we use Brazil nuts, not just to give a creamy texture but to provide a detoxifying selenium boost. They're also great for a last-minute smoothie as they don't require pre-soaking. For a final hit of goodness, we add flaxseeds, rich in omega-3 fatty acids, and coconut oil to give a sustained release of energy and balance the sugars in the fruit.

BERRY BRAIN BOOSTER

SERVES 2 (400ML EACH)

150g fresh or frozen blueberries (no need to defrost)
200g fresh or frozen strawberries (no need to defrost)
25g Brazil nuts (about 8) or 1½ tablespoons almond butter
1½ teaspoons coconut oil

5 tablespoons full-fat probiotic yoghurt
1 tablespoon flaxseeds or chia seeds
1 teaspoon ground cinnamon
A good pinch of sea salt
400ml water

1 Add all the ingredients to a high-powered blender and blend until smooth. Pour into glasses to serve.

VARIATIONS

+ You can substitute the Brazils for cashews, almonds or macadamia nuts, or use different nut butters.

+ For a dairy-free option, leave out the yoghurt or use coconut yoghurt instead.

TIPS

+ If blending in a food processor, use almond butter and ground chia or flaxseed.

+ If you're not planning on drinking your smoothie straight away, it may thicken up, so a quick stir or blast in the blender will sort that out. Alternatively, let the smoothie set for a few hours in the fridge to enjoy it as a chilled, creamy pudding!

If you rely a little too heavily on that morning cup of joe, then this is the recipe for you. Ground chicory has a rich, nutty, bitter flavour which will make weaning yourself off coffee that little bit easier. This caffeine-free alternative is far better for you than drinking standard 'decaf' which, unless Swiss water-filtered, can contain up to 30 per cent caffeine as well as chemicals from the decaffeination process. Add your favourite milk to make it creamy, or drink it black if you like, but definitely try this Chicory Bullet – our take on a 'Bulletproof Coffee', which is prepared with a hint of coconut oil and grass-fed butter or ghee to reduce the consequential energy crash that a caffeine-hit induces. It's also a great way to get some good fats in, so we've adopted the technique for our morning hot mug of chicory, for the sustained boost of energy you won't get from coffee.

CHICORY BULLET WITH CINNAMON

SERVES 2 (250ML EACH)

2 tablespoons
    ground chicory
    or Swiss water-
    filtered
    decaffeinated
    coffee (see
    recipe intro)
½ teaspoon ground
    cinnamon
½ teaspoon vanilla
    extract (optional)
1 tablespoon
    coconut oil
    or butter or
    2 teaspoons
    ghee
500ml just-boiled
    water
Milk or almond
    milk, to serve
    (optional)

1   Add the chicory or coffee to a cafetière with the cinnamon, vanilla extract (if using) and coconut oil, butter or ghee. Top with the just-boiled water and leave to brew for 5 minutes.

2   Pour into mugs and stir, adding milk or almond milk, if desired, for a creamy bullet. The oil will rise to the surface unless properly mixed, making the drink very hot, so be careful when taking the first few sips.

Sipping this blissful bedtime hug in a mug is going to set you up for sweet dreams. Lavender has been used for years to help people relax and unwind. Carob adds a chocolatey maltiness, while being naturally free of stimulating caffeine, and the coconut milk supplies satiating good fats to stave off any late-night hunger pangs. If you find the coconut milk too rich, you can always use almond milk or half and half instead. Dried lavender is easy to find but this is just as delicious without, and cocoa powder makes a good substitute for the carob during the day – just remember that carob isn't as bitter as cocoa powder so you'll need to add a little more maple syrup.

LAVENDER AND CAROB BEDTIME 'HOT CHOCOLATE'

SERVES 2 (250ML EACH)

1½–2 tablespoons
    carob or cocoa
    powder
½ teaspoon dried
    culinary lavender
½ teaspoon
    vanilla extract
½ tablespoon
    maple syrup
A pinch of sea salt
1 x 400ml tin of
    full-fat coconut
    milk or use
    almond milk
100ml water

1   Over a medium heat, whisk all the ingredients together in a small saucepan until the carob or cocoa powder has dissolved and the mixture is smooth.

2   Continue whisking the mixture, letting it simmer very gently for a couple of minutes to infuse the lavender.

3   Remove from the heat, let it cool slightly and pour into mugs. You can strain it if you want to, but we quite like having the lavender in the mug.

There is no need for cough syrup or central heating with this strong ginger and lemon concoction! Our recipe is based on the traditional Salabat tea from the Philippines that our mum and aunties would make us drink to ward off colds and flu. We really simmer the ginger for maximum effect and include the lemon peel too. It's fantastic as a general pick-me-up or after-dinner digestif, and if it's a cold we're busting then we allow it to cool down and swirl in some raw honey for its antibacterial and antiviral properties – manuka would be a great choice here. Served hot or chilled, this is a spicy, soothing tea to nourish your body and lift your mood at any time of day.

SALABAT

SERVES 4 (200ML EACH)

1–2 lemons
750ml water
120g (14cm piece)
    fresh root ginger
    (unpeeled if
    organic), sliced
1 tablespoon raw
    honey (optional)

1 Juice the lemons and set aside. Slice up the leftover peel and bring to the boil in a large saucepan with the water and ginger.

2 Reduce the heat, cover and simmer gently for about 10 minutes, topping up with more water if necessary.

3 Strain the tea into a pot or mugs and allow to cool slightly. When at drinking temperature, add the lemon juice and sweeten with a little honey if desired.

TIP

+ Refill the pan of lemon peel and ginger and simmer again for a weaker tea that's still good.

A rich, jewel-coloured cocktail, this is a real show-stopper that will tantalise the taste buds and pep up even the most retiring wallflower at a party. Made from beetroot and celery juice – as delicious and uplifting as a cleansing juice, minus the vodka of course!

BEETROOT BLOODY MARY

MAKES ABOUT 800ML
SERVES 4 (200ML EACH)

4 medium beetroots
4 celery sticks, plus
    extra (optional)
    to garnish
1 lemon (unpeeled
    if organic)
2 limes (unpeeled
    if organic)
2 teaspoons (peeled)
    grated fresh
    horseradish
    (see tips below)
1/8 teaspoon cayenne
    pepper, or a dash
    of Tabasco sauce
1/4 teaspoon
    Himalayan salt
    or sea salt
1/8 teaspoon white
    pepper
100ml vodka
150ml water
Ice cubes, to serve

OPTIONAL
EXTRAS
Splash of port
Dash of
    Worcestershire
    sauce
Splash of
    sauerkraut or
    pickle juice
Pitted olives,
    pickles, sprigs
    of fresh herbs,
    celery stick,
    to garnish

1   Wash the beetroots, celery and citrus fruits and chop to fit your juicer. Juice together, then add to a large jug with the rest of the ingredients except the ice. Add any optional extras and stir to evenly combine.

2   Serve in tall glasses over ice and garnish to your heart's delight – anything goes!

TIPS

+   If you can't find fresh horseradish use a teaspoon or more of horseradish in a jar, to taste.

+   Serve as a mocktail – it's so hearty you won't miss the vodka.

This quick cocktail is based on the 'Tom Collins' – a traditional London tipple consisting of gin and lemonade. It is an alcoholic favourite of ours when catering or hosting events. Light and refreshing with a bit of kick, it's perfect to get your party off to a flyer. If you have a gluten intolerance, make sure you buy potato-based vodka as opposed to wheat-based. Choose naturally sparkling water, as opposed to carbonated natural water, for a better taste and the mineral goodness that comes with it.

HEMSLEY COLLINS

**SERVES 2
(ABOUT 85ML EACH)**

50ml vodka
40ml lemon juice
20ml raw honey
   (runny)
75ml sparkling
   water
Ice cubes, to serve

1 Mix together the vodka, lemon juice and honey, or shake together in a cocktail shaker.

2 Pour into ice-filled glasses in equal measure, top with the sparkling water, stir and serve.

PLANNING AHEAD

Everything is easier with a plan! At the front of the book we included our one-week reboot plan to set you on your way (page 21). Here we share steps for our Sunday Cook-Off and outline two of our favourite weekly menus for eating well. Don't worry if you can't follow the plans to the letter; just adapt them to work for you. Eating well for life should be simple and flexible.

SUNDAY COOK-OFF

The Sunday Cook-Off is your chance to plan and prepare key ingredients and make snacks and meals to set you up for the week. While you're preparing your Sunday lunch or supper, make full use of the hot oven and any spare shelf space to cook up vegetables for future meals, being more time- and energy-efficient. If you're having a roast on Sunday, use the bones to make broth and turn any leftover meat and veg into a packed lunch or weeknight supper. You'll feel better prepared and ready to face Monday morning mayhem.

The most useful things to do ahead of time are soaking and/or cooking quinoa, making broth, soup or a stew, and blending dressings. Of course, the Cook-Off doesn't have to be restricted to Sundays – we all have different schedules so find the time for a Cook-Off that suits you and your family best.

As you get into the swing of things you can gear your weekly shop or weekend farmers market visit towards your Sunday Cook-Off – and even start activating ingredients the day before. In the menu plans on the following pages we give suggested Sunday Cook-Offs to help make things more manageable but these are just suggestions – do what's best for you.

TWO WEEKLY MENU PLANS

Use the following weekly menus on rotation, if you like, so that planning, shopping and cooking meals for you (and your family) is as fuss-free as possible.

We've chosen some of the easiest recipes in the book, most can be made ahead and many will provide leftovers to either use up later in the week or freeze for a future date. Both plans work for **two hungry adults**. If you are cooking for one, either halve the quantities in the shopping list and recipes or follow the plans and freeze the extra food for another week.

Don't forget that it's not just soups and stews that make a great hot lunch. Use your thermos to pack other leftover suppers, such as Chinese-style Beef and Broccoli (page 212) or Chicken Comfort Pie (page 191), too. Just don't forget to reheat them first! And if you end up going out for dinner, turn the meal you've made into tomorrow's lunch or freeze it ready for another day.

Make sure your shopping is in by Saturday evening then use the Sunday Cook-Offs to help you get ahead for the week. Note: the following shopping lists are designed for those starting from scratch – use up what you have in your cupboards first if you already have some of these ingredients.

SHOPPING LISTS

WEEK 1

Fresh fruit/veg
mushrooms (50g)
cherry tomatoes (50g)
asparagus (50g)
2 medium cabbages
/pak choi
2 heads broccoli
broccoli/purple
sprouting broccoli
/asparagus/green
beans (300g)
1 bulb fennel
1 cucumber
8 spring onions
kale (300g)
watercress (300g)
baby spinach (100g)
and 200g fresh
/frozen spinach
2 bunches celery
1 celeriac/2 small
swedes/2 turnips
3 medium courgettes
1 red pepper
10 large carrots
8 onions
4 bulbs garlic
5 lemons
3 avocados
250g fresh/frozen
berries

Fresh herbs/spices
1 large piece ginger
1 small bunch parsley
/thyme/rosemary
1 bunch basil
1 large bunch
coriander and
1 large bunch
coriander
/mint/basil

Dairy/meat
1 small pot coconut
yoghurt/full-fat
probiotic yoghurt
1 small block
Parmesan
5 medium eggs
1.8kg whole chicken
500g minced beef
250g onglet steak
2 x 300g salmon fillets
4 rashers unsmoked
bacon
3kg beef/lamb bones
/chicken carcass

Dried herbs/spices
1 jar each of ground
cinnamon; ground
turmeric; chilli
powder; dried
thyme; dried
oregano; dried
basil; cayenne
pepper; sweet
smoked paprika;
Chinese five-spice
powder; caraway
/fennel seeds;
garlic powder
1 pack bay leaves
sea salt
black pepper
/ peppercorns
1 bottle vanilla extract

Nuts/seeds
/dried fruit
chia seeds (150g)
black sesame
seeds (30g)
small packet mixed
nuts or seeds

Bottles/jars/tins
200g coconut oil
/butter/ghee
buckwheat/soba
noodles (300g)
dried red lentils (500g)
2 x 400ml tins
coconut milk
quinoa (300g)
chestnut flour (100g)
coconut flour (1 tbsp)
6 anchovies/8 pitted
olives in oil
capers in brine (1 tbsp)
1 tube tomato puree
3 x 400g tins tomatoes
1 x 400g tin cannellini
/butter beans
1 x 400g tin chickpeas
quality miso paste
(1 tbsp)
1 jar raw honey
1 bottle each of maple
syrup; ACV; tamari;
fish sauce; EVOO;
toasted sesame oil
bicarbonate of soda

WEEK 2

Fresh fruit/veg
small bag green
salad leaves
5 lemons
3 limes
2 large bananas
2 apples
kale (about 50g)
4 spring onions
14 onions
1 red onion
6 bulbs garlic
3 red peppers
2 romano peppers
1 bunch celery
1 celeriac (600g)
1 leek
7 large carrots
5 medium courgettes
3 heads cauliflower
1 head broccoli
1 red chilli
1 bulb fennel
200g green beans
250g mushrooms
mixed root veg
(beetroot/swede
/celeriac/squash,
about 600g)
1 large butternut
squash
spinach (about 300g)
and spinach/chard
(about 200g)
3 avocados
watercress (50g)

Frozen veg
frozen peas (100g)

Fresh herbs/spices
1 large piece ginger
1 small bunch mint
1 very large bunch
parsley
1 very large bunch
coriander
1 small handful thyme
1 small handful
oregano
4 lemongrass stalks
2 kaffir lime leaves

Dairy/meat
1 small pot coconut
yoghurt or full-fat
probiotic yoghurt
1 small block Cheddar
1 block feta
1 block Parmesan
250g ricotta
20 medium eggs
1.7kg chicken thighs
3kg beef/lamb bones
/chicken carcass
350g white fish fillets
6 rashers
unsmoked bacon
1 handful chicken
livers (optional)
8 medium sausages
(at least 97% meat
content)

Dried herbs/spices
1 jar each of ground
turmeric; ground
cinnamon; oregano;
ground cumin;
ground coriander;
sweet smoked
paprika; chilli flakes
garam masala or
medium curry
powder (2 tsps)
1 pack bay leaves
sea salt
black pepper
/peppercorns

1 small bottle
vanilla extract

Nuts/seeds
/dried fruit
chia /flaxseeds (1 tbsp)
ground flaxseeds
(250g)
white sesame seeds
(1 tbsp)
raisins (160g)
4 dried pitted dates

Bottles/jars/tins
300g coconut oil
/butter/ghee
hazelnut butter (100g)
coconut flour (4 tbsp)
quinoa (700g)
bicarbonate of soda
make sure you have
plenty of: maple
syrup; ACV; tamari;
fish sauce; EVOO;
flaxseed oil and
raw honey
cocoa powder (40g)
English mustard
/powder (2 tsps)
1 tube of tomato puree
8 pitted olives in oil
sundried tomatoes
in oil (120g)
6 x 400g tins tomatoes
3 x 400g tins
cannellini beans
3 x 400ml tins
coconut milk
1 x 400g tin
black beans

Note: shopping lists
do not include snacks
so pick what you
fancy from the menu
plans (overleaf) and
add the ingredients
you need to your
shopping basket in
addition to what is
listed here.

MENU PLAN 1

	BREAKFAST	LUNCH	DINNER
SUNDAY	One Pan Full Monty Breakfast (page 46)	Slow-cooked Chicken Pot Roast with Sweet Paprika and Cayenne (page 185)	Green Goddess Noodle Salad (page 250) *Soak 300g quinoa in the morning (page 341). Make Chia pudding and Quinoa Courgette Toast in the evening (pages 39 and 32). Put Bone Broth on overnight (page 63).*
MONDAY	Berry and Coconut Chia Pudding	Leftover Green Goddess Noodle Salad	Cream of Tomato Soup (page 85)
TUESDAY	Leftover Berry and Coconut Chia Pudding	Chicken and Sesame Noodle Pot (page 76) *using leftover meat from Chicken Pot Roast*	Quick Coconut Dahl with Zingy Slaw (page 78)
WEDNESDAY	Quinoa Courgette Toast (with your choice of topping)	Leftover Quick Coconut Dahl with Zingy Slaw	Courgetti with Quick Chickpea Tomato Sauce (page 229)
THURSDAY	Leftover Quinoa Courgette Toast	Leftover Cream of Tomato Soup	Chinese-style Beef and Broccoli (page 212)
FRIDAY	Ginger Zinger Smoothie (page 324)	Leftover Chinese-style Beef and Broccoli	Leftover Quick Coconut Dahl with Zingy Slaw
SATURDAY	Chestnut Pancakes (with your choice of filling, page 30)	Powerhouse Steak and Kale Salad (page 219)	Spicy Miso Salmon with Broccoli Rice (page 170)

SNACK IDEAS:

A slice of Quinoa Courgette Toast, Bone Broth with miso stirred in, a Ginger Zinger Smoothie, Nicky's Chocolate Chip Cookies (page 302), a boiled egg and some leftover Chickpea Tomato Sauce, Tummy Tonic Juice (page 321), Sri Lankan Squash Croquettes (page 98) or leftover Chestnut Pancakes with a sweet or savoury filling.

MENU PLAN 2

	BREAKFAST	LUNCH	DINNER	SNACK IDEAS:
SUNDAY	Apple and Bacon Muffins (page 118)	Chicken Comfort Pie with green salad (page 191)	Moroccan Meditation Stew (page 72) *Put Bone Broth on in the morning and soak 700g quinoa (page 63 and 341). You could make a batch of Flaxseed Buns today too, if you have time (page 136).*	Tahini Date Fridge Fudge (page 287), leftover Apple and Bacon Muffins, leftover Cinnamon, Raisin and Quinoa Breakfast Muffins, Caroby Fruit and Nut Balls (page 305), Blueberry Muffins (page 308), Multiseed Crackers spread with butter or coconut oil (page 127), Drink Your Greens juice (page 323) or crudités with Spicy Turmeric and Red Lentil Dip (page 269).
MONDAY	Hemsley Green Machine (page 323)	Leftover Chicken Comfort Pie with green salad	Squash and Ginger Soup with Lemony Coriander Oil (page 82)	
TUESDAY	Hemsley Green Machine	Leftover Moroccan Meditation Stew	Fish Amok Cambodian Curry (page 176) with Broccoli Rice (page 170)	
WEDNESDAY	Cinnamon, Raisin and Quinoa Breakfast Muffins (page 36, freeze any leftover muffins)	Flaxseed Bun Open Sandwich (Egg, Mayo and Watercress) page 143)	Quinoa Biryani (page 255)	
THURSDAY	Leftover Flaxseed Buns (with avocado or BBtella, page 293)	Leftover Moroccan Meditation Stew	Quick Sausage Ragu with Celeriac Spaghetti (page 198, freeze the leftovers)	
FRIDAY	Leftover Cinnamon, Raisin and Quinoa Breakfast Muffins	Leftover Flaxseed Bun (½ each) with leftover Squash and Ginger Soup	Slow-cooked 'No-fry' Chicken Curry (page 197) with Cauliflower Rice (page 240)	
SATURDAY	Huevos Rancheros with Guacamole (page 50)	Quinoa-stuffed Romano Peppers (page 255)	Courgette and Cannellini Bean Lasagne (page 226, freeze the leftovers)	

STOCKING YOUR KITCHEN

We've been delighted to see how much easier it has become to find all of the ingredients we champion – the tide is turning. The internet is a wonderful shopping resource where, with a single click, you can buy ingredients that aren't available locally and find bargains to order direct to your door. Buddy up with friends and family for the store cupboard ingredients you know that you'll use regularly and use this chance to get deals by buying in bulk as we do; this way you can save money while upgrading the quality of the food you eat. Ask your local shops and supermarkets to consider stocking the products you need – the more people ask, the more likely they will be to stock the item in question. We've seen it happen all over the country – your spending power will ensure that your voice will be heard.

As well as savvy shopping, making the best use of your store cupboard, fridge and freezer will make your life easier too. See the 'Sunday Cook-Off' (page 334) for how we get ahead on the working week by spending a few hours on a Sunday preparing ingredients for filling our fridge and freezer. While we love foods like bee pollen and avocado oil, they are not our everyday essentials and you won't find them

on our weekly shopping list. The following tables show the ingredients that we often use.

Other than the fresh staples (eggs, greens, lemons, herbs, etc.), which can be bought weekly, we recommend buying everything in bulk to store in the cupboard, fridge or freezer. Build up these supplies and you will always be able to make something nourishing and delicious. You can then supplement these staples with fresh, seasonal produce (tomatoes, butternut squash, celeriac, etc.) during your weekly shop or as you go.

Remember to research any new items or brands so that you are sure of what you are getting. Some varieties of buckwheat noodles (also known as soba) have wheat added to them, for instance. It's always best to check the labels.

FRESH STAPLES	STAPLES FOR THE FREEZER	DRIED BEANS, FRUITS, NUTS AND SEEDS	FLOURS AND POWDERS	OILS (COLD-PRESSED), VINEGARS, NUT BUTTERS	TINS AND PRESERVES	DRIED HERBS AND SPICES, CONDIMENTS, NATURAL SWEETENERS
Bones	Bones	Lentils (Puy /French, green, brown, red)	Chestnut flour	Extra-virgin olive oil (EVOO)	Coconut milk (full-fat) and almond milk	Dried herbs (oregano, parsley, basil, rosemary, thyme, bay leaves, etc.)
Butter and cheese	Berries	Mung beans	Chickpea flour (or gram/garbanzo /besan flour)	Flaxseed oil	Tinned fish	Ground spices (chilli, cayenne pepper, turmeric, cardamom, cumin, smoked paprika, coriander, cinnamon, allspice, etc.)
Yoghurt (full-fat probiotic and coconut)	Bananas (sliced)	Dried fruits (goji berries, dates, raisins, etc. – sulphur dioxide-free)	Coconut flour (expands three times in size when cooked, hence cannot be substituted 1:1 with other flours)	Sesame oil	Beans (aduki, black, cannellini, butter, borlotti, etc.)	Whole spices (fennel, caraway, mustard seeds, etc.)
Eggs (medium, at room temperature)	Kale	Dried seaweed (wakame, dulse)	Buckwheat flour	Apple cider vinegar (ACV) (raw, unfiltered)	Chickpeas	Pepper (black and white)
Leafy greens (watercress, spinach, lettuce, etc.)	Spinach	Pseudocereals (amaranth, buckwheat (not flakes), quinoa)	Ground almonds	Balsamic vinegar	Tomatoes	Sea salt (or rock salt, such as Himalayan – not table/low-sodium salt)
Garlic and onions	Peas	Quinoa flakes	Ground flaxseed (or linseed)	Red wine vinegar	Sundried tomatoes	Mustard (Dijon, English, wholegrain)
Fresh root ginger and turmeric	Broad beans	Buckwheat (soba) noodles (100% buckwheat)	Bicarbonate of soda	Tomato purée	Olives	Tamari (gluten-free Japanese soy sauce)
Fresh herbs (parsley, coriander, basil, mint, etc.)	Green beans	Nuts (e.g. almonds, hazelnuts, walnuts, pine nuts, Brazils)	Carob and cocoa/raw cacao powder	Nut butters	Capers	Raw honey
Lemons	Mackerel fillets	Whole seeds (chia, flax, sunflower, hemp, poppy, black/white sesame)	Superfood powders (maca, spirulina, acai, chlorella, lucuma, baobab, etc.)	Tahini (try light first before dark)	Pickled jalapeño peppers	Maple syrup
Miso paste (traditionally fermented)		Desiccated coconut		Vanilla extract (not essence)	Tamarind paste	Dark (85% cocoa solids) chocolate

ORGANIC: TO BUY OR NOT TO BUY?

Organic is a complex issue because the word 'organic' is both a certification and a way of describing anything grown or reared in a more natural way than industrial methods. In the supermarket look for labels such as 'organic certified', 'biodynamic certified' and 'GM-free' because these are indicators that what you're buying is chemical-free and naturally grown or reared – the way food should be. Don't assume that unlabelled (or sometimes labelled 'conventionally grown') supermarket produce is grown without chemicals. Chemical-laden, mass-produced food should not be the norm; neither should naturally grown produce be exclusively for the wealthy. Not all food will carry a label, of course. Produce from local farmers, grocers and butchers may be naturally grown or reared but just not labelled as such. They often have the advantage of being cheaper as they will have natural imperfections.

Here are some tips for buying natural food on a budget. Prioritise which foods to purchase based on the amount of pesticides they're likely to contain.

+ Animal products such as dairy (cheese, butter, yoghurt – always full-fat), eggs and meat should always be organically reared, wild or equivalent, to avoid the addition of hormones, antibiotics and steroids and to ensure the animals they came from were fed a diet that is natural to them and free from pesticides.

+ High surface area. Crops with a relatively high surface area relative to their mass (berries, tomatoes, leafy greens, courgettes) should be grown in an organic way too, as a greater proportion of the crop is exposed to pesticide spraying when grown by conventional farming methods.

+ Better flavour. Organic food is grown slowly and as a result produces a better flavour.

+ Thin skin. Prioritise anything with a thin skin – if you are going to eat the skin of the fruit or vegetable, then purchase organically grown. A lot of goodness is contained in the skin, so for organic root vegetables wash the earth off but don't peel. If you are going to peel veg, then non-organic is an option – wash it thoroughly when you get home. For non-organic root vegetables, such as beetroots and carrots, pesticides are concentrated around the top, so chopping 1cm off the top will help.

+ Naturally grown. Be sure to ask around at farmers' markets for naturally grown foods /unsprayed produce, which are often cheaper than those that are certified as organic.

+ Checking online. You can also keep up to date with the produce that contains the least and highest amount with an online search and buy accordingly: www.pan-uk.org/food/best-worst-food-for-pesticide-residues.

+ Don't be disheartened if you cannot make all of these changes. Simply try to get the best-quality food you can source and afford. By washing and peeling non-organic fruit and vegetables, you will be well on course.

WASHING FRUIT AND VEGETABLES

Be sure to wash fruits and veggies before eating, especially if eating them raw. Even food that's been grown organically will have become contaminated with bacteria and dirt during handling, transportation and storage. For any fruit and vegetables that are eaten unpeeled, such as apples, make sure you give them a really good wash to help remove any residual pesticides on the skin. You can also fill a large bowl with water and add 1 tablespoon of lemon juice and 2 tablespoons of vinegar or bicarbonate of soda before adding your fruit or veg. Leave to soak in the bowl for 20 minutes before rinsing thoroughly. Alternatively, pour the mixture into a squirt bottle and spray directly onto fruits and vegetables, scrub with a vegetable brush as needed (i.e. not on soft fruits like berries!) and rinse well.

A NOTE ON ACTIVATING

For anyone who regularly eats whole nuts, seeds, pseudocereals and dried pulses such as lentils, 'activating' them first is important in order to reduce the phytates in them – compounds that bind to certain dietary minerals, slowing their absorption. Pre-soaking these ingredients is a traditional way of making them more digestible.

We take shortcuts when we can – one-pot cooking means fewer pans to wash up, and cooking in bulk to save time – but we don't stint when it comes to activating. It's an easy and worthwhile habit to get into: just soak these raw wholefoods (see exceptions in the table below) in double the volume of water overnight, or for a minimum of 8 hours, for most, before rinsing them. Adding salt to the water for soaking nuts and seeds, and lemon juice or apple cider vinegar for soaking pseudocereals, helps the process. This pre-soaking also makes nuts and seeds easier to blend for smoothies and dips, and helps pulses and pseudocereals cook more quickly. For any recipes that require 'crispy activated' nuts and seeds (those that have been soaked and then dried), a dehydrator comes in handy. (Dehydrate at 45°C for 12–24 hours, depending on the size of the nuts or seeds. You can also dry them in the oven at fan 180°C/Gas mark 6 for 10 minutes, though they will no longer be raw.) Do this in bulk, and store in an airtight container somewhere cool or in the fridge or freezer to get ahead.

The table below lists the various wholefoods that we activate. For convenience, use tinned beans instead of dried ones. Just be careful to select brands containing no additives, including sugar; if any salt is included, make sure to adjust the seasoning in the recipe. Always drain the beans and rinse thoroughly before using. If you are using dried beans remember you still need to cook them after activating them! We stick to dried lentils in our recipes as they're much quicker to cook – and red lentils don't need activating.

+ **NO TIME TO ACTIVATE?** Uncooked lentils and beans nearly always need to be soaked before cooking but in the case of nuts, seeds and pseudocereals you can still make the recipe without activating. Just be sure to rinse pseudocereals really well, adding more liquid for cooking and allowing extra cooking time. Even soaking for an hour or so will be better than nothing, but try activating next time.

	NUTS	SEEDS	PSEUDOCEREALS	PULSES
SOAK OVERNIGHT /FOR 8 HOURS MINIMUM	Almonds, hazelnuts, peanuts, walnuts, pecans, macadamia nuts	Hemp, pumpkin, sunflower, sesame	Buckwheat groats, quinoa, amaranth	Puy/French, green and brown lentils, mung beans, chickpeas and other dried beans
EXCEPTIONS	Cashews (soak for 2–3 hours) Brazils, pine nuts (no need to soak) Ground almonds (no need to soak)	Chia seeds, flaxseeds (usually soaked as part of the recipes e.g. for smoothies)	Roasted buckwheat groats (kasha), quinoa/buckwheat flakes or flour	Red lentils (no need to soak) **NB:** Use cooked tinned chickpeas and beans, for convenience

KITCHEN ESSENTIALS

BAKING PARCHMENT. Avoid 'non-stick' liners and aluminium foil. Line baking tins and trays to stop food sticking using unbleached, metal-free baking parchment, which you can also use for wrapping leftovers. Look for muffin cases made of baking parchment for easy removal.

BAKING TINS, SHEETS AND TRAYS. For baking and roasting, use stainless steel, ceramic or lead-free, enamel-lined bakeware. Line all other bakeware with baking parchment to avoid toxic PTFE and PFOA.

CANTEENS. Use stainless-steel canteens for carrying water, smoothies and juices when you are on the go. Buy food-grade stainless steel so it doesn't react, and double check that there is no plastic liner.

CHOPPING BOARDS. Avoid plastic and choose wood and bamboo, which are naturally antibacterial. After washing and drying, use a leftover halved lemon to deodorise them.

FLASKS. Stainless-steel vacuum flasks are perfect for keeping food hot or cold for transporting to work. Make sure there is no plastic liner.

FOOD PROCESSOR WITH A RANGE OF ATTACHMENTS. Grate a mountain of cauliflower or broccoli into rice, whip up cakes and blitz cabbage into slaw in no time. Use the small bowl insert for blending dips, pestos and dressings.

GLASSWARE. Toxic BPA found in the plastic used for some lunchboxes and food-storage pots can leak into food, so we use lidded glass bowls and dishes instead, for more liquid foods, and plastic containers lined with baking parchment for storing things like cookies, cakes and muffins. Save glass jars for storing dips, dressings and sauces and even soups, smoothies and juices. Heatproof jars are good for making noodle pots (page 75) to take to work. Containers made of ovenproof glass can also go straight into the oven – an added benefit.

KITCHEN SCALES. We like compact digital scales for ease and accuracy.

KNIVES. One big, one small and one serrated for soft foods should be all you need. You'll need a knife sharpener too – a blunt knife is not as safe and will slow you down.

POTS AND PANS. Use stainless-steel pots or pans and a ceramic frying pan to avoid toxic substances found in other types of modern cookware. Try the new generation of 'green cookware' instead. We highly recommend a 4-litre pot with a lid for making broth, stews and big batches of soup.

SPATULAS. Use a wooden one for cooking and a silicone one for scraping out bowls, blenders and food processors.

SPIRALIZER. This turns vegetables – such as carrots, courgettes, cucumbers, squash and celeriac – and apples into spaghetti-like noodles. A julienne peeler makes a good alternative, or you can try a standard vegetable peeler for different shapes.

ALSO USEFUL:

Of the items listed below, the two we would recommend most are, number one, a high-powered blender and, number two, a slow cooker.

BLENDER. Use a high-speed blender to make light work of blending raw veg like kale and beetroot for smoothies and grinding nut milk and flours such as ground flax. Hand-held stick blenders are great for softer ingredients. Check the power of the blender suits your requirements before you invest in one. For smoothies, you can use a food processor for blending softer ingredients, though you might not get such a smooth finish. We indicate in the relevant recipes when to swap harder ingredients for softer ones if using a food processor.

DEHYDRATOR. This machine gently dries out food at a very low temperature. Very handy for dehydrating 'activated' nuts and seeds (page 341) to make them 'crispy', for fruit and vegetable 'crisps' and for making raw crackers and granolas.

JUICER. The slow-grinding action of a masticating juicer (also known as a cold-press juicer) ensures that more of the goodness from your fruit and veg makes it into your juice. You can also use it to make nut milks and butters.

MANDOLIN. Great for finely slicing fruit and vegetables quickly, but not needed if you have a spiralizer.

MEASURING SPOONS. If you don't have proper measuring spoons, the temptation is always to use an ordinary tablespoon from the cutlery drawer to measure ingredients. While this may work well enough for some recipes, most baking requires precise measurements. Check you are using the right-sized spoons: 1 teaspoon = 5ml, 1 tablespoon = 15ml. Look for stainless-steel measuring spoons that are hardwearing – starting with a ½ teaspoon measure, right up to a full tablespoon. Unless a recipe indicates otherwise, make sure your spoonfuls are level – don't heap or compact them, especially when it comes to ingredients like coconut flour where a little goes a long way.

SALAD SPINNER. Important for making good salads – you don't want soggy leaves!

SLOW COOKER. Throw in the ingredients for a stew, soup or bone broth in the morning and it's then ready when you get home from work, or get it going the night before for a hot breakfast when you wake. An ovenproof casserole with a lid, for cooking stews or casseroles in the oven, makes a good alternative otherwise.

WATER FILTER. Tap water typically contains chloride, fluoride, traces of heavy metals, nitrates, pesticides and hormones. We recommend a water filter to remineralise your tap water, but a filter jug is a good starting point.

H+H LIVING

GOOD + SIMPLE HABITS

You might not expect this from a cookbook, but the truth is you cannot depend on just food alone to make you feel good. A holistic approach is one that encompasses mind, body and lifestyle beyond what is simply served on your plate. Once you address one area in your life, you soon notice what else isn't falling into line. Start today with some of these simple changes and you'll feel better immediately; the rest you can incorporate as and when you're ready. You owe it to yourself to slough off bad habits and replace them with healthy new ones. Your new happier and healthier life begins right now!

+ Drink water first thing. Start the day with a glass of room-temperature or warm water to flush the system. If you like, add the juice of half a lemon, then rinse out your mouth and wait at least 20 minutes before brushing your teeth.

+ Take regular time out. This may sound like the most unachievable change, but in our experience taking time out makes extra time. For 2 minutes a day, close your eyes and shut out external stimulation, breathe deeply and slowly to oxygenate your blood.

+ Enjoy your lunch. Try to get away from your desk for lunch and spend an extra 10 minutes over it. Concentrate on the act of eating rather than trying to do other things at the same time.

+ Gentle exercise. Make time to head outside and get some fresh air. Go for a walk, do some gentle yoga, or make your way to work on foot. Don't punish yourself at the gym. Gentle exercise will release the same good vibes as an intense workout and help you to ease into the day.

+ Switch off from tech. Try 'no screen evenings' and totally switch off from tech. Socialise instead, enjoying the company of your friends /family, read, paint, indulge in other hobbies or do a little cooking.

+ Wind down before bed. Give yourself a wind-down routine – aim to go to bed an hour earlier, have a 'digital detox' and give your eyes a rest from TV, phones and computers at least 2 hours before bed. Dim the lights and light some aromatherapy candles to set the mood and help your body and mind wind down – particularly important if you are suffering from stress or anxiety.

+ Night-time routine. Be sure to drink some water before hitting the hay. And remember to remove any make-up and cleanse your skin so that, with a good night's sleep, it's refreshed for the next day.

NATURAL BEAUTY AND CLEANING PRODUCTS

As you eat more naturally, try expanding this approach into other areas of your life. It will reap huge benefits for your general well-being. Get into green/chemical-free beauty products and cleaning products for the home. These don't have to be expensive – use a homemade blend of equal parts almond or jojoba oil with unrefined sesame oil as a nourishing body moisturiser post-bathing.

We also like using organic coconut oil as a massage oil and a face cleanser. Simply massage it into your skin and then remove with a warm damp cloth. It's great for removing eye makeup too. For a homemade face toner, brew a small cup of chamomile or green tea and store in the fridge for a few days in an airtight container.

Bicarbonate of soda and vinegar (don't use your ACV – normal vinegar will do) make kinder traditional alternatives to the harsh and toxic household cleaners of today. For the bathroom, kitchen and other areas, use a separate microfibre cloth that you can throw into the wash for an economical, effective and environmentally-friendly way to clean your house easily.

FEELING STRESSED, TIRED OR LOW?

Try these few tips and tricks:

+ Smiling reminds your body that everything is going to be OK!

+ A quick nap. Meditation is also a fantastic reset, but if you're feeling flaky, then a snooze or even a lillle lie-down will be a massive help. Learn some deep-breathing techniques that you can do anywhere.

+ Lavender oil. Add a few drops of lavender essential oil to the edge of your pillow to soothe and relax you when you're sleeping.

+ Positive reappraisal. Too often we give ourselves a hard time and dwell on the negatives. Observation is a useful tool and so is appreciation, so look back on the day, think about how you're feeling and make a mental note of anything that you would do differently next time.

OVERDONE IT?

After a big night out or a heavy working week, adopt these easy steps to get yourself back to a good place. Avoid stimulants like caffeine, sugar, 'hangover food' or 'hair of the dog' and be gentle with yourself.

+ Good hydration. Start off/wake up with an alkalising lemon water and then keep drinking water and herbal teas throughout the day. If you can get a fresh coconut (full of electrolytes and minerals), all the better!

+ Bone broth. Having some quality Bone Broth (page 63) at the ready is key to kicking post-party binging. We've always got a pot on the go, and a mug of bone broth with a squeeze of lemon juice and a little sea salt will soothe your stomach.

+ Make eggs with a soft yolk (to preserve anti-oxidants and heat sensitive nutrients), cooking them sunny side up in coconut oil for better absorption of those plentiful fat soluble vitamins found in the yolks. Serve with avocado and plenty of watercress and greens.

+ Have a bath. Take an Epsom salts bath or boil up some ginger to make a strong tea and add to the bath to help you sweat out any toxins. Dry body brushing and tongue-scraping will help to further rid the body of toxins.

+ Bed is best. Sleep is free and nothing else beats it, so put on your favourite pyjamas, sip a herbal bedtime tea and go to bed.

EATING WELL ON THE GO

AT WORK

Pack a snack, along with your lunch, so you aren't tempted by crisps and chocolate bars before you get home for dinner. Remember: leftover stews and soups are easily heated up and transported in a flask. For good packed lunches and snacks try our sandwiches (page 138–143), Blueberry Muffins (page 308), Caroby Fruit and Nut Balls (page 305), Power Salad in a Jar (page 160), noodle pots (page 75–77) and Sri Lankan Squash Croquettes (page 98).

TRAVELLING

When it comes to eating when you're travelling, the only challenging part is being unprepared and stuck somewhere where real, wholefoods don't exist. Take a fresh dish or two, such as a smoothie (pages 324–325) or Green Goddess Noodle Salad (page 250), as well as foods that keep well and can be eaten with your fingers: Cinnamon, Raisin and Quinoa Breakfast Muffins (page 36), Tahini Applejacks (page 124), Multiseed Crackers (page 127) or Lemon and Cranberry Biscotti (page 306). Good portable snacks also include apples, cheese, avocado, raw chicory or Little Gem lettuce, nuts and dried fruit. For long trips to unfamiliar places, we like to have some non-perishables with us, including superfood powders such as spirulina, maca and baobab, to give us vitamins when fresh food is not so readily available; and tinned sardines and biltong (dried beef strips), which offer a good source of portable protein that you can keep in your handbag. Make a travel jar of our Quinoa Kettle Porridge (page 29) for a hot breakfast in hotel rooms as well as at work. And keep hydrated with lots of water.

HOTELS + RESTAURANTS

Not able to prepare your own food? Then apply the 'Better Than' rule (page 15) and look for the best option available: search for real-food restaurants and sources at your destination (researching these before you travel, if necessary); ask the hotel to clear your

mini bar to avoid temptation – which will also leave you space to stock up on your own snacks/drinks; and keep hydrated. If you're ducking into a supermarket, pick up a pot of hummus made with extra-virgin olive oil, and a whole red pepper or courgette. Give it a wash if you can and then dunk it into the hummus for a vitamin-rich, giant crudité. If you pass an artisanal delicatessen, pop in and get some good cheese to eat with apples and raw veggies, as above.

Just as you would at home, allow plenty of time between supper and bedtime for a good night's sleep, so make an early reservation at the restaurant, avoid eating too much or too quickly – don't be tempted to fall into pace with your companions, enjoy every bite and you'll feel better for it. Mix and match the menu to suit – choosing, for example, the wild fish from one dish and pairing it with the vegetables from another.

For hotel breakfasts, ask for your eggs to be fried in butter rather than vegetable oil or choose poached or soft-boiled and pair with a side salad. Avoid the bread basket, sip water and remember that too much alcohol as well as too much food will disrupt sleep, which is not such an issue if you're on holiday but not great on a work trip if you have an early start! If you can't finish your meal, then ask for a doggy bag and take it home or keep it in your hotel fridge for the next day – eateries are all too happy not to waste good food.

INDEX

ACKNOWLEDGEMENTS

10 9 8 7 6 5 4 3 2 1

Ebury Press, an imprint of Ebury Publishing,
20 Vauxhall Bridge Road, London, SW1V 2SA

Ebury Press is part of the Penguin Random House
group of companies whose addresses can be found
at global.penguinrandomhouse.com

Copyright © Hemsley + Hemsley 2016
Photography © Nick Hopper 2016

Jasmine and Melissa Hemsley have asserted
their right to be identified as the author of this
Work in accordance with the Copyright,
Designs and Patents Act 1988

First published by Ebury Press in 2016

www.eburypublishing.co.uk

A CIP catalogue record for this book
is available from the British Library

Design: Imagist

ISBN: 978 1 78503 160 1

Colour origination by Altaimage, London
Printed and bound by Firmengruppe APPL,
aprinta druck, Wemding, Germany

Penguin Random House is committed to a
sustainable future for our business, our readers
and our planet. This book is made from Forest
Stewardship Council® certified paper.

MIX
Paper from
responsible sources
FSC® C018179

For more info, product recommendations, and stockists'
details check out www.hemsleyandhemsley.com.

Thanks firstly to Nick Hopper, creative director and co-founder
of H+H who wears many hats – not least the one of photographer!
We couldn't do a thing if it weren't for the rest of Team H+H
– our very own Eva Ramirez, Sjaniel Turrell, Nicky Smiles,
Nina Fitzpatrick and Taylor Kelly.

Thank you to Ebury Press who made the book happen –
especially the hard work and endless patience of Lizzy Gray,
Laura Higginson, Sarah Bennie, Kealey Rigden, copy editor Kate
Parker, proofreader Anne Sheasby and designer David Eldridge.

Our epic shoot team who bring this book to life – Uyen Luu,
Jenny Brown, Ellie Dunbar, Lauren Hunter, Kitty Coles, India
Whiley Morton and Laura Jacobs. Then there's our brand
and book design team, Colm Roche and Rose Brissenden
at Imagist who keep it looking slick.

Thank you to some wise old owls Susie Pearl, Professor
Tim Spector, Raj Bhachu, David Bond, Tara Donovan and
Rachel Lovell for helping us keep it real. And of course to our
recipe testers who've always got our backs – Shelley Martin
Light, Jessica Malik, Mellany Robinson, Carine Dauphin,
Evangelina 'mum' Hemsley, Laura Segura Ramirez,
Lenie Sanchez, Jo Cura, Sima Bibi and Maria Francolini,
Liam Hart and Henry Relph.

Last but not least, the biggest thanks to all our family,
friends, supporters and followers, who made *The Art Of
Eating Well* such a success and inspired us to work harder
and come back with a bang!